Community *Energy* Workbook

A Guide to Building a Sustainable Economy

Rocky Mountain Institute
By Alice Hubbard and Clay Fong

1739 Snowmass Creek Road
Snowmass, Colorado 81654
(970) 927-3851

A project cosponsored by the U.S. Department of Energy
through the Urban Consortium Energy Task Force

Rocky Mountain Institute is an independent, nonprofit research and educational foundation whose mission is to foster the efficient and sustainable use of resources as a path to global security.

We undertake to use professional care in our research and publications and to verify our information from sources believed to be reliable. Please contact Rocky Mountain Institute with any corrections or comments for future editions.

We do not imply endorsement of any product, service, or company mentioned in this publication. The information and statements contained herein do not necessarily represent those of funders or reviewers of this publication.

Rocky Mountain Institute dedicates this publication to the memory of Jack Evans, founder of the Golden Rule Foundation, in recognition of his contributions to sustainable energy and the betterment of humanity.

RMI also acknowledges the generous support of:
The Golden Rule Foundation
Allen-Heath Memorial Foundation
GAG Charitable Corporation
Merck Family Fund
Educational Foundation of America
W. Alton Jones Foundation
Eugene B. Casey Foundation
U.S. Department of Energy through the Urban Consortium Energy Task Force
U.S. Environmental Protection Agency

Book (not cover) Design: Robert Maraziti/Aspen Marketing+Design
Desktop Publisher: Kate Mink
Design Assistance: Kelly Alford
Illustrations: Curt Carpenter
Photographs on page 99: Roy Willey
Copyediting: Paul Andersen

ISBN 1-881071-04-9

Acknowledgments

Numerous people graciously shared their expertise, ideas, time, and resources to create this publication.

The first thank-you goes to the many citizens of the Roaring Fork Valley of Colorado, who have shown how citizens can play an active role in shaping their community's energy future and allowed us to learn from their efforts. Bill Stirling, who started the Energy 2000 Committee, contributed irreplaceable talent, vision, and energy and played an invaluable role by championing the cause of energy efficiency. We thank the members of the original steering committee: Lee Cassin, Peter Dobrovolny, Steve Standiford, Marty Finkelstein, Bob Gish, George Newman, Michael Tierney, Steve Seifert, Lee Halland, and the close to one hundred people that were involved in energy planning task forces. Thank-you also to those who carried the effort on to create the Community Office for Resource Efficiency, in particular: Lynne Haynes, Joel Scott, Vitashka Kirshen, Dianna Beutas, Marianne Williams, Jim Pokrandt, Randy Udall, and the staff of Holy Cross Electric Association, Aspen Municipal Utility, Rocky Mountain Natural Gas, and elected officials of City of Aspen, Snowmass Village and Pitkin County, Colorado.

This publication also benefited immensely from:

Patty Cantrell, former RMI researcher, who played a critical role in developing the overall framework of the book, and in particular, the Energy Picture section.

Skip Laitner, of Economic Research Associates, who generously shared his expertise and insight on the community economic benefits of sustainable energy policies and community-based energy programs.

Craig Hibberd, Energy Services Manager for the Salt Lake City Office of U.S. D.O.E.'s Western Area Power Administration, who provided helpful comments, information, and ideas for developing public participation tools for energy planning.

Thanks also goes to Paul Aldretti, formerly of the Colorado Office of Energy Conservation; Karl Wunderlich, Economist, Western Area Power Administration; Hervey Scudder of The Catalyst, and Mark Monroe for reviews and helpful comments.

We also thank former and current colleagues at RMI, who offered ideas, suggestions, and help: Bill Browning (who wrote an earlier version) Kate Mink, Michael Kinsley, Hunter Lovins, JoAnn Glassier, Ross Jacobs, Daniel Yoon, Don Chen, Linda Baynham, Rick Heede, Owen Bailey, Maureen Cureton, Brady Bancroft, Jeanette Darnauer, Richard Malik, Jill Dominique, Joe Romm, Andrew Jones, and RMI Volunteers Jon Vogel, Dan Frey, Elaine Bueschen, and Liz Mason.

The authors also thank all the people who have been working to make communities more energy efficient over the last 20 years, creating examples of what works, and generously sharing their experiences. While these people are too numerous to name, many of the organizations that they represent, or publications that they have written, are listed in the resource section in this book.

And finally, this publication owes its completion to the irreplaceable encouragement, ideas, patience and lost week-ends contributed by Colin Laird, Alice's husband.

Community *Energy* Workbook

Workshop B: Discovering Opportunities

Workshop C: Creating Project Ideas

Workshop D: Selecting Energy Plan Projects

Bringing It All Together

Turning the Plan into Action

What's Worked in Other Places? The Task Force Packets

Appendices

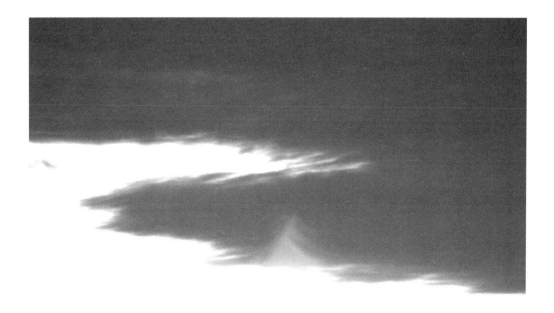

Building a Sustainable Economy

Some people believe that addressing environmental problems can only be done at the expense of the economy. Numerous communities are proving them wrong.

By investing in energy efficiency and renewable energy communities across the country are solving environmental problems and building stronger economies:

➤ An energy efficiency program started in 1974 by the municipal utility in Osage, Iowa, (pop. 3,500) keeps an additional $1 million a year in the local economy. This program, which relied on simple tools like caulk guns, duct tape, insulation, light bulbs, and education, has created an annual community economic stimulus equal to $1000 per household.[1]

➤ In Ellensburg, Washington, (pop. 12,000) energy efficiency programs begun in 1989 will result in an additional $6.84 million in industrial output. This savings is enough to support approximately 18 jobs per year between 1990-1999.[2]

➤ Since the establishment of energy management programs in the early 1980's, residents, businesses and agencies of San Jose, California have cut more than $5.5 million from annual energy bills and saved enough energy each year to power 7,600 homes.[3] San Jose predicts its sustainable energy programs will produce a county-wide $33 million increase in wages and salaries, and a net employment gain of 1,753 job years over a ten-year period.[4]

These successes represent a mere taste of the enormous economic potential of investing in sustainable energy practices. A vigorous national commitment to energy efficiency and renewable energy would save the U.S. tens, even hundreds of billions of dollars a year, create millions of new jobs, and strengthen local economies.

All these economic benefits come not at the expense of the environment, but at a net gain. Meeting energy needs efficiently and tapping renewable sources addresses one of the most environmentally damaging and costly human activities: the production and consumption of energy. Conventional energy practices are causing global climate change, oil spills, air pollution, acid rain, and scarred landscapes.

This workbook challenges you and other community residents to ask new questions about how your community meets its energy needs. It provides tools to discover the economic and environmental benefits sustainable energy practices can bring to local residents and businesses. And most importantly, this workbook offers a framework for your community

> **A vigorous national commitment to energy efficiency and renewable energy would save the U.S. tens, even hundreds of billions of dollars a year, create millions of new jobs, and strengthen local economies.**

to begin today to build a sustainable economy with energy efficiency and renewable energy.

Ask new questions

We can save billions of dollars by asking new questions about the way we meet energy needs. The conventional approach has asked: "How do we get more barrels of oil? How do we generate more kilowatt hours of electricity?" Yet nobody wants barrels of sticky black goo or raw kilowatt hours for their own sake. What we are really after are the hot showers and cold beer, lighting, productivity, mobility, comfort, and the other "end-use" services that energy provides.

Instead, we could ask: "How can we provide these hot showers and cold beer in the cheapest and most efficient way, counting all financial, social, and environmental costs?" Answering this question opens up a wealth of win-win environmental and economic opportunities. Taking advantage of these opportunities is also much more profitable than developing expensive new energy sources. This "end-use/least-cost" approach can cost-effectively reduce energy use by typically at least a third, and up to 90% in some cases, with the same or improved quality of service.

Take lighting, for instance. Although many assume the typical household incandescent bulb is the only way to get light, there are other ways to meet that objective with less energy and money. Replacing ordinary incandescent light bulbs with compact fluorescent lights (CFLs) saves 3/4 of the electricity and provides the same or better quality light. Because CFLs last 8 to 10 times as long, they also cut the costs of buying and installing replacements.

To tap even greater savings, we can design buildings that require little or no electrical lighting in the daytime. It's cheaper to construct and operate a super-efficient building that maximizes sunlight than it is to use conventional design approaches and pay the resulting electricity bills.

Asking questions about how we meet our lighting needs adds up to big results. The Environmental Protection Agency has helped some businesses cut lighting bills by up to 90%,[5] while improving lighting quality. These enhanced work conditions noticeably reduced absenteeism and increased productivity. The EPA maintains that lighting improvements could save as much as 50% of all electricity used for lighting across the country. These energy savings would allow consumers nationwide to save $18.6 billion on their utility bills, free up $60 billion for other economic purposes, avoid the cost of building new power plants, and prevent 200 million tons of CO_2 from entering the atmosphere.

Lighting is just the beginning. Exploring how we can create comfortable indoor climates reveals other areas of money-saving opportunities. Well-insulated buildings that are heated by the sun or cooled by natural means are more efficient and cost-effective than heating with electricity or using air conditioners. Such buildings are also more pleasant and healthy places in which to live or work. Since electricity is a highly refined energy source best suited for performing sophisticated tasks like running computers, using it to provide heat is like using an eighteen-wheeler as a personal car.

Matching tasks with the appropriate kind of energy and then using that energy as efficiently and cost-effectively as possible can lead to significant savings in all end-uses. America can save more than half of all energy used to cool and heat buildings, heat water, refrigerate food, and run motors for industrial processes.

This end-use/least cost approach for delivering energy services can deliver a healthy dose of economic benefits. Thanks to the use of more efficient automobiles, buildings, computers, appliances, and factories, the U.S. has already reduced energy expenditures by more than $150 billion a year since 1973 levels.[7] While part of this energy bill reduction is attributable to the economy shifting from manufacturing to services, at least 75 percent of these savings are due to increased energy efficiency.[8] As impressive as these improvements are, far greater savings remain untapped. A transition to efficiency and renewables would result in billions of dollars freed up for domestic investment, over a million new jobs created by 2010,[9] new export opportunities, a healthier environment, and greater comfort and productivity. All this from asking a few new questions about how best to meet our energy needs!

Tap local economic opportunities

Billion dollar economic benefits at the national level, as reported by national statistics, don't always mean more money on main street. However, improving local energy practices will create the tangible economic benefits that are sometimes missing from reported improvements in the national economy.

In a typical town, 70 to 80 cents of every dollar[10] spent on energy immediately leaves the local economy. Finding ways to reduce these costs and plug these leaks initiates a series of local economic benefits.

When households, businesses, and government cut energy expenses, they have more disposable dollars to spend on other priorities. Local schools can spend more money on education instead of on lighting classrooms. Businesses can increase productivity instead of pouring money out their windows. And families can increase their quality of life instead of worrying about high heating bills.

In addition to these direct benefits, the money saved from reduced energy bills circulates in the community economy, creating additional benefits. Depending on the type of products made and sold locally, and the degree to which residents and businesses make purchases locally, a "multi-

In a typical town, 70 to 80 cents of every dollar spent on energy immediately leaves the local economy. Finding ways to reduce these costs and plug these leaks initiates a series of local economic benefits.

plier effect" creates a ripple of benefits throughout the community.

Sustainable energy practices can also directly generate new jobs and businesses. They require an investment in insulation, efficient light bulbs, solar water heaters, super-efficient windows, and other technologies, as well as new skills and services. Local businesses can offer these products and services and benefit from the increased demand for them. If such products and services are unavailable in your area, community entrepreneurs can create new jobs and businesses to meet the demand.

Build real wealth

Improving how we use energy may seem like an "experts only" issue, to be handled by utility planners, the federal government, and various energy professionals. The good news is that there *are* no experts when it comes to implementing sustainable energy practices. Citizens and businesses don't have to wait for anyone else to lead the way.

You can start right now in your community to put energy efficiency to work. Homes, neighborhoods, workplaces, shopping centers, schools, transportation systems, and public buildings are all cash cows waiting to be milked. Some people in your community may have already independently tapped efficiency opportunities in their homes and businesses and reaped the rewards.

While energy efficiency and renewable energy have tremendous economic and environmental advantages, there are barriers to their implementation. Some of these barriers originate at a national level, such as lack of market incentives for efficiency, cost assessments that don't count environmental and social harms, and subsidies that favor inefficient energy practices.

Other barriers exist right in your community. Many people have not taken advantage of energy opportunities because they don't know they exist, it's difficult to get upfront financing, or they just don't have the time. Furthermore, institutions that shape overall community energy use, such as utilities and the building industry, may not yet see how promoting sustainable energy practices can benefit them.

Joining forces with other citizens creates tremendous opportunities for addressing these issues. Pooling resources and efforts, communities can develop programs that will make it easier to either overcome barriers, or succeed in spite of them. Rather than working individually to change light bulbs in one home or business at a time, a joint effort enables individuals to create a ripple of long-term energy improvements throughout the community.

By working with other citizens to make your community as energy-efficient as possible, and by tapping renewable sources, you are bringing the idea of a sustainable economy to life. Rather than being caught in the trap

Homes, neighborhoods, workplaces, shopping centers, schools, transportation systems, and public buildings are all cash cows waiting to be milked.

of creating ever-greater supplies, whether they be energy, highways, or consumer goods, developing a sustainable economy means remembering to ask, "What are we *really* after?" and "What's the *best* way to provide it, counting all costs and benefits?" By working together to answer these questions citizens can create the *real* wealth that makes communities good places to live, for this generation and the ones to come.

Developing sustainable energy practices in your community will help you create a thriving economy and a healthy environment today, and build a vibrant foundation for tomorrow. This workbook offers a way to get started.

Endnotes:

1. Renew America, *Searching for Success: Environmental Success Index,* Washington D.C., Renew America, 1991 p. 1.

2. William Wildprett and Michael Grady, *Encouraging Local Economic Development through Energy Conservation.* Northwest Policy Center, University of Washington. 25th Annual Pacific Northwest Regional Economic Conference Proceedings, 1991

3. Energy Task Force of the Urban Consortium, *The Sustainable City Project: A Tri-City Collaboration for Developing and Implementing Sustainable Urban Energy Practices,* Energy Task Force of the Urban Consortium, Portland, OR; San Francisco, CA; San Jose, CA, 1991 pp. 45-46.

4. Energy Task Force of the Urban Consortium, p. 70.

5. United States Environmental Protection Agency, Office of Atmospheric Programs, *1992 Accomplishments and Prospects for 1993,* Washington DC, EPA, 1992 p. 2.

6. *Ibid.,* p. 1.

7. Richard Heede, *The NES Strikes a Dry Hole.* Natural Resources and Environment. Vol.6 #2, Fall 1991.

8. Skip Laitner, *Energy Efficiency and Economic Indicators: Charting Improvements in the Economy & the Environment.* American Council for an Energy Efficient Economy, December 1994.

9. Howard Geller et al., *Energy Efficiency and Job Creation,* Washington D.C., American Council for an Energy Efficient Economy, 1992 p. iii.

10. *The Jobs Connection: Energy Use and Local Economic Development.* Cities and Counties Project, U.S. Department of Energy. National Renewable Energy Lab, July 1994.

The phrase "real wealth" is borrowed from Tom Bender's winning entry to the American Institute of Architect's contest on sustainable communitites, entitled *Building Real Wealth.*

How does Osage save over $1 million each year?

Here are some of the ways Osage, Iowa has become the most energy efficient community in the country:

➤ Newspaper articles, advertisements and a utility newsletter keep residents informed about ways to increase energy efficiency.

➤ Utility representatives speak to local service clubs on the value of weatherization. This effort reaches 15% to 20% of the town's adults.

➤ To identify inefficient appliances, utility customers borrow electric test meters for free.

➤ All new gas and electric customers must conform to minimum insulation standards before the utility will sell energy to them.

➤ The utility produced infrared aerial and ground scans that showed heat loss in local buildings.

➤ Customers gauge home and business heat loss with infrared scanners and blower-door tests.

➤ The utility promotes an energy efficiency curriculum for schools.

➤ With the help of the local Junior Chamber of Commerce, the utility provides weatherization services to low-income households.

➤ The utility supplies efficient light bulbs, shower heads, faucet aerators and efficiency handbooks to customers.

➤ Industrial customers can take advantage of energy checks by professional engineers.

➤ The utility pays businesses two years' interest on the cost of making efficiency measures.

Wes Birdsall, the retired Osage Utility director responsible for the program, has said these measures have created the following kinds of benefits:

➤ All new construction has exceeded utility insulation standards.

➤ Installation of compact fluorescent lights has reduced coal consumption by 200 tons, CO_2 pollution by 750 tons, and acid rain-causing emissions by 10 tons.

➤ A sock factory cut the cost of knitting a dozen socks from $.48 to $.34 and has increased its production 295% and workforce 290%.

➤ The average Osage resident uses 25% less electricity than the state average and at a 37% lower utility rate.

Since 1980, despite growth in the town's three largest industries, the utility has kept growth in energy demand below three percent. It has also cut gas rates 5.5 % and reduced electric rates five times, for a 19 % total cut.

> **Osage residents use 25% less electricity than the state average.... Since 1980, despite growth in the town's three largest industries, the utility has kept growth in energy demand below three percent.**

From the White House to your house

In an effort to lead by example, the Clinton Administration has launched the "Greening the White House" project. Targeting residential quarters, office spaces, and public areas, the project will work to reduce White House resource consumption by 30%, with special attention paid to energy efficiency.

By Earth Day 1994, the project had already completed 50 initiatives to improve the environmental performance of the White House. Initiatives have included lighting retrofits, building envelope improvements, and procurement practices that encourage the purchase of efficient equipment. These products include Energy Star computers and a "Golden Carrot" refrigerator that is over 25% more efficient than 1993 Department of Energy standards and contains no CFCs.

Early results indicate that the project will exceed the 30% resource reduction goal. A lighting retrofit in the White House's West Wing should result in a 50% to 75% energy savings from improved lighting, with a three-year payback period. Installing efficient windows in the solarium and greenhouse should boost window performance 70% to 85% and reduce cooling loads.

A main goal of the "Greening the White House" project is to create an environmentally-sound showcase for citizens to learn about resource-efficient technologies and measures.

To reach its aggressive goals, the project is using a new design approach that brings together the knowledge and experience of a wide range of experts. Traditional design approaches often require building professionals to address their own specialty, without regard for combined effects and overall functionality. This approach can lead, for example, to an architect creating a striking building, which in reality is extremely difficult to ventilate and heat. The White House project has offered an opportunity for architects, interior designers, facilities managers, cooling and heating engineers to all work together to achieve the best results possible.

A main goal of the project is to create an environmentally-sound showcase for citizens to learn about resource-efficient technologies and measures. Project staff are developing a computer "workshop in a box" so that citizens and design professionals around the country can learn how to replicate project results. The National Park Service, one of the agencies managing the White House, is also developing ways to share project results and techniques with the complex's 1.2 million annual visitors.

Climate Change Action Plan calls on citizen ingenuity

"America's most important assets are its people—decent, hard-working, creative and concerned. When that talent is focused through our economic and political system to solve a problem, it can accomplish great things...The (Climate Change Action) plan harnesses economic forces to meet the challenges posed by the threat of global warming. It calls for limited, and focused, government action and innovative public/private partnerships. It relies on the ingenuity, creativity, and sense of responsibility of the American people."

- The Climate Change Action Plan

Over 50 countries have ratified a world treaty to protect the earth's atmosphere. Denmark, Germany, Austria, and Australia have commited to reducing CO₂ levels by at least 20% from 1988 levels by the year 2005.

Over 50 countries have ratified the Framework Convention on Climate Change, a world treaty to protect the earth's atmosphere. The U.S. Climate Change Action Plan (CCAP) charts how the U.S. will meet its commitment of reducing greenhouse gas emissions to 1990 levels by the year 2000.

Denmark, Germany, Australia, and Austria have committed to reducing CO_2 levels by at least 20% from 1988 levels by the year 2005. Communities worldwide have already created programs that address local contribution to climate change. Portland, Oregon, a member of the Urban CO_2 Project and the Sustainable Cities Project, has developed a plan to reduce CO_2 emissions to 20% lower than 1988 levels. Other cities setting CO_2 reduction goals include Bologna, Italy; Ankara, Turkey; Toronto, Canada; Helsinki, Finland; and San Jose, California.

Communities will need to play a critical role in addressing climate change issues. Organizing Energy Town Meetings can be a potent tool to raise understanding of climate change issues and the economic opportunities of implementing programs to reduce CO_2 emissions. Holding the energy planning workshops and creating an energy action plan offers a way to harness the citizen ingenuity in your community and achieve the goals of the CCAP locally while tapping economic opportunities.

The CCAP offers a wide variety of programs to help businesses and communities increase energy efficiency, including programs aimed at increasing motor efficiency, industrial efficiency, building energy improvements, and utility use of integrated resource planning. For more information on some of these programs see page 253.

To learn what other communities are doing to address climate change issues, contact the US Climate Action Network or the International Council for Local Environmental Initiatives, listed on page 253 and 251.

A Framework for Local Success

Communities that are leading the way in improving their economy through better energy practices have several assets in common:

➤ **Widespread awareness of energy alternatives:** In many communities, residents seldom think of energy issues, much less see improved energy use as a means to a stronger economy. In places that are making improvements, awareness of energy alternatives is becoming so commonplace that people are incorporating cost-effective efficiency methods into everyday practice.

➤ **Incentives to change:** Community members see it is in their best interest to take advantage of energy efficiency for economic, environmental or other reasons. Rather than an issue that only a few citizen activists care about, improving energy use becomes a community priority directly tied to existing important local goals and concerns.

➤ **Community and political support:** Good ideas without community and political backing often go nowhere. Strong and enthusiastic support from elected officials, civic leaders, and the community at large plays a critical role in turning good ideas into lasting local change.

➤ **Strong local leadership:** Someone in the community, or some organization, has a vision of how local energy use and the economy could be improved. They've taken an active, persistent role in turning community potential into reality.

➤ **Ability to mobilize resources:** Education and the resulting awareness of energy alternatives is not enough. Successful energy-efficient communities have made the most of available resources to help residents and businesses overcome barriers such as lack of upfront financing or technical expertise.

➤ **An effective organization to carry the effort on, year after year:** This organization might be the local utility, a community development corporation, local government, a nonprofit energy center, an energy service company, or a variety of organizations working together. While individual actions are critical to success, institutions and organizations create a reliable base to mobilize the necessary resources to make improved energy use an ongoing priority for years to come.

If your community currently lacks these assets, this workbook offers a framework for developing them. If your community has some of them, the workbook approach can help you build on them to become yet another

It works!

As the result of citizens using this workbook's approach in Pitkin County, Colorado, three utilities and three local governments created a community energy office. By holding annual energy town meetings and energy planning workshops the Energy 2000 Committee succeeded in putting energy efficiency on the local agenda and creating an energy action plan. The plan recommended that an energy office be established to mobilize resources, coordinate projects, develop long-term energy policies, and provide ongoing leadership. Energy Town Meetings have become a local tradition, and a way for citizens to celebrate energy improvements each year, and set goals for the future.

energy and economic success story.

In the following pages, you'll find detailed suggestions and materials to gather information on the local energy picture, prepare for and conduct an Energy Town Meeting, and hold a series of energy planning workshops. These steps will create the conditions you'll need to improve your energy and economic picture.

Invest in a community approach for long-term benefits

This approach relies heavily on citizen participation. Some people in your community may be skeptical of getting citizens involved in energy planning or economic development. You can point out a few things to them:

A citizen-based approach to energy planning will help your community achieve the best results possible. First, the process itself increases residents' awareness of energy alternatives and how to implement them. The community becomes more aware of the opportunities of energy efficiency and the costs of current energy use. Second, a citizen-based approach draws on the knowledge and insights of a wide variety of people, resulting in solutions that are more responsive to real conditions. Finally, a participatory approach creates the community and political commitment necessary for creating long-term energy and economic improvements. If you want to see real energy improvements, you have to get people involved.

Organizing energy town meetings, energy task forces, and energy workshops will require a lot of time and cooperation from many community members. Sometimes you might wonder if it's worth all the effort. You might start wishing you had a utility director like Osage, Iowa's Wes Birdsall or a small group of knowledgeable people to plan your community's energy future. But very few towns have a Wes Birdsall, and he dedicated 15 years to achieve his results. Furthermore, a key component of his approach was speaking to every community group and hundreds of citizens, to increase their awareness of energy-saving measures and how they could take advantage of them. Very few communities have a small group of people wise enough to develop a plan that considers all the real-world conditions that will affect implementation. And without community or political support, there's no guarantee that even the best plan will be put to work and make any difference whatsoever. Ultimately, investing the time and effort into a community-based approach will give your community the best chance at improving your local energy and economic picture.

Build upon and improve the workbook framework

This workbook is just a starting point. You'll find step-by-step suggestions and outlines of how to approach the entire energy planning effort. The level of detail and specificity is provided only as a way to get you started. The

> **The workshops provide a framework for citizens to go beyond talk of what could be and on to develop projects tailored to local conditions with direct local benefits.**

suggested agendas are meant to be built upon, improved and tailored to meet your community's particular concerns and conditions. Find ways to make the energy picture information especially relevant to your community. Organize variations of the workshops, and variations of the entire process. If you don't have the time or the resources to conduct the entire process, organizing just the Energy Town Meeting will result in increased awareness of the opportunities presented by sustainable energy practices.

Let us know what works, what doesn't, and what kind of results you achieved. You can use the "Talk to Us" form in the back of the book. We're eager to add your community to the growing list of energy and economic success stories!

Tailor the Energy Town Meeting and the planning workshops to fit your community's concerns and conditions.

Overview of Workbook Planning Steps

Start by building the energy steering committee

A steering committee representing different local interests will guide the energy planning process. This committee manages the planning effort, from securing initial sponsorship of local groups to getting the first energy projects off the ground.

Draw the local Energy and Economic Picture

To build community support and identify incentives for improving energy use, find out how much energy your community is consuming and what that means for the economy and the environment. The Energy Picture section, starting on page 37, helps you figure the total local energy bill and put it in a community context.

Mobilize the community for energy planning

A well-attended Energy Town Meeting and a solid core of workshop participants are critical to the planning effort's success. An effective education campaign will achieve these ends, as well as create broad local awareness of energy alternatives.

Organize and hold the Energy Town Meeting

The goal of the initial organizing process is to hold a successful Energy Town Meeting. Designed to be fun and informative, this event should attract wide media coverage, put energy on the community's agenda, and launch the energy planning workshops.

Create energy task forces

At the town meeting, create task forces to address community energy sectors: Residential; Commercial/Industrial; Transportation. Task forces can begin by discussing the services they need energy to deliver and more efficient and renewable alternatives for meeting them. Task force participants learn about the many opportunities for delivering energy services more efficiently and tapping renewable sources. The session should conclude by posing the question: How do we put these alternatives into place?

Each Task Force conducts four workshops

Workshop A — What do you have to work with?
> By examining the three factors of people and organizations, energy finance, and government, participants identify assets, opportunities, and barriers for improving local energy use.

Workshop B — Discovering opportunities

➤ To make the most of local resources, task force members look for connections between assets, opportunities, and barriers identified in Workshop A. By studying other towns' successes, task forces explore how to address local barriers.

Workshop C — Creating project ideas

➤ Participants use Workshop B connections and lessons from other communities to brainstorm project ideas. They then briefly consider what they need to make projects happen and gather more information for Workshop D, if necessary.

Workshop D — Selecting Energy Plan projects

➤ Task forces examine project ideas from Workshop C, select a complementary mix of priority proposals, and prepare to present them to other task forces at the next meeting. This mix of proposals makes up the energy action plan.

Bring it all together to create the Energy Action Plan

In the last planning meeting, all task forces compare action plans. The task forces identify projects that complement and conflict with each other. They then draft a local energy action plan by merging all task force plans.

Turn the plan into action

This step is the most important in the entire process. Implementing simple, high-visibility projects immediately following the final workshop shows task forces the positive results of their work. This momentum encourages participants to pursue more difficult projects that pave the way for measurable improvements in the local energy picture. Find ways to measure and celebrate successes. Hold yearly events that track progress made in improving the local energy and economic picture.

Anchor the plan within local organizations

Communities with the most successful ongoing energy projects have a local organization whose mission is to improve local energy conditions. Such organizations include utilities, nonprofit energy centers, community development corporations, energy service companies, and local government. A long-term, collaborative effort among such groups is critical for putting the resources in place to turn the plan into action.

Launching Your Effort

How can a few people take a good idea and turn it into a community-wide effort? Here's a step-by-step approach to launching a community-wide energy and economic development campaign.

CONTENTS

Develop an Energy Steering Committee

A steering committee representing a range of community interests will lead the energy planning effort. The steering committee will be responsible for gathering the local energy picture information, securing initial support and sponsorship for the planning effort, and preparing for the Energy Town Meeting and workshops. This section outlines how to develop this committee and set it to work.

CREATING A TOOL FOR CHANGE

➤ **Find citizens to start the committee**

➤ **Recruit key interests**

➤ **Hold the first energy committee meeting**

➤ **Develop a lasting and effective committee**

Find citizens to start the committee

The first step to building the energy steering committee is finding several citizens eager to take a leadership role to improve community energy use. Rather than relying on one person to start a steering committee, several enthusiastic individuals will make the task much easier by dividing responsibilities.

If you are a member of an existing community organization, you can propose energy and economic development as a project for your group to pursue. Group members can then help launch the effort.

To pitch the idea to your existing community organization:

➤ Discuss how other communities have strengthened their economies with energy efficiency by drawing on examples from the introduction. Talk about the advantages of putting efficiency to work in your community.

➤ Discuss how an energy efficiency campaign needs to be a community-wide effort to get the best results. Establish that pursuing energy as an economic development tool offers an opportunity to work with diverse local groups to achieve a common goal.

➤ Propose that your organization approach other community groups to develop an Energy and Economic Development Steering Committee to initiate a community-wide energy planning process.

➤ Ask if there are people in your organization that are interested in helping to launch an energy-efficiency effort in your community.

➤ If your group gives the go-ahead, ask for volunteers to help organize the initial energy committee meeting.

If you are not a member of an existing organization, think of groups who can provide individuals or staff that could help form the core group. Your local utility, the chamber of commerce, local government, or an environmental organization could play this role. Contact a staff person or organization leader and pitch the idea of using energy efficiency as an economic development tool. Ask if their group is interested in initiating a local energy and economic development effort. If they are, ask to make a presentation at their next meeting. Use the approach outlined in the above paragraph for your presentation.

Recruit key interests

A broad coalition of interests, rather than a single group or several similar groups, will be most effective at involving a variety of citizens and mobilizing the necessary community resources. Working to develop this kind of coalition at the very beginning of the planning effort will help ensure success.

Meet with those who have offered to help start the steering committee to familiarize them with the energy planning process. Referring to the Overview on page 14, discuss the workbook approach for developing an energy action plan so that they understand what lies ahead.

Next, use page 21 to brainstorm which groups and individuals would be useful to have on the steering committee and who would be important to involve in future steps.

Some potential committee members may not have given energy issues much thought, or may have never considered participating in an economic development effort. Discuss ways to tie the goals of improving the local economy through better energy use into potential committee members' areas of interest or concern.

Divide the names on the list so that those present can share in the task of contacting the individuals or groups. Invite them to an organizing meeting with either a phone call or letter. Here are a few points you can make when approaching individuals and groups:

➤ Many communities have significantly improved their economy by finding ways to use energy more efficiently.

➤ Depending on the group with whom you are speaking, mention ways the effort ties into their concerns. Stress affordable living for groups that deal with low-income issues. Sustainable economic development should appeal to environmental groups. Business stability will interest merchants associations, and so forth.

➤ Point out that a variety of organizations are interested in developing a local energy plan to improve the economy and are going to meet to get the effort started.

➤ Invite your contact or a representative of their group to attend the meeting, letting them know their participation is vital for the success of the effort.

➤ Ask potential participants if they know of other people or organizations who may be interested in serving on the energy committee.

If people seem reluctant or disinterested in participating on the steering committee, offer to make a brief presentation about energy and economic development to their group, or put them on the list to be contacted at later stages in your effort.

Who cares about energy?

Most people could care less about energy. But they do care about a strong economy, clean air, thriving businesses, affordable housing, better transportation, a healthy community, and a variety of other issues that can be influenced by changing the way we use energy. Think of the issues that potential steering committee members care about, and how energy issues are connected to them. Use these connections to show how creating a more sustainable energy future can support a variety of community goals.

The steering committee: who to involve

Use this checklist to explore who to involve in the energy steering committee. Look for ways to connect energy and economic development issues to various organizations' and people's interests.

	Connecting issues	Contact person Telephone	Who will contact?
Respected, active citizens			
Chamber of Commerce / Business groups			
Environmental groups			
Design and building industry leaders			
Neighborhood / community organizations			
Schools / teachers / student leaders			
Civic organizations and service clubs			
Utility representatives			
Local government staff: Planning / Building			
Environmental			
Economic development			
Federal agencies serving your area			
People with computer, media, or PR skills			
Other			

Hold the first energy committee meeting

The goal of the first steering committee meeting is to familiarize participants with energy efficiency as an economic development tool, inspire them to start a community efficiency effort, and determine whether there is enough interest to move forward. To prepare for the meeting, the core group of volunteers should:

➤ Develop an agenda. See page 24 for a sample.
➤ Set a convenient meeting time and place.
➤ Prepare meeting materials. It may be helpful to have several copies of the workbook, as well as copies of the introduction and the planning overview (page 14) for each participant.
➤ Select a facilitator or split the task among volunteers.

Develop a lasting and effective committee.

An effective energy steering committee will be the driving force behind a well-organized energy and economic development effort. It will also be an important organization for carrying the effort beyond the planning phase. There are a few basic yet often overlooked methods for turning a group of volunteers into an effective, enduring organization.

Select an effective chairperson

The ideal chairperson is a good meeting facilitator, skilled at delegating tasks and monitoring progress. The chairperson should be a respected member of the community, able to serve as spokesperson for the planning effort, and skilled at building coalitions and collaborative efforts.

Build committee skills

Community projects can falter when a key individual leaves. Share tasks and cultivate skills to ensure that no one person is indispensable.

Establish set meeting times

Frequent meetings at regularly scheduled times give the committee continuity and stability. Keeping your meetings at the same time and place will encourage consistent attendance.

Communicate, communicate, communicate

Sending out agendas, meeting notes, and background materials keeps members informed and prepared for upcoming meetings. These mailings also lend professionalism to your efforts.

Make every meeting count

At each meeting, have an agenda and stick to it. See that the group makes decisions to move forward and that members leave with assignments to be completed within specific time frames.

Keep meetings concise and to the point

The people you will want on the steering committee are often the busiest people in town. Use their time wisely. Start and end meetings promptly. Keep meetings less than one hour unless participants agree to a longer meeting. Be aware of discussions that may be more appropriate for a later time.

Reinforce and celebrate the spirit of collaboration

To function as an effective coalition, it's essential that all groups receive credit for their participation in the effort. Publicize the diversity of people involved and make sure that single individuals or groups do not get credit for what is a collaborative endeavor.

Sample Agenda—First steering committee meeting

Five minutes

1. Introductions and welcome

Thank attendees for coming and make introductions. Summarize the goals of the meeting.

Ten minutes

2. Energy efficiency as an economic development tool

Describe some of the energy and economic community success stories presented in the *Community Energy Workbook.*

Ten minutes

3. Turning these ideas into local action

Briefly describe the Workbook framework as a way to increase community awareness of energy opportunities and to develop an energy action plan. Pass out copies of the planning overview from page 14, and discuss.

Ten minutes

4. Are people interested in launching a local effort?

Propose that your community pursue energy efficiency as an economic development tool. Ask participants if they and their organizations would be interested in joining a steering committee that leads the effort.

Twenty minutes

5. Preview first tasks and make assignments

After you have finished describing the following tasks and what is required to complete them, ask for volunteers.
- ➤ Form a subcommittee to complete the Energy Picture section.
- ➤ Take the Energy Picture results and talk to key community leaders and organizations. Find local organizations who can help sponsor the planning workshops and provide initial resources.
- ➤ Organize an outreach campaign, concluding with the Energy Town Meeting, the kick-off event for the planning workshops.

Five minutes

6. Wrap up and preview the next meeting

Ask attendees to ask their respective organizations to join the effort. Set a date for the next meeting to discuss support for the effort. Also set a date for the Energy Picture subcommittee to present its findings.

Set the Committee to Work

If you have held the first energy steering committee meeting and successfully recruited a variety of community interests to lead the effort, you've built the foundation for launching a successful planning process. This section outlines the steps the committee can take to get the rest of the community involved, put energy efficiency on the community agenda, and prepare to hold the planning workshops. The steering committee will need to meet regularly to prepare for and accomplish the following tasks.

FIRST STEERING COMMITTEE TASKS

➤ **Draw the Energy Picture**

➤ **Build support for the effort**

➤ **Line up resources**

Draw the Energy Picture

The first task for your steering committee will be to gather information on the local energy bill, its impact on the economy and the environment, and the economic benefits of more sustainable energy use. The Energy Picture section, page 37, provides the framework for gathering this information. Energy Picture results will be critical for generating news coverage of your efforts, persuading community leaders to support the planning process, and getting solid involvement in the energy task forces.

Since the steering committee has many responsibilities, recruiting several additional people to form a subcommittee to generate the Energy Picture will make the task easier. You may be able to recruit people to help from the following groups:

➤ Students and teachers
➤ Utility representatives
➤ Energy professionals, such as architects interested in sustainable design, electricians, and weatherizers.
➤ Economic / community development professionals, such as Cooperative Extension staff, Small Business Administration staff, and other local, state, or federal government staff working on development issues.

Ask potential volunteers if they would be interested in helping to determine the total local energy bill, examine its economic and environmental impacts, and explore the economic benefits of increased community energy efficiency.

Let potential volunteers know that developing the energy picture will be completed within a short time frame. Since developing the Energy Picture could sound quite daunting, also let them know that there are easy-to-use worksheets that will help the committee gather the information. Find someone who is willing to be the point person for developing the Energy Picture.

Refer to the Energy Picture section for specific directions on how to develop this energy and economic information. Make copies of the Energy Picture section for each person interested in helping to gather the information. Completing the entire Energy Picture section can be done in two to three weeks. Allow additional time to develop slides or other visual aids to assist in communicating the information at the Energy Town Meeting.

Build support for the effort

After the Energy Picture subcommittee has gathered the initial energy and economic information, the next step is using these facts to build support for the energy effort. There may be community leaders who do not have time to participate in the steering committee but whose support can make a difference in your success. These leaders can also provide advice and insight on how to make your effort as effective as possible. It's worth your time to inform each of them early on about what your group hopes to do, and to ask for their advice and support. These citizens may include:

➤ Former and current elected officials
➤ Local government staff
➤ Business leaders
➤ Citizen leaders active in community affairs and environmental issues
➤ Media representatives: reporters, news directors, editorial staff

Develop a list of a handful of these leaders and arrange for steering committee members to visit them one on one.

Briefly describe some of the energy and economic successes other communities have had, and point out the potential economic benefits of improving local energy use. Share a few Energy Picture summary numbers and potential economic benefits of increased energy efficiency. Describe how the steering committee wants to organize a series of community meetings and workshops to take advantage of these benefits in your town. Seek their advice with the following questions:

➤ What do they think of the idea?
➤ How would it work here?
➤ Who are the key people to get involved?
➤ Have there been any similar efforts in the past?
➤ Tell them that the first step will be to get sponsorship for the effort from local government or other organizations. Do they have any suggestions on how to secure sponsorship?

Line up resources

Holding an Energy Town Meeting and running the planning workshops will require resources such as a coordinator, facilitators, meeting spaces, writing materials, and postage. Having the resources on hand to make the workshops as effective and efficient as possible will make them more enjoyable and well-run, and will greatly enhance the success of your effort.

Ask some of the groups represented on the steering committee if they would be interested in providing some of the required resources including staff support, meeting spaces, and mailing privileges. The energy workshops will be most successful with the sponsorship of organizations such as the chamber of commerce, extension service, utilities, community foundations, schools, or local government.

Here's a list of the resources the steering committee will need to line up for the planning process. Since the Energy Town Meeting is the kick-off event for the planning effort, these resources will need to be in place by the time the event is held.

➤ **Coordinator**: The coordinator will ensure that the process stays on track, trouble-shoot problems, and support facilitators. The coordinator will make sure facilitators are prepared and in touch with the progress of the overall effort. Since this task is time-consuming, the effort will be more effective if there is a paid staff person to fulfill this role. The sponsoring organizations can be approached for either the funds to hire this person, or provide staffing as an in-kind contribution.

➤ **Workshop facilitators**: Each of the three task forces (which will be described later) needs a facilitator to run workshops. Facilitators do not need to be experts on energy or the economy. However, they should be experienced in conducting meetings and guiding a group through discussions and decisions. If you can't find experienced facilitators for each task force, other interested people can take advantage of this opportunity to gain practice in running meetings. Ask sponsoring organizations if they can contribute a staff person as a facilitator. Facilitators will need to prepare for workshops by reading all the workshop materials and reviewing the information on running the planning process in the appendix (see page 256). *The Facilitator's Guide*, available from Rocky Mountain Institute, is another helpful resource.

➤ **Workshop support staff**: The workshops will be most effective if each task force has access to staff who can type and send workshop results to participants to help them prepare for the next meeting. Since this task requires time and office equipment, the steering committee should enlist staff from an organization sponsoring the planning effort. Phone calls from this staff reminding task force members of upcoming workshops and events will significantly improve participation rates.

➤ **Meeting spaces:** You will need to find a large meeting hall for the Energy Town Meeting and appropriate meeting spaces for each task force to conduct their workshops.

➤ **Workshop materials:** Copies of worksheets and supporting materials, flip charts, markers and tape.

➤ **A small budget to cover postage and copying.**

Securing local government support

Securing local government endorsement and sponsorship of your energy planning effort is critical for improving the local energy picture. Since local government can determine building and land use practices, procurement and bidding policies, and building and operation standards for large public buildings, it can play a major role in improving the local energy picture over the long term. It can also play an important role in mobilizing the resources to implement the resulting action plan.

Developing solid local government support for the planning effort in the beginning will be far more effective than first developing a plan and later expecting government to promote and help implement it. Local government is often the most prepared to provide the financial support to hire a coordinator or allocate staff time to fulfill the coordinator, workshop facilitator, or other roles.

Here are a few tips on securing local government support for the energy effort:

➤ Make every aspect of your pitch organized and professional.

➤ Ask to meet with city or town managers before you pitch your proposal to elected officials. Managers often influence local government spending and priorities, and have insights on local decision-making. Find out the correct procedure for approaching officials with your presentation and request for support.

➤ Ask a supportive elected official for suggestions before making your official request to city council or county commissioners.

➤ Provide written, well-organized background information that concisely summarizes the local Energy Picture and the proposed planning process, along with potential benefits and results of pursuing a community-wide energy planning effort. Put your information into a problem/solution format that addresses the opportunities awaiting the community and local government by reducing the community energy bill. Use the energy picture information to discuss the economic impacts of energy use and refer to successes from other communities.

➤ Include a list of the resources (i.e., coordinator, facilitators, mailing privileges, etc.) required to make the effort a success.

➤ Emphasize the many different community interests represented by organizations promoting the effort.

➤ Collect sample yearly energy bills for several local government buildings or operations. Discuss how other local governments have made a commitment to increasing energy efficiency in public buildings and operations. Explain how the planning effort will help line up the resources to make energy improvements and help government lead by example.

➤ Offer a list of ways local government can help the effort be a success.

Checklist of resources to conduct the planning process

Resources and Staff Needed		Provider	Who / Where	Telephone
Workshop coordinator		_____		
Task force facilitators	Residential	_____		
	Commercial/Industrial	_____		
	Transportation	_____		
Support staff for task forces	Residential	_____		
	Commercial / Industrial	_____		
	Transportation	_____		
Operating expenses	Copying	_____		
	Postage	_____		
	Envelopes	_____		
Workshop supplies	Large flip charts	_____		
	Markers	_____		
	Worksheets	_____		
Meeting places for	Energy Town Meeting	_____		
	Residential Task Force	_____		
	Commercial / Industrial Task Force	_____		
	Transportation Task Force	_____		

Organize the Energy Town Meeting

You've worked to build the base for launching a community-wide energy and economic development effort. The next step: hold an Energy Town Meeting to inform the entire community of the effort and invite them to become involved. This section outlines the tasks the steering committee will need to carry out for this kick-off event. Subsequent workbook sections will provide more detailed information for carrying out these tasks.

ENERGY TOWN MEETING PLANNING

➤ **Logistics and materials**

➤ **Media and outreach campaign**

➤ **Program and presenters**

➤ **Optional energy-wise open house**

Prepare for the Energy Town Meeting

A successful Energy Town Meeting is informative, inspiring, and productive. The two-hour town meeting will:

➤ Present the local Energy Picture.

➤ Briefly share proven energy alternatives and community success stories.

➤ Offer a chance for citizens to improve the local energy and economic picture by asking them to join the energy task forces.

➤ Outline and begin energy planning steps.

The steering committee will need to meet to prepare for the Energy Town Meeting and divide responsibility for the following components of the event.

1. Logistics and materials (see below)
2. Media and outreach campaign (see below; mobilizing section, page 85)
3. Program and presenters (page 34)
4. Optional energy open house (page 35)

1. Logistics and materials

Set your meeting date and time so it doesn't conflict with other important events or regularly scheduled meetings. Allow enough planning time to thoroughly organize the event. See the sample media / organizing calendar on page 101 to get an idea of the time required.

Reserve a public meeting space that can accommodate the anticipated number of participants. Since the meeting will break into subgroups, be sure there is enough space for them to meet comfortably, either in nearby rooms, or in opposite corners of a large room. If you have an energy open house find a room that can accommodate both display/exhibitor tables and work areas for participants.

Materials needed:

➤ Sign in sheet with space for names, addresses and phone numbers

➤ Energy picture visual props (See the Energy Picture section)

➤ Large easel pads/flip charts for each task force

➤ Colored markers for each task force

➤ Meeting agendas

➤ Task force materials: participant planning workshop overview (page 115) and copies of task force packets.

2. Media and outreach campaign

The Energy Town Meeting offers an opportunity to conduct a full-scale energy outreach campaign. Referring to pages 85-101, a media subcommittee can develop an outreach strategy that will take the community by storm. In addition to raising general awareness, the goal of the outreach campaign is to put energy on the community agenda and pack the Energy Town Meeting room with interested citizens.

3. Program and presenters

The program and presenters subcommittee can refer to pages 103-107 for a sample meeting agenda and outlines for presenters.

While the agenda presented offers a logical way to present key information required for launching the workshops, you will need to tailor it to your community and find ways to make the meeting as interesting as possible. Involving local "celebrities" can add some interest, while finding a role for elected officials and other influential citizens will draw them into the effort and increase their support.

To produce an enjoyable and effective meeting, all presenters should meet at least a week before the meeting to rehearse presentations. Although most people will be very busy and feel this is unnecessary, it will make the difference between a long, boring meeting and a crisp, succinct performance. Establish firm time limits and have presenters run through their presentations to trim them to the allocated time. A meeting that drags on and on will sap all the interest and enthusiasm the steering committee has worked so hard to create.

4. The energy-wise open house (see page 35)

You can increase both turnout and effectiveness at the Energy Town Meeting with an energy-wise open house that showcases locally available energy-wise goods and services. While the open house is an optional part of the Energy Town Meeting, it's well worth the effort. Linking the meeting with energy-smart businesses, free information and local energy experts will make energy efficiency possibilities more tangible and inspiring. The open house can start an hour before the Energy Town Meeting.

5. Entertainment and contests

Another way to build attendance at the Energy Town Meeting and to make it more enjoyable is to provide entertainment such as live music during the open house. Holding a special event, like a race between non-gasoline powered vehicles (see page 99) to publicize the meeting will attract media coverage and build interest. Giving out awards at the meeting to local organizations, individuals, and businesses for energy successes will also increase attendance.

Optional energy-wise open house

Designate an open house coordinator and recruit additional volunteers to help with organizing.

Search the phone book for local energy-related businesses and organizations to invite to participate. Encourage these businesses to bring product samples and displays. Since these businesses can benefit financially from the open house, it is not inappropriate to ask them to pay a small display space fee.

Approach the following to attend:

➤ Retail outlets of weatherization materials, efficient light bulbs and fixtures, and other energy-smart products.

➤ All local utilities.

➤ Book stores which can display books on home energy savings, green architecture, and energy issues.

➤ Insulation companies.

➤ Recycling organizations/companies.

➤ Solar equipment and installation companies.

➤ Architects, contractors and builders.

➤ Public transportation representatives.

➤ Bicycle shops, alternative transportation advocates

➤ The state energy office.

➤ Any other organizations offering energy education, products or services.

To avoid logistical nightmares, make sure you have spaces reserved for participants and have arranged for any necessary equipment such as extension cords.

Ask sponsoring organizations to donate refreshments. If they can't, include food in your funding request to local government. Refreshments are an added draw and encourage people to linger.

If your community lacks local outlets for either efficient or renewable technologies:

➤ Contact the resources listed in this book (starting page 243) for brochures, publications, and videos.

➤ Order sample efficient light bulbs and efficient shower heads and make a display. Include posters on how much energy they save.

➤ Contact relevant companies in other parts of the state and see if they'd like to participate.

➤ Ask school science classes to prepare visual displays on sustainable energy topics.

Find ways to have fun

• **Organize a poster contest at local schools and display students' work at the open house.**

• **Ask local musicians to perform.**

• **Raffle off energy-efficient door prizes.**

• **Give rides in alternatively powered vehicles.**

• **Arrange hands-on demonstrations of solar water heaters and ovens, water-efficient shower heads, and efficient lighting.**

Drawing the Local Energy Picture

This section offers materials to create a profile of local energy use and its

impact on the economy and the environment. It also offers a way to sample

the economic benefits of community energy efficiency.

Directions and Background Information

How much does local energy use drain your community's economy? What are the hidden costs of this use? What are the economic benefits from using energy more efficiently? The energy picture section will help answer these questions, and put this information into a meaningful context for other citizens.

TO GET STARTED

➤ **General directions**

➤ **Energy Picture Summary forms**
    (to be filled in as you work through subsequent
    Energy Picture sections.)

➤ **How is energy measured?**

➤ **What kinds of utilities serve your community?**

➤ **What role will your utility play?**

The energy picture you develop using this workbook will estimate total local energy consumption and costs based on such numbers as utility energy sales and the number of registered local motor vehicles. Professionals use a similar method to develop community energy profiles. The figures resulting from this section won't be exact, but they'll demonstrate the magnitude of local energy costs and the potential for community-wide savings. At some point, your group may be interested in performing a more detailed analysis of the economic opportunities of community energy saving programs. Resources for performing such an analysis are listed on page 82.

General directions

1. Form a small group to share the task of developing the local Energy Picture. Volunteers from the energy steering committee can head this group and ask other community members to join them. This task is an ideal way to involve high school or college students. Ask teachers, professors, or student groups if they can help. A class could easily develop the Energy Picture as a school research project.

2. Designate a point person to keep track of what information each Energy Picture volunteer is gathering and to make sure the entire process is conducted in an organized manner.

3. Have all participants meet and review the Energy Picture steps. Provide participants with copies of the Energy Picture worksheets, starting on page 41.

4. To begin gathering information your group will need to make two decisions:

   A. Decide the boundaries of what you consider your community and keep your information geographically consistent. Are you considering only your town or the entire county? Sometimes information will be available for the county but not for your individual community; but there are ways to estimate municipal figures using available county information. Make your decision by determining what information would be most useful to the energy committee and the planning effort, and what will be the most feasible to find.

   B. Decide what year you will study. You will need to collect information for the last full year for which there are available figures. This will be your base year. Don't expect perfection here. It may be impossible to get every single piece of information for a given year.

5. Everyone enters the study year and study area on their copy of the energy picture summary forms, pages 41-43. Make sure everyone is using the same study year and study area when gathering information.

6. To start, focus on figuring the local energy bill. Divide up the information-gathering among participants. To avoid duplicating efforts or having several people calling the same place, you can divide things up into these categories:
   ➤ Population and total personal income
   ➤ Electricity information
   ➤ Natural gas information

Energy Picture steps

1. **Form the Energy Picture group.**
2. **Designate a point person.**
3. **Meet and review materials.**
4. **Determine study year and study area.**
5. **Divide tasks and complete the local energy bill section.**
6. **Meet and combine energy bill information.**
7. **Move on to the remaining sections, dividing tasks.**
8. **Summarize information.**
9. **Present findings to the entire energy steering committee.**
10. **Create energy picture presentation materials: large displays, charts, graphics, or slides.**

➤ Renewable energy information
➤ Other fuels: propane, heating oil, etc.
➤ Transportation fuel information
➤ Sample transportation fuel costs

7. Set a time for information gatherers to meet after they have gathered the initial energy information. At this meeting information gatherers will complete the energy bill section and move on to the remaining sections.

8. Allow at least three weeks to gather the energy information and complete the Energy Picture worksheets. The information required for this step should be readily available from the sources listed. But allow for delays, and allow at least another two weeks to create the Energy Picture presentation.

9. Make a presentation of the Energy Picture findings to the energy steering committee. See if they have suggestions for any additional information the Energy Picture subcommittee might want to pursue.

10. Develop visual prop to communicate Energy Picture findings at the Energy Town Meeting.

Where to find population and total personal income figures:
   After your group has determined the study year and study area someone can gather two pieces of information: **population** and **total personal income**

   ➤ To get population figures, call your local or county government. The clerk's office should have these figures. If they don't have them readily available, you can call your state government and ask for the office that deals with demographics.

   ➤ *Total personal income* is a statistic that measures the combined income (before taxes) received by all area residents from all sources (wages, salaries, rents, pensions, dividends, etc.) in a calendar year. Ask your local government for your community's total personal income for your study year. If your local government cannot readily provide you with this figure, contact the state local affairs or demographics offices. If this figure is unavailable for the year of your study, ask for an estimate based on the most recent census.

Energy Picture Summary:
Energy used by sector and energy type

As you collect your Energy Picture information, use these charts to summarize your findings for easy reference later on. The Local Energy Bill section starting on page 54 will help you fill in each blank.

Year of study _____ Area of study _____ Population of study area _____

Energy used by sector and energy type in millions of Btu

	electricity	natural gas	petroleum	other	Sector Total	Sector % of total
Residential						
Commercial						
Industrial						
Transportation						
Energy Type Total						
Energy Type % of Total						

Energy used by sector and energy type in dollars

	electricity	natural gas	petroleum	other	Sector Total	Sector % of total
Residential						
Commercial						
Industrial						
Transportation						
Energy Type Total						
Energy Type % of Total						

Energy Picture Summary:
Economic impacts and sample benefits

As you collect your Energy Picture information, summarize your findings for easy reference. Pages 62-69 and 76-82 will help you fill in information for the blanks below.

Year of study _____ Area of study _____ Population of study area _____

Economic impacts of local energy use

Total local energy bill _____

Local per capita share of the energy bill _____

Energy costs as a percentage of community's total personal income _____

# of work days to Energy Freedom _____

Energy Freedom Day _____

Interesting findings / comparisons _____

- -

Sample economic benefits from energy efficiency

If local schools increased energy efficiency by 20%, how much money would be available for other needs? _____

If local government increased energy efficiency by 20%, how much money would be available for other needs? _____

Sample 20% savings for several local businesses _____

How much additional money would your community have if it cut community energy costs by 10%? 20%? _____

_____

Note: When this saved money will be available will depend on length of paybacks and the financing methods used to make the initial efficiency investments. See the task force packets sections on finance for more information.

Energy Picture Summary:
Environmental costs

As you collect your Energy Picture information, summarize your findings for easy reference. Pages 70-75 will help you fill in information for the blanks below.

Year of study _____ Area of study _____ Population of study area _____

What's the original fuel source for your community's electricity supply? What are the environmental problems associated with these sources?

Primary source	Percentage of total mix	Pollution, wastes, and other environmental problems created by these sources of electricity:
Coal		
Nuclear		
Natural gas		
Hydropower		
Oil		
Wind / solar		
Efficiency		
Other		

Community contribution to climate change

Local CO_2 bill from energy use _____ lbs. CO_2

Environmental costs of local transportation fuel bill

How is energy measured?

As you find out how much energy your community uses, you will come across units such as kilowatt-hours (kWh), British thermal units (Btu), thousand cubic feet (mcf) and therms. You don't need to be an expert on these terms to gather your information, but, for the curious, here's an explanation of energy measurement units.

Measuring electricity

Electricity is commonly measured in watts and watt-hours. Watts describe the rate at which energy is being consumed or produced at a given moment; for instance, the power output of a generating plant, or the amount of energy a 100-watt light bulb draws at any given moment. Watts are used for ratings, as in "60-watt lightbulb".

Watt-*hours* measure the total amount of energy consumed or produced over time. This total is determined by the power consumption rate (watts) and how long the power is used. For example, a 100-watt bulb draws 100 watts. In one hour it uses 100 watt-hours. Since electricity is used for periods of time, measurements of electricity consumption are always in watt-hours.

One way to understand the difference between watts and watt-hours is to think of the distinction between miles per hour and miles traveled. Similar to mph, watts are a measurement of rate, while watt-hours, similar to number of miles traveled, measure a total amount.

Watts, kilos, megas, and gigas: What are they for?

> Watts and watt-hours are useful for describing small amounts of electricity, such as that used by lightbulbs or a radio.

> In describing more energy-consumptive appliances such as refrigerators and water heaters, kilowatts and kilowatt-hours are useful. One Kilowatt (kW) is 1,000 watts; one kilowatt-hour (kWh) is 1,000 watts consumed or produced in one hour.

> Measuring the output of power plants or the electricity required by an entire town requires a larger unit— the megawatt. One megawatt (MW) is 1,000,000 watts or 1,000 kilowatts. The average size of U.S. power plants is 213 MW.

> Gigawatts (GW) are useful for measuring the capacity of large power plants, or many power plants. A gigawatt is 1,000 megawatts, or 1 billion watts. The total generating capacity of all electric utilities in the U.S. in 1990 was 690 GW.

Efficiency generates kWh

- Currently, the 125 million refrigerators and freezers in U.S. homes require the entire output of 43 large power plants. If the current stock of refrigerators was replaced with the newest efficient models, it would be possible to eliminate almost 20 power plants.

- If all federally-owned and operated buildings made efficiency improvements in their lighting systems we could save 5000 GigaWatt-hours, which is enough electricity to power half a million average households for a year.

Measuring natural gas

Natural gas is measured either by volume (cubic feet) or by heat content (therms). Some gas companies use cubic feet (a box one foot high, one foot wide and one foot deep) as the standard measurement. Since a cubic foot of gas is not really very much, quantities are given in the hundreds ("Ccf") or thousands ("Mcf") of cubic feet. Some of you may wonder why this thousand isn't "k" like in kilowatt (kW). These volume measurements are using Latin roots: "mille," meaning one thousand (m), and "centi" meaning hundred (c). Kilo, mega, and giga are Greek roots.

Gas companies are increasingly switching to therms as the standard measurement because heat content is a more accurate way of quantifying amounts of natural gas. The amount of gas in a cubic foot will vary with temperature and pressure, and natural gas from various wells will vary in quality. A therm is defined as 100,000 Btu. One hundred cubic feet of natural gas, on average, is roughly equivalent to one therm.

The Btu

Each kind of fuel has a measurable amount of heat energy stored within. To compare or add up different kinds of energy sources, it's useful to convert to the energy industry's common unit, the British thermal unit.

➤ 1 Btu = the amount of energy required to increase the temperature of one lb. of water (one pint) by one degree Fahrenheit, or the heat produced from burning one match.

➤ 1,000 Btu = four-fifths of the energy contained in a peanut butter and jelly sandwich, or 250 calories.

➤ 100,000 Btu = one therm, or the energy of 80 peanut butter and jelly sandwiches.

➤ 1 million Btu(Mbtu) = 1.1 days of U.S. per capita energy consumption. Since 1 btu is not very much, energy usage is often measured in millions of Btu.

➤ 277 million Btu = U.S. per capita energy consumption, 1990.

➤ 23 million Btu = Chinese per capita energy consumption, 1990.

➤ 130 million Btu = Danish per capita energy consumption, 1990.

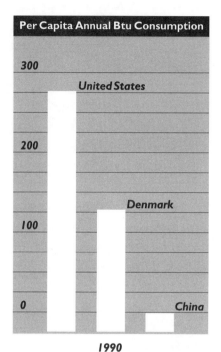

Per Capita Annual Btu Consumption

1990
(in million Btu)

CONVERTING INTO BTU		
To convert	**Multiply by**	**Equivalent Btu**
kWh electricity	3,413	
Mcf natural gas	1, 030,000	
Therms of natural gas	100,000	
Gallons of gasoline	125,000	
Cords of wood	14,000,000	
Gallons of propane	91,000	

What kinds of utilities serve your community?

The type of electric utility that serves your community, and the conditions under which it operates, will influence the role it plays in your energy and economic development effort. Below is a brief summary of the kinds of utilities that serve the U.S. Page 48 summarizes some of the circumstances that might affect your utility's role in an aggressive community energy-efficiency and renewables program.

There are 3200 utilities in the United States, and they come in four forms[1]. In 1990 there were:

267 for-profit, investor-owned utilities;

2011 publicly owned, municipal utilities;

953 cooperative systems;

10 federal power agencies.

As you gather your energy picture information, take note of the types of utilities serving your community. You can record this information on the energy suppliers form on page 55. To find out more about your utility and the conditions under which it operates, be sure to also talk to utility staff directly, and involve them early in your effort.

Investor-owned utilities

Like all private businesses, the objective of an investor-owned utility is to produce dividends for owners or shareholders and produce funds for reinvestment. Investor-owned utilities are regulated by state utility commissions, and generate and distribute more than 75 percent of all U.S. electricity. They operate in all states except Nebraska and are most common in cities and on both coasts. Several states have changed utility regulations so investor-owned utilities can profit by selling efficiency. Call your state energy office or Public Utilities Commission to find out if your state has these regulatory incentives.

Publicly owned utilities, or municipal utilities

"Munis" are nonprofit, local government agencies that usually serve customers at cost and return any excess funds to the community. Publicly owned utilities distribute about 14% of the nation's electricity. Most municipal utilities distribute, but don't produce power, although some larger ones also produce electricity. They obtain their financing from municipal funds and from revenue bonds secured by electricity sale proceeds. Some municipal utilities make a profit on power sales, and this money is used to fund other municipal programs. A 1992 survey of demand-side management (DSM) in public power found that less than half of the responding public utilities operate DSM programs (American Public Power Association, January 1992).

An Energy-Wise Muni

California's Sacramento Municipal Utility District is taking energy-efficiency measures to their full potential. SMUD plans to save 800 MW of capacity by the year 2000 through residential, commercial, and industrial efficiency improvements that target air conditioning, refrigeration and lighting. In 1994 SMUD budgeted about 8% of their $689 million operating revenues for efficiency programs. SMUD also plans to generate 400 MW from renewable programs, which include installing photovoltaic panels and 20,000 solar domestic water heaters on customers' homes by the year 2000.

Cooperative electric utilities

Cooperatives are owned by their members and are established to serve those members. Cooperative electric associations operate mostly in rural areas, distribute seven percent of the nation's electricity to 10.5 percent of the population, but serve nearly three fourths of the land area in the U.S. Cooperative utilities are generally governed by a locally elected board, and are funded by the Rural Electrification Administration, the National Rural Utilities Cooperative Finance Corporation, the Federal Financing Bank, and the Bank for Cooperatives, as well as their consumer owners. Rural cooperatives often own their own generating capacity.

Federal electric utilities

Federally operated utilities primarily produce and sell electricity wholesale to publicly owned and cooperative electric utilities and other nonprofit entities, as required by law. Power is generated by federally-owned power plants and marketed by federal power marketing administrations, such as Bonneville, Southeastern, Southwestern, Western Area, and Alaska. The federal power marketing administrations operate in all states except those in the Northeast, upper Midwest, and Hawaii. All federal power administrations have efficiency and renewable programs. If the utility serving your community buys power from a federal power administration it may have access to federally-provided technical assistance for designing energy efficiency programs. See page 51 for additional information.

Gas utilities

Most gas utilities are private companies which purchase natural gas from wholesale suppliers. Sometimes municipal electric utilities also sell natural gas to their customers, which makes it easier to design energy efficiency programs that affect both electricity and natural gas. There are currently over 1200 natural gas companies around the country, counting large transmission companies, local distribution companies, and municipals. In most states gas companies are regulated by the state utility commissions. Gas companies are just beginning to explore demand-side management supply options.

Source for description of utilities: Electric Power Annual 1990. For more information on energy statistics and other Energy Information Administration(EIA) publications, contact EIA's National Energy Information Center at (202) 586-8800 or write them at: National Information Center, Energy Information Administration, U.S. Department of Energy, Forrestal Building, Washington, D.C. 20585.

Co-op taps efficiency

Vermont's Washington Electric Co-op Inc. (WEC) expanded its power options by offering efficiency services to homes, businesses, schools and dairies. The co-op's demand-side management program, Efficiency Saves, offers information, audits, and financing. The program installs measures only if both customers and the utility save money and power. In some cases, the utility pays the whole cost of efficiency measures. WEC also offers incentives and assistance for efficient new residential and commercial construction.

What role will your utility play?

While spending less on energy makes economic sense for businesses and residences, your utility may or may not see that promoting efficiency and other sustainable energy practices is in their best interest. Some utilities operate under conditions where there is a great deal of incentive to support efforts to reduce energy demand. Others may operate under conditions, or have characteristics, that will make them less interested in, an aggressive community effort to increase energy efficiency and use of renewable power sources.

To find out how energy efficiency and renewable energy fits into your utility's priorities, see if you can find answers to the following two sets of questions.

1. If the answer is yes to any of the following questions your utility will probably be interested in being a partner early on in your energy and economic development effort:

➤ If your utility is regulated, has your state changed the rules by which utilities operate so that they can profit by selling efficiency? Are they rewarded for helping customers use energy more efficiently?

➤ Is there a pending need for a new source of power for the utility?

➤ Does the utility lack its own generating capacity, and must it buy its power from another supplier? How much must the utility pay for this power?

➤ Do the utility's leaders see demand-side management as a low-risk, low-cost source of power?

➤ Will the utility be required to develop an integrated resource plan (IRP)? Are there public participation requirements for developing this IRP?

➤ Is the utility a participant in the U.S. DOE/EPA Climate-Wise Pledge program? This program is designed to encourage voluntary emissions reductions under the Climate Change Action Plan. Call your regional DOE office (see page 253) for information.

2. If the answer is yes to any of this next set of questions, your utility faces disincentives for aggressively pursuing energy efficiency or renewable sources.

➤ If the utility owns its own generating capacity, does the utility currently have surplus power?

➤ Do the utility's leaders believe that selling less electricity will only decrease revenues and hurt the utility financially?

➤ If the utility is municipally owned, are utility sales a revenue source for other government expenses?

IRP creates incentives

An increasing number of utilities are required to develop "Integrated Resource Plans" (IRP's). IRP is a method of utility planning that weighs all options to provide energy services at the lowest total cost. This means that energy-efficient and renewable must be considered along with conventional power sources as part of the overall power mix. Both the National Energy Policy Act of 1992 and the Climate Change Action Plan include the goal of increased use of IRP. Some utilities are required to develop IRP's by their state, others must develop IRP's in order to continue to buy federally produced power. Public participation plays a critical role in helping utilities better analyze all supply options.

➤ Does the utility's wholesaler reward the utility for buying more power? For instance, does the utility get bulk rate prices, and if it decreases the amount bought, do unit costs increase?

➤ Are the utility's leaders skeptical of the results of demand-side management? Is it seen as ineffective or administratively inconvenient?

➤ If the utility is regulated, does your state still reward utilities for selling more power, and reduce their profit if they sell less?

➤ Does the utility report to a principal financing agency that views the utility's mission as promoting the increased use of electricity?

If the utility serving your community faces some of these disincentives, utility decision makers may not at first see how promoting energy efficiency or use of renewable sources is in the utility's best interest. Your community-based planning effort can be an effective means for removing some of these disincentives and for demonstrating how investing in efficiency and renewables can in fact serve the utility's needs.

If your utility needs examples of how other utilities are making efficiency and renewables work for them, listed below are a few organizations that can serve as resources. Some of these organizations can also assist you in demonstrating how efficiency and renewables can be a cost-effective power supply option for the utility.

Regional utility reform efforts

While you are working to increase use of energy efficiency and renewables at the community level, many groups are also working to change utility energy policy at the state, regional and national level. Contact the groups that are working in your region to encourage utility energy efficiency and renewable programs. Let them know about what you are doing at the local level and ask if they have any information that would be useful for your efforts. Below is a listing of 18 organizations that are involved in regional utility reform efforts. The states in parentheses are where the organization is focusing its efforts. If your region is not included in this listing, call the organizations working in nearby regions. They may be aware of similar efforts in your area.

Competing for customers?

One of the hottest debates in the utility industry involves the concept of competition for utility customers. Currently, utilities serving designated regions and customers cannot choose where they buy their power. Advocates of competition are proposing that the utility industry be restructured to allow large industrial customers to choose their source of electricity. Others maintain that the concept of competition will benefit customers and utilities only if performance criteria and ground rules are established to guide such a competitive environment.

Natural Resources Defense Council (CA)

Suite 1825

71 Stevenson Street

San Francisco, CA 94105

(415) 777-0220

Fax (415) 495-5996

Center for Energy Efficiency and Renewable Technologies (CA)

Suite 311

1100 11th Street

Sacramento, CA 95814

(916) 442-7785

Fax (916) 447-2940

Northwest Conservation Act Coalition (WA, OR, MT, ID)
Suite 1020
217 Pine Street
Seattle, WA 98101-1520
(206) 621-0094
Fax (206) 621-0097

Land and Water Fund of the Rockies (CO, NM, AZ, NV)
Suite 200
2260 Baseline Road
Boulder, CO 80302-7740
(303) 444-1188
Fax (303) 786-8054

Environmental Defense Fund-Texas (TX)
Suite A
1800 Guadalupe
Austin, TX 78701
(512) 478-5161
Fax (512) 478-8140

Citizens Energy Coalition Education (IN)
Suite 300
3951 N Meridian Street
Indianapolis, IN 46208
(317) 921-1120
Fax (317) 921- 1143

Izaak Walton League of America (MN, IO)
Suite 317
5701 Normandale Road
Minneapolis, MN 55424
(612) 922-1608
Fax (612) 922-0240

Minnesotans for an Energy-Efficient Economy
1916 Second Avenue South
Minneapolis, MN 55403
(612) 872-3295
Fax (612) 870-0729

Michigan United Conservation Clubs (MI)
PO Box 30235
2101 Wood Street
Lansing, MI 48090
(517) 371-1041
Fax (517) 371-1505

Center for Clean Air Policy (OH)
Suite 602
444 North Capitol Street
Washington, DC 20001
(202) 624-7709
Fax (202) 508-3829

Campaign for an Energy Efficient Ohio (OH)
Suite 120
400 Dublin Avenue
Columbus, OH 43215
(614) 224-4900
Fax: (614) 224-5914

Tennessee Valley Energy Reform (TVA states)
PO Box 8290
Knoxville, TN 37996
(615) 637-6055
Fax (615) 546-4479

Conservation Law Foundation of New England (MA, CT, VT, NH, RI)
62 Summer Street
Boston, MA 02108-1497
(617) 350-0990
Fax (617) 350-4030

Southern Environmental Law Center (GA, VA, NC)
Suite 14
201 W Main Street
Charlottesville, VA 22902-5065
(804) 977-4090
Fax (804) 977-1483

Legal Environmental Assistance (FL)
1115 North Gadsden Street
Tallahassee, FL 32303-6327
(904) 681-2591
Fax (904) 224- 1275

Pace University Energy Project (NY, FL, MI)
78 North Broadway
White Plains, NY 10603
(914) 422-4324
Fax (914) 422-4180

Alliance for Affordable Energy (LA)
604 Julia Street
New Orleans, LA 70130
(504) 525-0778
Fax (504) 525-0779

Federal power marketing administrations

Federal Power Marketing Administrations offer a variety of technical assistance and efficiency programs to the utilities that buy power from them. For example, the Western Area Power Administration (Western) loans its members infrared heat detection unites (for surveys of heat leaks from buildings), load management equipment, a toll-free hotline, workshops, and a peer-matching program which links interested utilities with those with successful efficiency programs. Bonneville Power Administration also offers a very wide range of programs to develop energy efficiency as a power source. Find out if your utility buys power from a federal power administration and see if they are taking advantage of resources for increasing energy efficiency and use of renewable energy.

Alaska Power Administration
Suite 2B
2770 Sherwood Lane
Juneau, AK 99801-8545
(907) 586-7405

Bonneville Power Administration
PO Box 3621
Portland, OR 97208
(503) 230-5101

Southeastern Power Administration
Samuel Elbert Building
Elberton, GA 30635-2496
(404) 283-9911

Southwestern Power Administration
PO Box 1619
Tulsa, OK 74101
(918) 581-7476

Western Area Power Administration
PO Box 3402
1627 Cole Boulevard
Golden, CO 80401
(303) 231-1513

Resources for utility sustainable energy programs

A variety of utility associations and information resource centers offer publications and training to both members and nonmembers. Find out if your utility is taking full advantage of services and publications for encouraging efficiency and renewable programs.

American Council for an Energy Efficient Economy (ACEEE)

Suite 801

1001 Connecticut Avenue NW

Washington DC 20036

(202) 429-8873

Fax (202) 429-2248

email Liz Burke%ccmail@pnl.gov

ACEEE has an extensive list of publications that examine effective utility energy efficiency programs and demand- side management techniques.

American Gas Association (AGA)

1515 Wilson Blvd.

Arlington, VA 22209

(703) 841-8400

AGA is composed of more than 250 gas utility and pipeline companies, accounting for over 90 percent of all gas delivered by the regulated gas industry in the U.S. AGA acts as a clearinghouse for gas energy information, educational materials, and publications on a variety of aspects of the gas industry.

American Public Power Association

2301 M Street, NW

Washington, DC 20037-1484

(202) 467-2900

APPA programs help publicly owned utilities *without* DSM experience to initiate cost-effective programs and aid publicly-owned utilities *with* DSM experience to expand cost-effective programs. APPA provides technical and program information on DSM management, publishes a variety of periodicals, conducts conferences/workshops and utility education courses.

Association of Demand-Side Management Professionals (ADSMP)

Suite 2315

7040 West Palmetto Park Road

Boca Raton, FL 33433

(407) 361-0023

Fax (407) 361-0027

ADSMP is an organization dedicated to the advancement of the Demand-Side Management Profession through the exchange of ideas, information and support on issues affecting demand-side management. Membership in ADSMP is necessary to gain access to its many services: a quarterly newsletter, an annual "yellow pages" of DSM professionals; training courses in DSM, and ADSMP publications.

Edison Electric Institute (EEI)

1111 Nineteenth Street, NW

Washington, DC 20036

(202) 828-7400

EEI is the trade association of investor-owned electric utilities, and provides information on energy efficiency, including a monthly newsletter, the magazine Electric Perspectives, and computerized services.

National Rural Electric Cooperative Association (NRECA)

1800 Massachusetts Avenue, NW
Washington, DC 20036
(202) 857-9500

NRECA offers management institutes, training and consulting services, women's and youth programs, and energy-efficiency campaigns. NRECA publishes the Rural Electric Newsletter 40 times a year, and the Rural Electrification Magazine monthly.

Electric Power Research Institute (EPRI)

3412 Hillview Avenue
Palo Alto, CA 94304
(415) 855-2000

EPRI provides information on all sectors of the electric utility industry, including a computerized data base of summaries of ongoing and completed research in the electric power industry. The Demand-Side Information Service data base encompasses end-use planning and high-efficiency heating and cooling equipment.

E source, Inc.

1050 Walnut Street
Boulder, CO 80302-5140
(303) 440-8500

E-Source is an information service providing up-to-date, comprehensive, independent information on the most efficient ways to use electricity. E-Source clients include utilities, government agencies, energy users, consultants, research institutions, and other organizations from around the world. E-Source services include a bimonthly newsletter, Strategic Issues Papers, comprehensive State of the Art manuals on energy efficiency techniques, and a yearly members' forum. Services are available through a membership subscription.

The Results Center

PO Box 10990
Aspen, CO 81612-9689
(970) 927-3155

The Results Center has over 100 profiles of the most effective energy efficiency programs in North America and Europe. Each profile includes background on program design, implementation, monitoring, evaluation, program cost, and lessons learned. Profiles are available through a subscription arrangement.

The Local Energy Bill

The following pages can be used to find out how much energy your community uses. You can also use these pages to find out how much electricity, natural gas, and other fuels each energy sector in your community uses in a given year.

Behind the scenes...

The Community Energy Bill you will develop in this section is based on end-use energy consumption. Because there are large energy losses during production, transmission, and distribution of electricity, the actual energy used by a community is greater than these numbers will convey. For every unit of end-use electricity, there are typically 3.2 units of primary energy consumed to make that energy available to local homes and businesses.

TO DEVELOP ENERGY BILL NUMBERS

➤ **Collect energy use figures from local suppliers**

➤ **Add up what each supplier sells to each sector**

➤ **Add up each energy type used**

➤ **Develop a transportation fuel use estimate**

➤ **Add figures together for the community energy bill**

Collect energy use figures from local suppliers

Using page 55, identify the natural gas and electric utilities that serve your community. Also identify other fuel suppliers, such as heating oil and propane companies, or wood providers. You can consult the yellow pages or ask local government which utilities and fuel suppliers serve your community.

Call each supplier and explain that you want to calculate local energy use, for a given year, in the residential, commercial, and industrial sectors in your study area. These three sectors are the most common categories of energy use. Include additional categories if your utility has records on them. Using the energy suppliers form to record your findings, ask the following questions:

➤ How much energy was sold to each sector for your study year? Ask for the amount in both the energy unit the utility uses, and in millions of Btu, so you can compare different quantities of varying energy types. If the utility is unable to give you the amount in Btu, you can use the conversion numbers on page 45.

➤ What was the total dollar amount of sales made to each sector during the study year?

➤ Some utilities may not record the energy they sell using the same boundaries that your group wishes to use. In this case, work with the utility to develop estimates of what they sell to your study area.

Energy sold by suppliers to your community

This form is for gathering information on energy sold to the residential, commercial and industrial sectors. Transportation information will be gathered using page 58. Make copies of this form if needed.

Study year _____ Geographic area of study _____

Amount sold per sector

Energy supplier _____

	kWh, therms, gallons, cords, etc.	MBtu	$
Contact person _____

Phone _____ Residential _____

Contact Date _____ Commercial _____

Energy supplied _____ Industrial _____

Type of utility _____ Other _____

Comments _____

- -

Amount sold per sector

Energy supplier _____

	kWh, therms, gallons, cords, etc.	MBtu	$
Contact person _____

Phone _____ Residential _____

Contact Date _____ Commercial _____

Energy supplied _____ Industrial _____

Type of utility _____ Other _____

Comments _____

Add up sector totals

To organize your numbers into energy end-use sectors, transfer page 55 results to the spaces below. If your study area has more than one supplier for each energy type, be sure to add up the amounts from each utility for each sector.

Residential	Amount	MBtu	$
kWh electricity			
mcf / therms natural gas			
Other (specify)			
Residential Total			

Commercial	Amount	MBtu	$
kWh electricity			
mcf / therms natural gas			
Other (specify)			
Commercial Total			

Industrial	Amount	MBtu	$
kWh electricity			
mcf / therms natural gas			
Other (specify)			
Industrial Total			

If there are additional categories that your utility tracks, such as agriculture, mining, and street lights, add those numbers up as well. It may make your task easier if you assign any additional categories to either the commercial or industrial sectors.

Add up each type of energy used

To find out how much total electricity, natural gas and other fuel (heating oil, wood, propane, etc.) is used, transfer the information gathered on page 55 according to type of energy. Make copies of this form as needed.

Electricity	kWh	Btu	$	% of total kWh
Residential				
Commercial				
Industrial				
Total				100%

Natural Gas	mcf	Btu	$	% of total mcf
Residential				
Commercial				
Industrial				
Total				100%

Other		Btu	$	% of total other
Residential				
Commercial				
Industrial				
Total				100%

Develop a transportation fuel use estimate

Record the information you gather in the steps below in the appropriate spaces on the transportation fuel summary sheet.

Before you start, check with planning staff in your area to see if a local transportation study has been conducted in the last several years. If one exists, be sure to get a copy since it may help you gather some of the following information.

1 Get an estimate of the number of vehicles in your area of study

The easiest way to estimate the number of local vehicles is to call the county clerk and ask for the number of registrations for your study area and year. Record that number on the transportation summary sheet, page 59 (see note below).

2 Find the average annual gallons consumed per vehicle

Check the Table on page 60 for the average number of gallons consumed by a vehicle in your state. If you have more exact information on how much fuel local vehicles consume in a year, use it instead. Otherwise, the estimates in this table provide acceptable numbers to work with, since driving patterns and fuel efficiency change slowly. Record the average gallons consumed in the appropriate spot.

3 Find the average price of a gallon of gas

Find the average price of a gallon of gas during your study year. Call several local gas stations and ask if they can tell you the average cost of a gallon of gas during your study year. If you can't get satisfactory numbers this way, try the Chamber of Commerce, local newspapers, or an automobile association.

4 Complete the calculations on page 59.

Optional: Gather transportation fuel costs from available vehicle and fuel records

Call the school district, local government, public transit agencies and other organizations with vehicle fleets and see if they can share their fuel cost records. Ask for the number of vehicles they have, total gallons of fuel consumed, and average cost per gallon during the year of your analysis. These numbers will make it easier to target specific areas where transportation fuel costs could be cut. You can also find out how much fuel is used for airports, freight, and water-based travel.

Record this information on the page 59 and calculate your fuel costs.

Optional: Gather information on use of alternative fuels

Call local governments, local fuel suppliers, and your state energy office to find out what kind of alternative fuels (ethanol, natural gas, propane, etc.) are used in your area.

Note: If the county clerk's office cannot give you figures corresponding to your study area (i.e., you are estimating the total energy bill of your town rather than the county, and no breakdown of municipal vehicle registrations is available from the clerk's office) you can approximate the number of vehicle registrations with this calculation:

municipal population x   county vehicles registered / county population = municipal vehicles registered

Transportation energy use summary

Use the numbers you found from the steps on the previous page to calculate estimates of total gallons consumed, the total transportation bill, and the equivalent in barrels of oil.

Study year _____   *Study area* _____

_____ **x** _____ **=** _____
Estimated number   **Average annual**   **Total gallons consumed**
of local vehicles   **gallons per vehicle**

_____ **x** _____ **=** _____
Total gallons consumed   **Average local**   **Annual transportation**
                              price per gallon   **fuel bill**

_____ **÷**   **42**   **=** _____
Total gallons consumed   **(number of gallons in one barrel)**   **Barrels of oil**

_____ **x** **125,000 Btu per gallon of gasoline** **=** _____
Total gallons consumed   **(138,700 Btu per gallon of diesel)**   **Transportation Btu**

Sampling of Transportation Fuel Bills

	# of vehicles	Gallons	Price/gallon	Fuel costs /year
Schools				
County Vehicles				
Public Transit				
Taxis				
Other				

Average annual gallons per vehicle by state

United States 1992

State	Average Annual Gallons per Vehicle	State	Average Annual Gallons per Vehicle
Alabama	822	Missouri	850
Alaska	587	Montana	625
Arizona	749	Nebraska	723
Arkansas	1,088	Nevada	903
California	688	New Hampshire	629
Colorado	592	New Jersey	643
Connecticut	584	New Mexico	774
Delaware	117	New York	641
District of Columbia	738	North Carolina	734
Florida	667	North Dakota	644
Georgia	745	Ohio	606
Hawaii	512	Oklahoma	650
Idaho	589	Oregon	648
Illinois	677	Pennsylvania	675
Indiana	746	Rhode Island	650
Iowa	596	South Carolina	842
Kansas	740	South Dakota	676
Kentucky	797	Tennessee	658
Louisiana	712	Texas	780
Maine	715	Utah	747
Maryland	649	Vermont	748
Massachusetts	707	Virginia	688
Michigan	657	Washington	604
Minnesota	679	West Virginia	809
Mississippi	822	Wisconsin	689
		Wyoming	967
		National Average	698

Source: Selected Highway Statistics and Charts 1992

U.S. Department of Transportation

Federal Highway Administration

To get most recent data available call (202) 366-5032

Add figures together for the community energy bill

Referring to the numbers developed on the previous pages, find the total community energy bill and the total amount of energy used, expressed in Btu.

Energy Sectors	$ Amount	% of total bill	Btu	% of total Btu
Residential				
Commercial				
Industrial				
Transportation				
Other				
Total energy bill		**Total Btu**		

Presenting the community energy bill

Making an over-size check and filling it in with the appropriate amount can be an effective and fun way to display your information at the Energy Town Meeting.

No. 2103

P. O. Box 1, Anywhere, USA _____ *19* _____

**Pay to
the Order of** _____ $ [   ]

_____ **Dollars**

Community National Bank
P. O. Box 100, Anywhere, USA

For: *Community Energy Bill* _____ _____

Economic Impacts of the Energy Bill

The following pages will help you examine and illustrate the magnitude of the community energy bill and compare the bill to other community expenses and income sources.

WAYS TO EXAMINE THE BILL'S BURDEN

➤ **Per capita share of the total energy bill**
If the community energy bill were divided evenly among local residents, how much would each person pay?

➤ **The energy bill versus personal income**
How much of your community's income is consumed by energy expenses?

➤ **The energy bill compared to employment payrolls**
How does the energy bill compare to the income generated in various local sectors of your economy?

➤ **Energy Freedom Day**
How many 8-hour work days would it take your community to pay off its energy debt?

Per capita share of the total energy bill

If the community energy bill were divided evenly among local residents, how much would each person pay? Figuring per capita share of energy expenses is one way to assess the energy bill's burden on your community and compare it to the amount of money spent on other local priorities.

Calculating per capita share of the energy bill

To calculate each resident's share of the total energy bill, divide the bill by the local population figure (see page 40).

Total energy bill _____

$$\frac{\text{Total energy bill}}{\text{Local population}} = \text{Per capita share of the energy bill} \underline{\hspace{2cm}}$$

Local population _____

People tend to confuse per capita figures with average use per person. When using this per capita figure, clarify that it is not the average of what any one individual spends on energy, but rather it is the amount each person in the community would have to pay if the energy bill were divided evenly among all residents.

Comparing energy expenses to other community priorities

Find other community per capita expenditures to use as a comparison. What is the per capita share of the education budget for your community? Parks and recreation? Arts?

	Total local budget	Per capita expenditure
Education		
Parks and recreation		
Arts programs		
Child care		
Other		

The energy bill versus personal income

One way for a community to become more prosperous is to find ways to increase income sources. Another way is to spend less money on necessities like energy, through resource-efficient measures. How much of a bite does local energy use currently take out of community income?

To find the size of the bite

You can put a number on the local energy bill by finding what portion of your community's total personal income is consumed by energy expenses.

> ➤ "*Total personal income*" (TPI) is a standard statistic that measures the combined income received by all area residents from all sources (wages, rents, dividends, etc.) in a calendar year. If this figure has not been gathered, ask your county clerk or town manager for your community's total personal income for your study year. If they cannot provide you with total personal income for that specific year, contact your state's local affairs or demographic office for an estimate. These offices regularly calculate projections of total personal income based on the most recent census.

To calculate the portion of your community's total personal income consumed by energy expenses, divide the energy bill by the total community personal income.

Total energy bill _____

_____ **=** **Energy bill as % of total personal income** _____

Total community personal income _____

While some local expenses drain incomes, they also can stimulate local economic activity and create future benefits. For example, money spent on food supports a number of local jobs at grocery stores, restaurants, and at any local food producers and processers. These businesses can then use those dollars to purchase other goods and services in the community, creating a ripple of local economic benefits, referred to as the "multiplier effect."

The money spent on energy, however, does little to spur local economic activity, since 70 - 80 cents of every dollar spent on energy immediately leaves the community. Energy bill money may support a few jobs at local utilities, but the majority of it goes to concrete, power lines, and transmission stations somewhere else.

The energy bill compared to employment payrolls

In some communities, residents are spending more on energy than the local economy receives from its largest employer or employment sector. Reducing the total energy bill through efficiency can have the same benefit to the local economy as recruiting a new employer.

How large is your community's energy bill compared to earnings in these sectors?

Contact your state department of labor and employment and ask for a report of the total dollars earned in different sectors of your local economy. Most states publish a Standard Industrial Classification (SIC) employment and wages report. This report contains information on the income generated by different sectors of your local economy, such as retail, construction, manufacturing, tourism and so forth.

Local Sectors	Sector Earnings	How does amount compare to energy bill?
Construction		
Retail		
Manufacturing		
Tourism		
Other		

You can also contact city and/or county government to see if they have local payroll records. How does the community's total energy bill compare to the payrolls of the area's major employers?

Major employers	Payrolls of major employers	Energy bill comparison

Energy Freedom Day

When people buy a new coat or a new stereo, they often gauge how expensive the item is by calculating how many days they must work to pay for it. You can use this technique to better understand the magnitude of the bill's size.

To calculate your local Energy Freedom Day

1 Figure your community's daily wage

Total personal income _____

_____ **= Community daily wage** _____

260 annual working days _____
(52 weeks per year) X (5 working days per week)

2 Determine how many 8-hour working days it takes to pay off the energy debt:

Total annual energy bill _____

_____ **= Number of work days to "Energy Freedom"** _____

Community daily wage _____

Using the calendar below, find your community's "Energy Freedom Day," by counting off the above number of working days to energy freedom (Monday through Friday) from the beginning of January. The calendar date at which you finish is your community's Energy Freedom Day.

JANUARY

M	T	W	T	F	S	S
				1	2	3
4	5	6	7	8	9	10
11	12	13	14	15	16	17
18	19	20	21	22	23	24
25	26	27	28	29	30	31

FEBRUARY

M	T	W	T	F	S	S
1	2	3	4	5	6	7
8	9	10	11	12	13	14
15	16	17	18	19	20	21
22	23	24	25	26	27	28

MARCH

M	T	W	T	F	S	S
1	2	3	4	5	6	7
8	9	10	11	12	13	14
15	16	17	18	19	20	21
22	23	24	25	26	27	28
29	30	31				

The concept of "Energy Freedom Day" was developed by Skip Laitner of Economic Research Associates. For more information on "Energy Freedom Day" see *Energy Efficiency and Economic Indicators: Charting Improvements in the Economy and the Environment* by Skip Laitner. American Council for an Energy Efficient Economy, 1995.

Energy Freedom Days compared

The number of days a community must spend working to pay off its energy bill will affect the overall vitality of its economy. Compare U.S. and Japan 1988[1] Energy Freedom Days, then see how your local Energy Freedom Day compares to that of your entire state.

Graph your Energy Freedom Day

Graph the number of days your community must work to pay off its energy debt on the chart below. You can turn to the next page to find the 1991 Energy Freedom Day for your state and graph that as well.

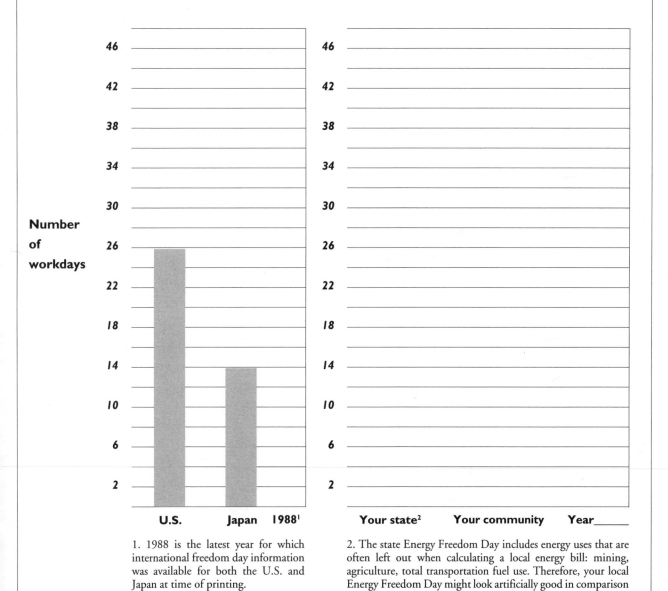

Number of workdays

U.S.   Japan   1988[1]

Your state[2]   Your community   Year_____

1. 1988 is the latest year for which international freedom day information was available for both the U.S. and Japan at time of printing.

2. The state Energy Freedom Day includes energy uses that are often left out when calculating a local energy bill: mining, agriculture, total transportation fuel use. Therefore, your local Energy Freedom Day might look artificially good in comparison to the that of your entire state.

Estimated Energy Freedom Days for 1991

Note: All values are in billions of 1991 dollars.

State	Income	Energy Bill	Freedom Day
AL	$63.8	$8.3	17 February 1991
AK	$12.4	$1.9	25 February 1991
AZ	$62.2	$6.4	07 February 1991
AR	$34.7	$4.7	19 February 1991
CA	$634.1	$47.5	28 January 1991
CO	$66.5	$5.4	30 January 1991
CT	$84.6	$6.2	27 January 1991
DE	$14.7	$1.4	04 February 1991
DC	$14.9	$1.1	27 January 1991
FL	$252.0	$20.3	30 January 1991
GA	$116.4	$12.5	09 February 1991
HI	$24.1	$2.0	31 January 1991
ID	$16.2	$1.9	12 February 1991
IL	$239.9	$21.5	02 February 1991
IN	$97.0	$11.9	14 February 1991
IA	$48.6	$5.2	09 February 1991
KS	$45.5	$5.1	10 February 1991
KY	$58.6	$7.2	14 February 1991
LA	$64.0	$13.2	17 March 1991
ME	$21.3	$ 2.5	12 February 1991
MD	$109.0	$8.0	27 January 1991
MA	$137.1	$10.6	29 January 1991
MI	$176.0	$16.8	04 February 1991
MN	$85.3	$7.6	02 February 1991
MS	$34.3	$4.9	22 February 1991
MO	$93.9	$9.4	06 February 1991
MT	$12.7	$1.7	18 February 1991
NE	$28.7	$3.1	09 February 1991
NV	$26.0	$2.4	03 February 1991
NH	$23.9	$1.9	30 January 1991
NJ	$197.1	$15.9	30 January 1991
NM	$23.0	$3.0	17 February 1991
NY	$407.9	$28.0	26 January 1991
NC	$114.2	$12.6	10 February 1991
ND	$10.0	$1.6	28 February 1991
OH	$195.5	$21.1	09 February 1991
OK	$49.7	$6.0	14 February 1991
OR	$51.3	$5.0	05 February 1991
PA	$231.1	$22.3	05 February 1991

Estimated Energy Freedom Days for 1991

Note: All values are in billions of 1991 dollars.

State	Income	Energy Bill	Freedom Day
RI	$19.1	$1.8	04 February 1991
SC	$55.1	$6.8	15 February 1991
SD	$11.4	$1.3	11 February 1991
TN	$81.7	$9.3	11 February 1991
TX	$300.6	$42.9	22 February 1991
UT	$26.2	$2.9	10 February 1991
VT	$10.1	$1.1	09 February 1991
VA	$127.5	$11.0	01 February 1991
WA	$99.8	$8.6	01 February 1991
WV	$26.0	$3.8	23 February 1991
WI	$89.7	$8.2	03 February 1991
WY	$8.1	$1.5	09 March 1991
US Total	$4,833.5	$467.1	05 February 1991

Source: Skip Laitner, Economic Research Associates, 1205 Collingwood Road, Alexandria VA 22308-1729

Environmental Costs of the Energy Bill

In addition to economic impacts, local energy use has environmental and social costs. Most of these environmental and social costs are not accounted for by energy prices. Find out some of these hidden costs to develop a more complete picture of the local energy bill.

EXAMINING UNCOUNTED COSTS

➤ **Start asking "Where" and "How?"**
Trace all local energy use to original fuel sources and locate the final resting point of any wastes or pollutants produced.

➤ **Map your community energy system**
To give people a better understanding of where your community gets its energy, and some of the environmental costs involved, display your findings on a large map.

➤ **Graph your community's electricity fuel mix**
What are the original fuel sources for your community's electricity, and how much does each contribute? Is your community using a mix that produces the least environmental cost? How is this likely to change in the future?

➤ **Examine transportation fuel environmental costs**
Petroleum-powered transportation creates some of the most perceptible environmental costs of community energy use, since fuels are burned in local streets. Find out what is being spewed into your local air, and in what quantities.

➤ **Calculate the community CO_2 bill**
The U.S. has made an international agreement to stabilize U.S. CO_2 emissions to 1990 levels by the year 2000. Reaching this goal will require that every community do its part. How much CO_2 is your community currently responsible for?

This section emphasizes the environmental costs of electricity and transportation fuel use because they generate the most significant environmental impacts, and you can do something about them locally. This does not mean that other energy sources do not also have environmental costs. If another fuel or power source is a particular problem in your area, gather more information on its specific environmental costs. For more information on the environmental costs of energy look for additional information from the resources listed starting page 243.

Start asking "WHERE?" and "HOW?"

Where does the energy used in your community come from? What kinds of impacts are created by extracting or processing it, and where do wastes or pollutants end up? The questions below can help you trace some of this essential information.

1   Where are the utilities that supply your community with electricity based?

2   Where are the power plants that supply your community with electricity? What are they powered by?

3   Where does the fuel source for this electricity originate? (i.e. where is the coal or uranium mined?) How does it get from its original source to the power plant?

4   What are some of the environmental costs (i.e. health concerns, damaged landscape, loss of habitat, etc.) caused by obtaining the original fuel source?

5   What pollutants or wastes are produced by the power plants supplying your community with electricity? Where do the pollutants or wastes produced end up?

6   How does electricity make its way from the power plant to where it is used in your community? Are there any health-related concerns related with how the electricity is transmitted to your community? How much energy is lost between producing the electricity and when it finally shows up in your community?

7   Where does the natural gas used in your community originate? How does natural gas make its way to your community? What are the environmental costs of supplying your community with natural gas?

8   Where do other heating fuels used in your community originate? What environmental costs are associated with these fuels?

9   Where does the gasoline sold at local stations originate? Where are the gasoline companies based? How does the gasoline sold at local pumps make its way to your community? What are some of the environmental costs of getting gasoline from its original source to local gas stations?

10 Where are the renewable energy sources used in your community located? What are some of the environmental costs of these renewable sources?

Where to find out

You can start your search by talking with the energy suppliers that serve your community. Organizations that focus on energy issues in your state or region may also be able to help you (see page 49 for a list of some of these organizations). If they are unable to provide all the answers, call your state energy office for suggestions of who might know the answers.

Map the community energy system

Using a large map of the world, and copies of the cards below, map your community energy system. The finished product can help give people a better understanding of the environmental costs of current energy use.

1 Where are the utilities that supply your community with electricity based?	**6** How does electricity make its way from the power plant to where it is used in your community? Are there any health-related concerns related to its transmittal?
2 Where are the power plants that supply your community with electricity? What are they powered by?	**7** Where does your community's natural gas originate? How is it transmitted? What are the environmental costs of supplying your community with natural gas?
3 Where does the fuel source used at the power plants originate? How does it get from its original source to the power plant?	**8** Where do other heating fuels used in your community originate? What environmental costs are associated with these fuels?
4 What are some of the environmental costs caused by obtaining the original fuel source?	**9** Where does the gasoline sold at local stations originate? What are the environmental costs of producing and transporting gasoline to your community?
5 What pollutants or wastes are produced by the power plants supplying your community with electricity? Where do the pollutants or wastes produced end up?	**10** Where are the renewable energy sources used in your community located? What are the environmental costs of getting these energy sources to your community?

Graph your community's electricity fuel mix

What are the original fuel sources for your community's electricity, and how much does each contribute? Is your community using a mix that incurs the least environmental cost? How is this likely to change in the future?

What sources contribute to your electricity?

Ask your electric utility for the original sources of the electricity they sell. What percentage of your community's electricity does each source contribute? Draw a bar graph that corresponds to this fuel mix.

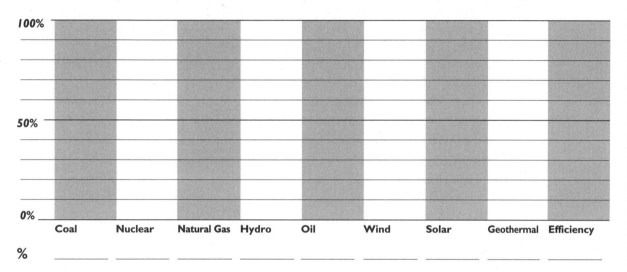

% _____ _____ _____ _____ _____ _____ _____ _____ _____

How could this fuel mix change over the next ten years? Call your state energy office to see what the renewable energy potential is for your area. If they cannot help you, ask them to refer you to someone who can. If energy efficiency or demand-side management is not currently considered a supply option by your utility, ask them what role it will play in future supply plans. How does your local electric power mix compare to the U.S. as a whole?

Sources of U.S. electricity

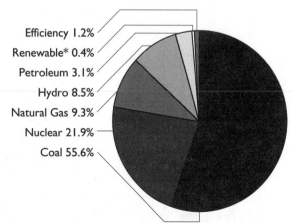

*Renewable sources include geothermal, solar, wood, waste biomass, and wind. *Source:* Monthly Energy Review 11-93. Efficiency data is from Electric Power Annual 1992, Table 65. Both publications are available from Department of Energy, Energy Information Administration.

Examine transportation fuel environmental costs

Petroleum-powered transportation creates one of the most perceptible local environmental costs of community energy use since fuels are burned on local streets rather than at a distant power plant. Find out what is being spewed into your local air and in what quantities.

What do tailpipes leave behind?

Using the total number of gallons used in your community (page 59) you can develop an estimate of pollutants released into the local air by transportation fuel.

Total Gallons	X Emissions emitted / gallon	= Total lbs. of emissions
	x .15 lbs. hydrocarbons	lbs. of hydrocarbons
	x 1.1 lbs. carbon monoxide	lbs. of carbon monoxide
	x 19.8 lbs. carbon dioxide	lbs. of carbon dioxide
	x .07 lbs. nitrogen	lbs. of nitrogen
	x .004 lbs. benzene	lbs. of benzene

The above pollution estimates represent only what happens locally, not counting a host of other environmental costs, such as the impacts of drilling in fragile wildlife areas, coastal oil spills, pollution from refineries, and gas that leaks from community gas stations, to name a few.

What do these emissions do to air and health?

Hydrocarbons: In the presence of sunlight and nitrogen oxides, hydrocarbons react to form ground-level ozone, a component of smog. Ground-level ozone is highly toxic and irritates the eyes, nose, throat and lungs. Transportation sources cause 40% to 60% of the pollution that produces ozone.

Carbon monoxide: Carbon monoxide limits the blood's capacity to absorb oxygen, causing headaches, drowsiness, aggravation of heart and respiratory problems, and in some cases, death. Vehicles cause 70% to 80% of carbon monoxide emissions.

Carbon dioxide: Nearly a third of carbon dioxide (CO_2) emissions come from the use of transportation fuels, making them the single largest source of CO_2, which is the major cause of global climate change.

Nitrogen: By itself, nitrogen is nontoxic, but it combines with oxygen to form nitrogen dioxide, one of the main components of smog. At high concentrations, NO_2 is potentially toxic and damaging to plants.

Benzene: The U.S. Environmental Protection Agency has identified benzene as an "air toxic:" a substance that can have either an immediate or a long-term harmful effect on human life or health. Benzene is a known carcinogen.

Calculate the community CO_2 Bill

Atmospheric concentration of CO_2, the main contributor to climate change, has increased by about 25 percent since 1800. World emissions have risen sharply over the last decade. The U.S. has made an international agreement to stabilize U.S. CO_2 emissions to 1990 levels by the year 2000.

How much CO_2 does your community contribute?

To develop an estimate of your community CO_2 bill, enter your community energy totals in the spaces below and multiply by the amount of carbon dioxide produced per energy unit.

	Community energy totals (x lbs. of CO_2 produced per unit used)		Total lbs. of CO_2 produced per energy type
Natural gas	mcf _____	x 124.6 lbs.	
	therms _____	x 12.1 lbs.	
Transportation fuel	gallons _____	x 22.0 lbs.[1]	
Electricity	kWh _____	x 1.89 lbs.[2]	
	Total CO_2 Bill		_____

This figure does not include other CO_2 sources, such as methane, other locally used fuels, or the use of halocarbon products.

[1] Carbon dioxide emissions vary for various transportation fuels. 22 lbs. per gallon is the average.

[2] Carbon dioxide emissions per kWh vary depending on the fuel source. The figure used here (1.89 pounds of CO_2 per kWh) is the national weighted average of CO_2 emissions per kWh of all fuel sources, including the energy used in transmision and distribution of electricity. The emissions per kWh range from 2.86 pounds of CO_2 for every kWh produced by coal-generated electricity, to zero pounds produced by wind, solar or efficiency-generated electricity. To get a more exact estimation of CO_2 produced by your community, contact Rocky Mountain Institute for the amount of CO_2 released by each fuel source.

[3] To find out more about tracking local CO_2 emissions, contact the Cities for Climate Protection Campaign at the International Council for Local Environmental Initiatives. The Campaign has publications that can assist your community in developing CO_2 reduction targets, and developing aggressive CO_2 reduction strategies. Their number is listed in the resources section under ICLEI. Also see page 10 for a description of the Climate Change Action Plan and what several communities are doing about global climate change.

See pages 253-255 for additional resources.

Economic Benefits of Community Energy Efficiency

What do retrofits, efficient technologies, and local renewable energy sources have to do with a more prosperous economy? This section will help you explore how sustainable energy strategies strengthen the local economy.

COMMUNITY ENERGY EFFICIENCY WILL

➤ **Plug the leaks**

Energy savings will ease the drain on public and household budgets, freeing up money for other priorities.

➤ **Support existing businesses**

Energy efficiency measures will strengthen businesses by trimming operating costs and creating new local markets.

➤ **Encourage new local enterprise**

A community energy program can stimulate business start-ups such as those providing energy-smart goods and services.

➤ **Multiply local savings**

By implementing the first three approaches your community will keep money previously spent on energy circulating in the local economy. As this money is reinvested it creates additional jobs and supports other local businesses.

The numbers you will develop on the following pages will provide a very rough estimate of the community economic benefits of implementing energy efficiency. These numbers are intended to help illustrate the opportunities awaiting your community. You may want to later take advantage of more sophisticated tools for assessing the economic benefits of investing in energy efficiency measures. See page 82 for these resources.

Plug the leaks

Although overlooked in most economic development efforts, reducing the drain on public and household budgets goes a long way toward boosting local economic health.

Using public money wisely

Rather than slashing school budgets and cutting back on important services, local government can create additional funds by using resources as efficiently as possible. Because energy efficiency improvements generate significant cash surpluses, cutting energy costs is one of the best places to start.

Contact the institutions listed below and ask what their total energy bills were for your study year, or what their average annual bills have been in recent years. Find out how much additional public money would be made available through a simple 20% savings. Find a way to give these amounts meaning by comparing them to other needed expenditures, such as a teacher's salary or new computers for the public library.

	Annual Energy Bill	20% energy savings*	What savings could pay for
All local school buildings			
City-owned buildings			
County-owned buildings			
City vehicle fleet			
Streetlights			
Local federal buildings			
Water treatment plant			
Other			

* Investing in the initial energy improvements will require a certain amount of upfront funding. See the Task Force Packets for a sampling of how energy users have covered the upfront financing costs. Length of paybacks will vary.

Plug the leaks

Household economies are an important part of the local economy. Finding ways to ease household energy burdens creates more disposable income and makes the community better able to withstand hard times.

Creating homegrown economic development

Energy efficiency measures such as improved insulation, wrapping water heaters, and lighting retrofits can easily trim most household energy bills by more than 20%. To see the effect these energy savings programs can have on local households, find out the annual energy bills for the following types of households and calculate a 20% annual savings.

To gather household energy use figures: Call your utility first to see if they keep records on average energy use for the various kinds of households listed below. If they do not, ask people in your group if they have records of their annual energy bills. Be sure to gather information from people living in different kinds of housing.

Call a typical apartment complex or condominium project for your community. Explain that you are gathering information on local household energy use and ask if they could share information on the energy costs for their buildings.

Gather sample transportation fuel costs by asking several members of your committee to calculate their costs, given their average weekly mileage and average fuel costs.

	Sample Energy Bill	20% Annual Savings*
Average local household		
Sample Apartment Complex		
Household Transportation		
Mobile Home		
Other		

See the Residential Task Force Packet for information on how energy savings of 20% and more can be achieved. The number you will be developing here is the total of energy saved, but does not include the money that would be required to finance the improvements. See the Task Force Packets for examples of how energy users have covered the upfront financing costs.

Support existing businesses

Existing businesses are your community's most valuable economic asset. Trimming energy costs will improve local businesses' bottom line and increase their stability, and can free up funds for improvements, additional jobs, or employee raises.

Potential savings for local businesses

Find out the annual energy bills for the following types of businesses in your community. To get this information, call the businesses listed and ask to speak with the manager. Explain that your group is gathering information on energy use in your community to improve the economy through energy efficiency.

	Annual Energy Bill	20% Savings*
Grocery store		
Lodging		
Retail shops		
Light industry		
Restaurant		
Farm		
Commercial office space		
Other		

See the Commercial/Industrial Task Force Packet for information on how energy savings of 20% and more can be achieved. The number you will be developing here is the total of energy saved, but does not include the money that would be required to finance the improvements. See the Task Force Packets for examples of how energy users have financed energy improvements.

Encourage new local enterprise

To receive the greatest economic benefit from energy improvements, find ways to meet increased demand for products and services locally. If some energy products and services are not yet available, entrepreneurs have an opportunity to open businesses or expand an existing line of services.

Availability of efficient and renewable products and services

Use the checklist below to survey the current availability of a sampling of products, services, and skills that can help improve your local energy picture.

Products or Services	Locally Available?	Nearest Location?
Water-efficient shower heads		
Energy-efficient lighting		
Weatherization materials		
Water heater blankets		
Energy audit and retrofit services		
Super-efficient windows		
Insulation contractors		
Solar hot water systems and installation		
Solar electric systems and installation		
"Green" building design services		
Energy-efficient appliances		
Energy-efficient heating and cooling systems		
Efficient vehicles		
Bikes and bike servicing		

Multiply local savings

Reducing energy costs for businesses, households, and government is like developing a new source of community income. Besides the direct benefits to those with lower energy bills, this saved money can be reinvested in the community, supporting jobs in other sectors of the local economy.

A dollar saved is more than just a dollar earned

The economic gain from energy efficiency goes beyond the direct benefit of lower energy bills, or income to retailers and installers of energy saving measures. If the money that is freed up by lower energy bills is reinvested in the local economy it creates a ripple of additional benefits, known as the multiplier effect. More than 90% of the new jobs created from efficiency improvements are the result of re-spending the money gained through energy savings (for more information see the publication "Energy Efficiency and Job Creation" listed on page 82).

The size of the total multiplier effect of energy efficiency measures in your community depends on the extent to which:

➤ local businesses can supply energy-efficient goods and services;
➤ energy-efficient technologies are retailed, wholesaled, or manufactured locally;
➤ residents shop locally, and the extent to which consumer needs can be met locally;
➤ the money from energy savings is invested in the local community.

In short, the more purchases and investments are made locally, the more money circulates in the local economy, and the greater the multiplier effect.

Find your local multiplier

Different communities and regions of the country have varying economic multipliers. Find out what the average multiplier is for your community or county by calling your state economic development, state demographics office, or your state Cooperative Extension program. If local or county level data is unavailable, ask if they have data on state multipliers.

How will energy savings multiply in your community?

What total economic benefits will be generated by a community-wide investment in energy efficiency? To find a more exact answer to this question you will need to use some of the tools listed on page 82. However, you can use the chart below to glimpse a *rough* estimate of the additional money that will be added to the local economy if the community energy bill were reduced by 5% or 10%.

Community energy bill	x % savings	= total savings	x local average multiplier	= total additional money
	x .10			
	x .20			

Getting a more complete picture

Making energy improvements creates a series of changes in the local economy. To estimate the full range of economic consequences of community energy improvements, several kinds of effects and impacts must be examined. For example, an initial investment in energy improvements creates three kinds of effects:

➤ Direct effects: The initial investment in energy improvements will directly benefit a variety of people who play a role in the energy improvement. For example, when a business invests in an energy-efficient lighting system the direct effects would include the increased income to the lighting consultant who designs and installs the new system.

➤ Indirect effects: Direct effects indirectly benefit other people and businesses that provide supplies or services to the initial business. Additional income for the lighting consultant could mean more money goes to an advertiser or the wholesaler who sold products to the lighting consultant.

➤ Induced effects: Additional economic benefits are "induced" as the employees of the businesses experiencing the direct and indirect effects spend their wages throughout the economy. Employees of the lighting firm spend their paychecks at local restaurants, local retailers, and so forth.

An energy improvement investment may also have impacts on the economy. These impacts include such things as the loss of revenue to conventional energy suppliers.

To get a full picture of how all these economic consequences of improved energy use add up for your community, you may want to take advantage of the resources listed below.

Additional resources for estimating the economic benefits

The preceding pages offer several ways to get a preview of the economic benefits of investing in energy efficiency measures in your community. There are several computer-assisted techniques for developing more refined estimations of the economic benefits stemming from various energy managment strategies. These techniques are able to consider a wide range of effects and impacts of investing in energy efficiency and develop estimates that take a wide variety of interactions into account.

➤ OPTIONS has been used by many communities to examine a variety of community goals relating to energy efficiency, including desired environmental benefits, job creation goals, and required investment levels. OPTIONS can be obtained from the Iowa Association of Municipal Utilities, 325 Insurance Exchange

Building, Des Moines, Iowa 50309, 515-282-0904. For more
information on using OPTIONS in your community contact Skip
Laitner, who developed the program, at Economic Research
Associates, 1205 Collingwood Road, Alexandria, VA 22308-1729,
(703) 780-6407.

➤ IMPLAN, short for "IMpact Analysis for PLANning." Developed
by the U.S. Forest Service, IMPLAN is available for use on
personal computers from the University of Minnesota's Department of Agricultural and Applied Economics, 1994 Buford
Avenue, St. Paul, MN 55108 (612) 779-6638.

➤ RIMS II, the U.S. Department of Commerce's Regional Input-
Output Modeling System uses county-level data. To find out
about RIMS II, obtain a copy of *Regional Multipliers: A User
Handbook for the Regional Input-Output Modeling System*, available
from the Government Printing Office (Stock No. 003010002271)
for $13.00. (202) 783-3238.

For further reading:

*America's Energy Choices: Investing in a Strong Economy and a Clean
Environment.* Published by the Union of Concerned Scientists, 26
Church St., Cambridge, MA 02238. 1991.

The Economic Impacts of Renewable Energy Use in Wisconsin. Steve
Clemmer, Wisconsin Energy Bureau, 101 E. Wilson Street, 6th
Floor, Post Office Box 7868, Madison, WI 53707-7868. 1994.

*Energy Efficiency and Economic Indicators: Charting Improvements in
the Economy and the Environment.* Skip Laitner. American Council
for and Energy-Efficient Economy, 1001 Connecticut Avenue
NW, Washington D.C. 20036. 1995.

*Energy Efficiency and Job Creation: The Employment and Income
Benefits from Investing in Energy-Conserving Technologies.* Howard
Geller, John DeCicco, and Skip Laitner. American Council for an
Energy- Efficient Economy, 1001 Connecticut Avenue NW,
Washington D.C. 20036. 1992.

Energy Efficiency Strengthens Local Economies and *The Jobs Connection:
Energy Use and Local Economic Development.* Produced by the
Cities and Counties Project, U.S. Department of Energy, c/o
National Renewable Energy Lab, 1617 Cole Boulevard, Golden,
CO 80401-9889.

*Powering the Midwest: Renewable Electricity for the Economy and the
Environment.* Michael Brower, Michael Tennis, Eric Denzler, and
Mark Kaplan. Union of Concerned Scientists, 26 Church St.,
Cambridge, MA 02238. 1993.

Mobilizing the Community

A well-attended Town Meeting and a solid core of workshop participants are critical to your effort's success. An effective outreach campaign will achieve these ends, as well as create broad local awareness of energy alternatives.

Involving Individuals and Organizations

Most of us don't think about energy issues until prices increase dramatically or international conflict reminds us of our dependence on foreign oil. Most communities also aren't aware of the economic opportunities available from energy efficiency. Given that improved energy use is not in the forefront of public consciousness, getting people to give up their time to develop a community energy and economic action plan can be challenging.

While it may take some effort, a wide variety of community members will become interested in the topic of energy if it is made accessible and relevant to their concerns. Many people do not participate in community affairs simply because they have never been asked. Personally asking people to participate, and connecting the effort to their concerns, will result in a solid base of planning workshop participants and tangible improvements to your community's energy and economic health.

RECRUITING WORKSHOP PARTICIPANTS

- ➤ **Who to target**

- ➤ **Contact checklist**

- ➤ **Encouraging active participation**

- ➤ **Sample invitation**

Who to target

A variety of workshop participants from the following general groups can ensure a successful energy planning process.

1. Community-minded people and organizations:
➤ Neighborhood and civic groups
➤ Environmental interests
➤ Affordable housing groups
➤ Minority groups
➤ Social service groups
➤ Students

While these people may not have a background in energy issues, they will contribute greatly to the planning effort. Their perspective will help the workshops result in energy projects that work for the entire community.

2. People who have professional experience with energy issues:
➤ Facilities, building, and property managers
➤ Electricians, contractors, architects, engineers, and builders
➤ Energy efficient or renewable product retailers

These participants will provide an important perspective on the realities of implementing sustainable energy measures, and what is needed to make them common practice.

3. People and organizations with the power to initiate changes within institutions and industries that can have a major impact on improving energy use:
➤ Utilities that serve your community
➤ Building and design industry leaders
➤ Financial institutions
➤ Economic development leaders
➤ Local government staff of relevant departments, such as planning, public works, building, and environment.

When these organizations, and the people involved with them, become interested in making your community more energy efficient, they can create significant improvements in a short period of time. If it's initially difficult to get full participation from these entities in your community, the workshops and the resulting citizen-based plan can succeed in creating support for the effort from these groups at a later time.

Encouraging active participation

Community residents may not immediately come out of the woodwork to attend the Energy Town Meeting or join an energy task force. The following approaches can help you find ways to stimulate people's interest in energy issues and build participation in the planning workshops:

➤ Some people might be interested because the effort offers a chance to learn new skills, others because it ties into professional interests, and others because of environmental or economic concerns. How can the planning effort be made relevant to the interests of the people on the list?

➤ Some people will participate if they are designated as representatives of specific groups in the workshops. For instance, if you invite a builder's association to designate a representative so their point of view is included, one of their members might be assigned to attend the workshops.

➤ Look for the best way to contact potential participants. A letter or phone call from a friend, neighbor, co-worker, or respected community leader can be more effective than an invitation from a stranger. Find out if members of the steering group personally know some of the people you hope will attend, and have them make the contact. If no one in your group knows the person, send a letter signed by a respected community leader.

➤ After sending out initial invitations to the town meeting, follow up with a phone call to as many participants as you can. A personal contact can transform a potential no-show into an enthusiastic participant.

➤ As you near the Town Meeting, double check to see that you have invited representatives of all important community groups and perspectives, and see if you have a rough idea of who plans to show up. Don't hesitate to follow up with last minute phone calls to potential participants.

Energy Town Meeting contact checklist

Use the checklist below to make sure you have contacted a wide variety of organizations and people about the Energy Town Meeting. Think of ways to connect meeting topics to their interests and concerns.

	Contacted?	Connecting issues?	Representative Attending?
Architects			
Banks / credit unions			
Builders / contractors			
Business owners			
Chamber of commerce			
Churches			
Civic / service organizations			
Developers			
Elected officials			
Electricians			
Environmental groups			
Energy-related businesses			
Ethnic community groups			
Government agencies			

(Forest Service, Soil Conservation District, Cooperative Extension, Small Business Administration)

Hardware / appliance stores			
Home owners			
Housing groups			

(continued on next page)

Energy Town Meeting contact checklist *(continued)*

(continued from previous page)	Contacted?	Connecting issues?	Representative Attending?
Landlords			
Libraries			
Low-income assistance groups			
Manufacturers			
Media			
Neighborhood associations			
Plumbers			
Property and facilities managers			
Realtors			
Renters			
Utility staff			
Other			
Local government departments			
Building			
Planning			
Economic development			
Local schools and colleges			
Teachers			
Students			
Facilities managers			

Sample invitation to participate

Dear Community Resident,

You are cordially invited to the Jarlsberg Energy Town Meeting at 5:30 p.m., Wednesday, October 16, at the Jarlsberg High School Gymnasium.

Fact Our county's 1993 energy bill was $12.7 million greater than the total 1993 wages and salaries of our entire county logging industry.

Fact Retrofitting all U.S. buildings with today's most energy-efficient lighting technologies could avoid the emission, on average, of more than one-half billion tons of CO_2, the number one green house gas culprit, and six million tons of sulfur dioxide, which causes acid rain.

Fact By saving just five percent of our current energy bill, Gouda County could keep $1.8 million in the local economy every year!

Come find out how you can make energy efficiency work for you and your community! The agenda for the evening will cover:

➤ Gouda County's current energy picture: what it means for the local economy and the environment.

➤ Community energy success stories: what others are doing to improve their energy and economic future.

➤ Overview of some of the latest energy-smart technologies: how they deliver what we need with far less energy.

➤ Determine whether Gouda County should work to take advantage of the benefits of energy efficiency, and discuss how to go about doing this.

Local organizations and businesses will have practical information and energy-saving products on hand, starting at 5:00 p.m. and continuing throughout the evening.

Fact Cookies will be served.

Your participation is essential! We hope you can come!

Sincerely,

For the Jarlsberg Energy and Economic Development Committee

Working with the Media

Your energy and economic development effort should take full advantage of the power of the news media. Not only can the media inform the entire community about the economic opportunities of sustainable energy practices, but they also can play an important role in encouraging citizen involvement. This section offers tips on making the most of media resources and getting the coverage you need for success.

MAKE THE MOST OF MEDIA RESOURCES

➤ **Take stock of local media resources**

➤ **Getting your message across**

➤ **Sample media campaign materials**

Take stock of local media resources

A large part of a successful media campaign involves simply taking full advantage of every kind of media available. Create a complete local media contacts list by referring to the phone book and recording the necessary information below. Call all media outlets to find out the appropriate contact person, deadlines and the best times to call them.

Outlet Name	Contact Name	Telephone	Deadline	Release Sent?
Newspapers				
Radio				
Events Calenders				
Television				
Organizational Newsletters				
Other				

Getting your message across

Meet the press

It can be worthwhile to meet with an editor of your local newspaper early in your organizing process. Cover the following points in your visit:

➤ Describe how other communities have used energy efficiency and renewables to improve the local economy.

➤ Share the energy picture summary information (pages 41-43). Stress potential local economic opportunities. Explain that your group wants to tap this potential for economic development through energy efficiency.

➤ Community awareness is vital to the effort's success. Ask how your group can collaborate with the newspaper to increase awareness.

➤ Challenge the newspaper to increase energy efficiency and detail their efforts in a special series or section.

This meeting can help make your newspaper more aware of the planning effort, and how energy efficiency helps the community. Building a relationship with your local newspaper early on makes it more likely that editors will assign reporters to cover the energy planning effort and provide editorial endorsements later on.

Just like everyone else, reporters rarely think about local energy issues. They may not see how improved energy use is relevant to community concerns, or why it's something the public would want to know about. Your biggest challenge will be turning your effort into an issue the media wants to cover. Finding ways to make your effort newsworthy, developing partnerships with media, and presenting a professional image will help get the coverage you need.

Make energy issues and events newsworthy

When reporters look for story ideas, they often seek a current events or human interest angle. Here's a few news angles that can help promote your efforts:

➤ Economic development is always an issue of interest to local papers. For many, the connection between improving energy use and economic development is not readily apparent. Make the most of the information that you gathered in the Energy Picture section to illustrate this connection.

➤ Compare your estimates of total local energy costs to other community expenses or income sources, such as the county's annual budget and the payrolls of major local employers.

➤ Gather local energy success stories from businesses, homes and government. Reporters like stories of tangible successes that prove energy efficiency works.

➤ If your planning effort has a broad base of community support, stress the collaboration of different organizations, especially if they have previously been on opposite sides of community issues.

➤ Tie into national and international news events.

➤ Keep your message positive, emphasizing the economic opportunities that exist through improving energy practices. It's too easy for newspapers to play up the bad news regarding energy use. They often miss the many opportunities to improve energy practices and the positive steps residents in your community are taking.

➤ Humor can spice up a story that might otherwise be ignored. An occasional pun or one-liner can make a story memorable to both the reporter and the public.

➤ Determine your message before the media does. Some media representatives will tend to report on your energy efforts based on their memories of the 1970's energy crisis, using terms such as "conservation" and stirring up images that any effort that aims to encourage less energy waste means community deprivation and heavy-handed regulations. Other reporters and editors will be determined to look for controversy rather than celebrate civic-minded volunteerism and collaboration. To avoid headlines such as "Citizen planners attack local utility," or "Energy planning aims to control wasteful citizens," develop positive themes and use them repeatedly in your media materials and annoucements. While the media may find controversy attracts an audience, such headlines can damage your efforts to build long-term, broad based collaborative efforts to improve local energy use.

➤ Hold a news conference to kick off the planning workshops and the Energy Town Meeting. Discuss the local energy bill, its impacts on the local economy, and potential economic benefits. Announce that the Energy Town Meeting will be a chance to learn more and begin to turn energy saving ideas into action. Prepare media packets with easy-to-use fact sheets, news releases, and event schedules to distribute to reporters. If your town only has a few media outlets and news conferences are not a common occurrence, visiting each media source individually will be more effective.

➤ Furnish easy-to-use information for busy reporters.

➤ Create photo opportunities that relate to fun human interest angles. Hold a "No-Gas Dash" race or other attention-grabbing contests and invite local media representatives to participate.

Doing better or doing without?

What's the difference between conservation and efficiency? While the difference can seem minor, these two words can evoke different reactions, which in turn can create different levels of support for your efforts. Conservation often means doing with less: freezing in the dark, turning the thermostat down and putting on a sweater. Efficiency means having the same level of comfort (if not more) with less energy. Using "energy efficiency" rather than "conservation" will make it easier to reassure people that your effort aims to improve their quality of life, not reduce it.

Develop partnerships with media sources

See if a local media outlet will co-sponsor the energy town meeting and any other initial organizing events. A co-sponsorship will ensure news coverage by the media sources, and offer access to advertising you might otherwise be unable to afford. Co-sponsorships can range from financial assistance to a special advertising rate.

Developing a partnership with a local radio station is one of the most effective ways to reach your community. Radio station co-sponsorship can result in meeting announcements during the peak listening hours of 6-10 a.m. and 4-6 p.m., live coverage of promotional events, and on-site interviews with key attendees at the Energy Town Meeting. Some radio stations have even had "Alternative Energy Days" and played songs on the theme.

TV station co-sponsorships can result in promotional announcements and highlights of events on the evening news. Your local cable TV system may also have a community-access channel that can broadcast the Energy Town Meeting and other events.

Your local newspaper could be another sponsor. Besides running promotional advertising, the local paper could print an Energy Town Meeting supplement, presenting in greater detail the information developed in the Energy Picture section.

Present a professional image

➤ Develop news releases following the format of the sample on page 97. Double-space the document and put the most important information first (who, what, when, where, why). Ideally, the release is less than two pages. Include a contact name and phone number. If appropriate, print releases on letterhead.

➤ Send your news releases to the appropriate contact ten days before your event. To avoid confusion, do not send releases to more than one person at a given media outlet.

➤ Be aware of deadlines and do not call reporters near deadline. Find out what days of the week are the best time to contact them.

➤ Since reporters get many news releases, don't be afraid to follow up with a phone call (but not on deadline) to make sure they have received it. Don't be surprised if they haven't seen your release. If they haven't, offer to fax them another. Make your call far enough in advance of any event so they can plan to attend.

➤ Return reporter calls immediately.

➤ Select an articulate spokesperson for interviews. This spokesperson should say what you want people to know in short, brief sentences. If you say more than necessary, your message may be lost.

For Immediate Release: Contact: Arthur Asagio
September 25   555-1234

CITIZENS INVITED TO SHAPE JARLSBERG'S ENERGY FUTURE

Increasing Jarlsberg's energy efficiency by just five percent will mean local citizens can annually keep an extra $4 million in the local economy, and protect the environment at the same time.

How can we take advantage of this opportunity? Jarlsberg residents will have the chance to play a part in developing a plan to increase energy efficiency at the Jarlsberg Energy Town Meeting on October 5, 1996 from 5:30 pm to 7:00 pm at the Grand Hotel. Local energy organizations and businesses will be available to provide information and product displays of energy efficient and renewable technologies.

"With more efficient energy use, the United States could cut its total energy bill in half by using technologies now on the market. That puts millions of dollars a year back into the U.S. economy," said Jarlsberg Energy Committee chair Sue Stilton.

"That figure is the sum of local savings from individuals and institutions who put efficiency and renewable energy to work for them in each community," she said. "We invite residents to get involved in helping Jarlsberg take advantage of these opportunities."

Jarlsberg has an annual local energy bill of $80 million for energy consumed by residents, businesses, and government. That energy bill is more than all the annual earnings of Jarlsberg's largest employers.

With currently available energy-efficient and renewable energy technologies, homes and businesses can significantly reduce energy costs. According to a study conducted by the energy committee, Jarlsberg's government currently spends $347,000 in energy bills for city-owned facilities. "This drain on public finances could easily be slashed by 15 percent," said George Gruyere, Jarlsberg High School science teacher and committee member. "The Jarlsberg economy could reap a profit while reducing our contribution to energy-related problems like acid rain and global warming."

Speakers at the Energy Town Meeting will present information on what local energy use means for the economy and the environment; what other communities have done to reap the economic benefits of energy efficiency; and potential energy saving opportunities for Jarlsberg. Citizens will then create energy task forces as a first step in creating a local energy plan.

"This is the community's chance to take a good look at Jarlsberg's energy costs and set an energy efficiency course that will be good for our economy and good for the environment," said Arthur Asagio, Chair of the Chamber of Commerce. The Energy Town Meeting will also feature music by the Happy Enchiladas and refreshments donated by local businesses.

For more information, contact Arthur Asagio at 555-1234.

–30–

PUBLIC SERVICE ANNOUNCEMENT

Use between 9/25 and 10/5

93 words

20 seconds

Contact:

Arthur Asagio 555-1234

PUBLIC SERVICE ANNOUNCEMENT

ENERGY TOWN MEETING

Come to the Jarlsberg Energy Town Meeting, Wednesday, October 5, to find out how to make energy efficiency work for you, the local economy and the environment. Talk with energy experts, see the latest in energy-efficient and renewable technologies, and help decide what Jarlsberg should do to shape its energy future. The Jarlsberg Energy Town Meeting will be held October 5, 5:30 PM to 7:00 PM at the Grand Hotel. Come at 5:00 p.m. for an Open House, including energy demonstrations, prizes, and refreshments. For more information, contact Arthur Asagio at 555-1234.

- 30 -

Building a High Profile

The third component of an effective outreach campaign is creating a splash around town. Break up residents' daily routines with exciting and entertaining reminders of the upcoming events, inviting people to attend the Energy Town Meeting and join in improving energy use and the economy.

CREATING A HIGH PROFILE

➤ **Take it to the streets**

➤ **Hold attention-grabbing events**

➤ **Sample planning calendar**

Take it to the streets

Most people are far too distracted by everyday concerns to think about improving the way their community uses energy, much less do something about it. Break through peoples' preoccupation with daily concerns and motivate them to act by finding fun and creative ways to capture their attention. Hang banners across main thoroughfares, post colorful flyers on lamp posts and store windows, and find friendly people to stroll around at busy times with sandwich boards announcing events.

Hold attention-grabbing events

Make the news and capture people's attention by organizing events to publicize the Energy Town Meeting and planning workshops.

➤ Organize an Energy Awareness Week with a different theme for each day, such as energy efficiency, renewable energy, and transportation. The week could include demonstrations of energy efficient and renewable technologies, and tours of facilities that have put these technologies to work. Handing out solar-baked cookies on busy streets and offering rides in alternatively-powered vehicles will catch people's attention. These events can lead up to the week's focal point, the Energy Town Meeting.

➤ Hold a "No Gas Dash" or "Efficiency Grand Prix" in which non-motorized or energy-efficient modes of transportation (bicycles, pedestrians, rollerbladers, and buses) race a car (preferably a gas guzzler!). Enlist local celebrities or elected officials to play a role in the event. Design the race course to wind through busy streets to a decorated finish line in a prominent part of town. Include parking and doing an errand as part of the race.

➤ Create events with an eye for photo opportunities. Photos of energy-related events can land in the paper or on the evening news and help promote the upcoming Energy Town Meeting.

➤ Run special features on energy issues in local newspapers.

➤ Run an efficiency raffle. With the help of local business or co-sponsors, distribute raffle tickets for prizes to be awarded at the Energy Town Meeting. Prizes could include compact fluorescent lights, bus passes, and free energy audits.

Sample media/publicity planning calender

At least a month before the Energy Town Meeting:

- Gather mailing lists of all possible interested organizations.
- Develop media contact list.
- Meet with radio station to arrange cosponsorship.
- Start contacting providers of energy-efficient products and services for the Open House.
- Develop a list of names and addresses of key people to invite. Begin to personally contact.
- Meet with local editor to discuss local energy planning effort.
- Send announcements of the Energy Town Meeting to organizations early enough to put in their monthly newsletters.
- Send announcements to all published events calendars.

SUNDAY	MONDAY	TUESDAY	WEDNESDAY	THURSDAY	FRIDAY	SATURDAY
		Create lists of organizations to contact. Brainstorm connecting issues. Write letters of invitation targeted at specific groups.		Write news release with Energy Picture information. Develop easy-to-use fact sheets on the local Energy Picture.	Send letter of invitation to groups and individuals.	
	Notify paper of press conference.		Hang banner across Main Street. Start posting flyers all around town.			Post flyers all around town.
	Call media about news conference. Radio ads begin.	News Conference. Radio ads.	Articles announcing meeting appear. Begin follow-up phone calls to invite people.	Begin follow-up phone calls to invite people. Radio ads continue.	Radio ads continue.	
	Efficiency Grand Prix Live radio coverage of event. Radio ads. Editorial column reminds people of Energy Town Meeting and encourages people to participate.	Photo and reminder of Energy Town Meeting appears in paper. Phone trees to remind people to attend. Radio ads.	Alternative Commute Day: Free breakfasts Live radio interviews. Radio ads. ENERGY TOWN MEETING	Follow-up articles covering the meeting and announcing the planning workshops.		

Energy Town Meeting

A successful Energy Town Meeting is informative, inspiring, and
productive. This festive event presents sustainable energy opportunities
and offers citizens the chance to get involved to make them happen.

AGENDA

1 Welcome and preview

2 Presentation of the Local Energy Picture

3 The economic opportunities of sustainable energy
practices

4 Vote: Should we work to tap these opportunities?

5 Let's do it!: Overview of planning steps

6 Wrap up and schedule first task force meetings

Meeting Agenda

Five minutes

1. Welcome and preview

A host welcomes everyone, introduces speakers and previews the agenda.

Fifteen minutes

2. Presentation of the Local Energy Picture

Using visual props, the first speaker gives a summary of the local energy bill and its costs to the economy and the environment.

Fifteen minutes

3. The opportunities of sustainable energy practices

A second speaker relates energy and economic successes from other communities, and gives a brief sampling of local opportunities.

Five minutes

4. Vote: Should we work to tap these opportunities?

The host asks whether attendees think the community should develop a strategy to tap these opportunities. Ask for a vote with a show of hands.

Ten minutes

5. Let's do it!: Overview of the planning steps

Assuming there is strong support for a community effort to develop an energy strategy, a speaker gives a quick overview of steps the community can take to create a plan. The speaker briefly discusses how participants will form three task forces centered around the residential, commercial/industrial, and transportation energy sectors. These task forces will conduct a series of workshops to learn about sustainable energy alternatives, and barriers and opportunities for implementing them. Based on this information, participants will develop specific projects to put into action.

Ten minutes

6. Wrap up and schedule the first task force meetings

Announce task forces and introduce task force facilitators. Announce where each task force will gather to get started. Task force facilitators should hand out copies of the planning process overview, the first task force meeting agenda, and the Sustainable Energy Opportunities section from the appropriate task force packet. Task forces can briefly discuss who else might be important to involve in the task force, and decide who can contact these additional people. Schedule the time and place of the upcoming task force meeting and thank everyone for attending.

Meeting Materials

Copies for each participant:

• **Town Meeting agendas. Organizers can use the sample agendas to develop original agendas for attendees.**
• **Planning process overview, page 115.**
• **Sustainable Energy Opportunities from the Task Force Packets.**

For the Energy Picture presentation, presenters will need visual props to communicate the Energy Picture, including:

• **A large check to represent the energy bill**
• **Posters of the most important numbers**

Refer to page 256 for more information on meeting preparation.

Meeting Organizer Directions

A successful energy town meeting is informative, inspiring, and productive. The two-hour town meeting should:

➤ Increase awareness of the economic and environmental costs of local energy use;

➤ Demonstrate the economic oppotunities of community energy efficiency;

➤ Share proven energy alternatives and successes with attendees;

➤ Through a quick vote, gauge the community's commitment to tapping opportunities presented by sustainable energy practices;

➤ Outline the energy planning process so people know what's ahead;

➤ Establish times and places of the first task force meetings.

The town meeting will need individuals to play the following roles:

➤ A host who will run the meeting, introduce speakers and keep people within time limits.

➤ A speaker to present Energy Picture information.

➤ A speaker to present the opportunities of sustainable energy practices

➤ A speaker to introduce the energy planning process.

➤ Task force facilitators to meet briefly with task forces.

Dividing the agenda among different speakers in this way will add variety and increase participation. In addition, finding a role for elected officials and other influential people will help draw them into the effort and increase their support.

To help people prepare to play their role in the meeting, here is a rough outline for presenting the various sections of the agenda:

Presenting the Local Energy Picture

By this meeting, the media campaign should have communicated some of the most compelling energy-use statistics to the community. The town meeting will build on these numbers and put them in a meaningful context. Highlight the most striking numbers from the energy picture worksheets with visual displays that demonstrate the bill's cost to the economy and the environment. Here's a suggested outline for presenting the energy picture:

1) **Discuss the annual community energy bill**

➤ Give the total dollar amount of the bill. Posting an oversized check on the wall above the speakers will give your message a stronger visual impact.

➤ Briefly describe how energy use is divided into energy sectors and announce their totals.

2) **Discuss the bill's economic impact:**

➤ If each person had to pay an equal share, what would it be?

➤ What percentage of the community's total income is spent on energy?

➤ When is your community's Energy Freedom Day, and how does it compare to that of other communities or countries?

➤ Compare the bill to sources of community income or other community expenses.

3) **Discuss the environmental costs of the Local Energy Bill**

➤ Where does your community get its energy? (Refer to a large map developed by using pages 71-72.

➤ What are the environmental costs associated with your community's energy sources?

➤ How is the community contributing to climate change? What's the estimated local CO_2 bill?

➤ What are the environmental costs of the local transportation fuel bill?

Presenting the opportunities of sustainable energy practices

You can refer to the workbook introduction to prepare for this presentation. Overheads or slides summarizing examples will make the discussion more interesting. Make the presentation brief and upbeat. Here's a sample outline of points to make:

➤ Summarize a few examples of how other communities have used energy efficiency and renewables to strengthen their economy.

➤ How can sustainable energy practices generate such benefits? Summarize potential savings from several energy end uses, such as lighting, heating, and cooling. (See task force packets)

➤ Give brief examples of potential local benefits.

➤ Tapping these opportunities locally will create tangible benefits, such as business and household savings and a stronger economy.

Presenting the overview of the planning steps

After meeting attendees have determined whether they indeed want to work to develop an energy strategy, preview how the community can go about creating an energy action plan. This overview provides a brief introduction to the first task force meeting and lets people know what to expect. Referring to the planning overview that attendees have been given, explain that:

- ➤ Participants will form three task forces around the three main energy sectors: residential, commercial/large energy users, and transportation.
- ➤ These task forces will conduct a series of workshops to examine efficient and renewable alternatives, opportunities and barriers for implementing them, and other communities' successes.
- ➤ Based on this information, task force members will develop specific proposals to put into action. Then all task forces will present their individual action plans, and put them all together.

Tips for producing a successful Energy Town Meeting

The town meeting is in some ways a performance. Its purpose is to get people interested in taking an active role to improve energy use and the economy. A long, boring meeting with talking heads will do little to motivate people to give up their time to create a plan. Therefore, while the meeting will be packed with information you need to find ways to make the meeting as interesting as possible.

- ➤ Be brief! While the time allotments for each section of the agenda may seem tight, it is indeed possible to effectively cover topics in these suggested time periods. To speak longer than the suggested times will cause attendees to lose interest. Brief, clearly focused presentations keep the energy level high.
- ➤ Be upbeat! Stressing opportunities is far more persuasive than adopting a preachy tone and emphasizing the negative impacts of current local energy use.
- ➤ Find ways to add humor or an element of surprise. Information doesn't have to be boring. If presented effectively it can be inspiring! Be creative!

Energy Open House

If time and resources allow, organize an energy open house in conjunction with the town meeting. The open house provides an opportunity for citizens to see energy efficient lighting and solar water heaters first hand, browse among tables filled with energy information, and talk to local utilities about their efficiency programs. The open house also gives local vendors a venue to promote energy efficient goods and services. For more information on organizing this event, see page 35.

First Task Force Meeting

Meeting Goal: Participants begin the planning process by deciding who needs to be represented in their task force. They also begin exploring sustainable energy opportunities in their sector.

AGENDA

1 Introductions and meeting preview

2 What energy users does this task force include?

3 Discovering sustainable energy opportunities

4 Overview of planning steps

5 Schedule future workshops

Facilitator Agenda

Five minutes

1. Introductions and meeting preview

Welcome task force members and conduct a quick round of introductions. Pass out agendas and task force packets and briefly outline the meeting. Ask for a volunteer with legible writing to serve as the meeting recorder.

Ten minutes

2. What energy users does this task force include?

Discuss which energy users your task force will include and ask participants if relevant energy users, decision makers, and interests are represented in the task force. If not, how can you involve them?

Forty-five minutes

3. Discovering sustainable energy opportunities

Distribute worksheets and work through the questions. As suggested in the facilitators' notes, you may need to give examples to start discussion. Have the recorder write responses on the large sheets of paper.

After participants have exhausted what they already know, ask participants to add to their lists by referring to the Sustainable Energy Opportunities section in the task force packet.

Five minutes

4. Overview of planning steps

Given the significant potential for saving energy, what can we do to turn this potential into reality? Discuss how the proposed planning workshops will provide steps to help the task force develop specific projects that make the most of local resources and tap other communities' successes. These steps are: assess local opportunities and barriers for improving energy practices; examine what's worked in other places; and create and select priority projects.

Ten minutes

5. Schedule future workshops

At meeting's end, participants preview what will happen at the next meeting and the task force arranges a schedule for future workshops. Participants divide up names of additional organizations or interests that should be represented in the task force, and will contact them to invite to the next meeting. Ask for a volunteer to help the facilitator organize the group's meetings.

Meeting Materials

Each participant will need:
- A copy of the first task force meeting agenda adapted from the previous page
- A copy of the Discovering Sustainable Energy Opportunities Worksheet
- A copy of the appropriate task force packet

The facilitator will need:
- An easel and large pad of paper
- Large felt-tipped markers
- A sign-up sheet

Refer to pages 256 for more details on meeting material preparation.

Facilitator Directions

This first meeting gets the task force started by having participants get to know each other, begin talking about energy use in terms they know, and discuss two specific topics:

1. What energy users does this task force include?
2. What are the more sustainable ways of providing energy end-use services in this sector? (i.e., what's a better way to provide comfortable indoor climates? What's a better way to provide light?)

Here are a few notes on how to lead this discussion.

What energy users does this energy sector include?

Ask participants to briefly list what they think the task force's energy sector includes. Here are a few examples of what each task force includes:

Commercial / Industrial Energy Users
➤ Public buildings
➤ Manufacturers
➤ Retail stores
➤ Warehouses
➤ Street lights
➤ Farms
➤ Restaurants

Residential
➤ Apartment houses
➤ Single-family homes
➤ Mobile homes
➤ Condominiums
➤ Second homes

Transportation
➤ Private automobiles
➤ Public transportation
➤ Fleets: both public and business
➤ Taxis
➤ Rental cars

Based on this discussion, ask participants to identify people that are not present who could play an important role in improving the Energy Picture. Who would have insight on how energy is used in each of these sectors? How can the task force get these people involved?

> **Create task forces as needed**
>
> Your community may want to develop task forces to address specific needs within other groups, such as:
> • An agricultural energy-users group
> • A tourist accommodations group
> • A manufacturers group
> Smaller communities may also want to combine the residential and commercial/industrial task forces.

What are the more efficient and sustainable ways of providing energy end-use services in this sector?

This part of the meeting will set the stage for the planning workshops by familiarizing participants with the numerous efficient and renewable alternatives for delivering desired energy services. At the end of the workshop, participants will have a preliminary understanding of the many existing, yet untapped, techniques and technologies that can improve the local energy picture. They should also be asking themselves how the community can take advantage of these methods.

Another purpose of this exercise is to introduce participants to end-use/least-cost planning. While traditional energy planning stresses finding new supplies, end-use/least cost analysis identifies desired energy services, such as warm rooms and lighting, and the least costly ways to get them, counting all costs.

The worksheet provides a framework to focus the group's discussion and encourage participants to begin talking about energy use in terms they know. Participants do not necessarily need to complete the worksheet, but they can use it to follow along with the discussion. To answer the worksheet questions, consider the following:

1) **In this task force sector, what are the end-use services that energy delivers? Ask participants to think about basic energy end-use services such as:**
   ➤ Comfortable indoor climates (heating and cooling)
   ➤ Light
   ➤ Refrigeration
   ➤ Access to places and things we need

While the task force does not need an exhaustive list of end uses, try to have participants brainstorm all the basic ones for your energy sector.

2) **What are the technologies or measures used in this sector to deliver these services?**
   Participants answer this question by listing various technologies or measures (incandescent light bulbs, insulation, etc.) used to deliver end-uses.

3) **What are the types of energy and original energy sources used to deliver these services?**
   Participants answer this question by listing electricity, natural gas, and so forth, and the original energy source of the type of energy, such as coal or oil.

4) What are some of the problems and costs associated with these methods of acquiring services?

Costs can include energy bills, pollution, climate change, and the flow of money out of the community. Go through both the technologies and energy sources, and identify advantages and disadvantages of these methods. Have the group consider such questions as:

➤ Does a technology or measure use more energy than necessary?
➤ Does the original source have any negative side effects, such as pollution or high cash costs?
➤ Is the energy source the most economical and efficient way to deliver the end use?

5) Are there more efficient and/or renewable ways to fulfill your energy needs? What are they?

Go through the list of end-uses and ask participants if they can list alternatives that provide the same services with less energy. For example:

Comfort: Good insulation, weatherization, efficient windows, and efficient building design.

Light: compact fluorescent lights, day lighting, and occupancy sensors.

Access: Designing streets and communities so people can walk and bike to where they need to go.

For examples of more efficient technologies and measures, participants can refer as needed to the task force packets.

Schedule future workshops

Conclude the meeting by discussing task force logistics:

1) Distribute a sign-up sheet asking for names, phone numbers, and addresses and the best time to hold future workshops.
2) Set up meeting times and locations.
3) Ask for someone to volunteer to help the facilitator prepare for and organize the group's meetings.

Discovering energy-smart alternatives

Find more sustainable ways to fulfill end-use energy needs by examining the questions below.

1 In your task force sector, what are the energy end-uses?

2 What are the energy technologies used in this sector to provide these services ?

3 What are the energy sources used in this sector to provide these services ?

4 What are some of the costs (environmental, economic, and social) associated with these methods of providing these energy services?

5 Are there more efficient and /or renewable ways to fulfill your energy needs while cutting costs? What are they?

Energy End-use	Technology or Measures	Energy Sources	Costs	More Sustainable Ways
Lighting	Incandescent Light Bulbs	Coal-burning Power Plants	Air Pollution, Electric bills	Compact Fluorescent Bulbs, Daylighting

What's ahead: Steps to create an energy plan

1 First Task Force Meeting

Decide who needs to be represented in your task force to get the best results possible. Explore some of the many opportunities for increasing energy efficiency in your sector.

2 Workshop A: What Do You Have to Work With?

Identify opportunities and barriers to improving the local energy and economic picture by examining the three factors of people and organizations, financing, and government.

3 Workshop B: Discovering Opportunities

To make the most of local resources, look for connections among assets, opportunities, and barriers. Find out what other communities have done and how their successes relate to local conditions.

4 Workshop C: Creating Project Ideas

Combine what you've learned about the local situation and what's worked in other places to brainstorm project ideas. Then, consider how to turn these ideas into reality. Identify desired project results.

5 Workshop D: Selecting Energy Plan Projects

Evaluate project proposals and select the strongest projects for your task force's energy action plan.

6 Bringing It All Together

Meet with the other task forces and present plans. Identify complementary or conflicting projects, then combine findings to draft the community energy action plan. Establish steps for turning the plan into action.

7 Implement Projects!

Make sure the plan doesn't just sit on a shelf. Work to make all your good ideas a reality.

What Do You Have to Work With?

Workshop Goal: To identify opportunities and barriers to improving the local energy and economic picture, your task force will examine the three factors of people and organizations, financing, and government.

WORKSHOP A AGENDA

1 Review the first task force meeting and preview the workshop agenda

2 Assess local barriers, opportunities and assets in the following three areas:
   I. People and Organizations
   II. Financing
   III. Government

3 What else do we need to know? Who can find out?

4 Wrap up and preview the next workshop: Discovering opportunities

Facilitator Agenda

Twenty minutes

1. Review the first meeting and preview the workshop agenda

Welcome participants and conduct a quick round of introductions. Acknowledge any newcomers and briefly explain that the upcoming workshops are aimed at creating projects to put energy efficiency to work to strengthen the local economy. Briefly review points from the first meeting on possibilities for improving energy use in your task force sector.

Explain that while it's tempting to immediately develop specific projects, taking time to first assess local opportunities and barriers will ensure that the most effective projects will emerge. By examining the three energy factors of people and organizations, financing, and government, participants can identify significant opportunities and barriers to improving the local energy picture. This factor assessment will build the information base from which to create project proposals in future workshops.

Seventy-five minutes

2. Assess local barriers, opportunities and assets

Using the Factor Assessment Worksheets, and the accompanying questions for your task force, brainstorm assets, opportunities, and barriers for each of the energy factors. The group should spend about 25 minutes per factor. Ask a volunteer to record responses on large sheets of paper.

Five minutes

3. What else do we need to know? Who can find out?

The factor inventory may have raised questions that participants couldn't answer due to a lack of information. They may decide to gather additional information on some of these items. The task forces should determine who will be responsible for getting additional information.

Five minutes

4. Wrap up and preview the next workshop

Thank participants for coming and set the next meeting date. Give a brief preview of the next workshop by mentioning that participants will explore how to put identified resources to work to address barriers and improve the community's economic and energy picture. In the next workshop participants will also begin to assess projects that have worked in other communities for possible local implementation.

Facilitator Directions

The Energy Town Meeting and first task force meeting established that there are many opportunities for saving energy and tapping renewable sources. The million dollar question is "How do you put these to work locally?"

The three energy factors of people and organizations, financing, and government, will help task forces assess essential opportunities and barriers for turning energy-efficiency opportunities into reality. Participants will use Factor Assessment Worksheets and accompanying task force questions to focus their inventory of these three areas.

How to use the factor assessment worksheets

1) Introduce the factor assessment by using page 121 to describe the three factors areas. Describe what is meant by assets, opportunities, and barriers using a poster with the definitions from page 122. You can also use the Jarlsberg example on page 123 to illustrate how a factor assessment could look.

2) Large task forces may want to divide into subgroups of 5 to 7 participants. Each subgroup can assess at least one energy factor and then present their results to the entire task force. During this presentation, ask other task force members if they have anything to add to each subgroup's list.

3) Ask a volunteer to record the findings on large sheets of flip-chart paper, labeled Assets, Opportunities, and Barriers. Participants may also want to take notes on their worksheets.

4) Most people find it helpful to start with "people and organizations," which may be less intimidating than the financing or government factors. Everyone knows something about people and organizations.

5) Use the appropriate task force packet questions to help participants consider each factor. The thinking stimulated by these questions is more important than the answers they generate. If people run out of ideas, refer to the questions again.

➤ The lists you develop from brainstorming about each factor may not be of equal length. The first lists tend to be longer than the last ones. Participants shouldn't feel obliged to produce exhaustive lists, since the group can always add more suggestions later.

➤ When participants offer complex ideas, the recorder should find a brief phrase to summarize the thought. Another volunteer can record the full idea for later reference.

> The three energy factors of people and organizations, financing, and government will help your task force assess essential opportunities and barriers for turning efficiency opportunities into reality.

➤ The three factors offer a framework to guide your discussion of local resources and barriers. Participants may think of additional, important information that does not fit neatly in any of the three categories. Be sure to record this information and, if necessary, create an additional energy factor to cover these additional items.

➤ Keep the meeting moving and don't let it get bogged down in details. Since this workshop's purpose is to promote thinking about community energy issues, you should try to complete all three factors and not exhaustively discuss all local energy concerns.

➤ Most importantly, have fun! Establish an atmosphere of friendly and open brainstorming. Encourage people to take risks and share ideas by taking chances yourself and offering your thoughts.

Workshop variation

Since most of us rarely think about energy issues, some participants may want to learn more about the issues discussed before moving on to Workshop B. In that case, your task force can divide Workshop A into two meetings.

At the first meeting, the task force looks at each factor area. Participants then decide what additional information they need to adequately understand local conditions. The group may want to invite a guest speaker to the next meeting. A presentation from a utility staff person about current utility energy efficiency programs, or from a building code official, can help prepare participants for the next workshops.

Participants can also use the time between the two Workshop A sessions to find answers to some of the questions the group was unable to answer in their factor assessments.

The Three Energy Factors

Countless opportunities exist for improving the local economy through more efficient and renewable energy use. But the million dollar question is "How do we turn these opportunities into reality?"

Assessing the three energy factors will help you identify initial opportunities and barriers to improving the local Energy Picture. By identifying what you have to work with, your community can create projects that make the most of local conditions to turn the potential of efficient and renewable energy use into reality. The three factors are:

People and Organizations

While there have been many rapid advances in efficient and renewable technologies, it's up to people and organizations to put them to work. By examining opportunities and barriers associated with individuals and groups, your action plan can make the most of local skills and talents. This factor will help you identify and examine entities that can play a role in the effort. A small sampling of these players include:

> Businesses
> Architects and engineers
> Utilities
> Homeowners
> Community groups
> Schools
> Energy professionals

Financing

The upfront costs of efficient and renewable technologies, and a lack of initial financial incentives, are common barriers to instituting better energy practices. The factor assessment will help you identify financing options and examine financial barriers your community needs to address. Later, you can examine how other communities have overcome some of these barriers.

Government

Since local governments can enact codes, allocate funds, develop policies, and regulate land uses, they can have a far-reaching impact on the community energy picture. By taking stock of federal, state and local government's energy policies and resources, you can use the tool of government to improve your Energy Picture. You can also discover current rules and practices that perpetuate wasteful energy use.

How to assess the energy factors

To find out what you have to work with, use this framework and the questions beginning on page 127 to examine assets, opportunities, and barriers as they relate to the three energy factors.

Assets

What qualities, skills, unique characteristics, and resources exist in your community that could be put to work to make it more energy efficient? Assets include tangible resources such as money or programs, as well as abstract resources, such as leadership and concern for the environment.

Opportunities

What events, decisions, conditions or actions, could your efforts take advantage of? Opportunities differ from assets because they are temporary and must be acted on or missed. Sometimes, it's hard to tell the difference between assets and opportunties, so don't get caught up in debating which category a given idea may fall under.

Barriers

What obstacles, disincentives, and constraints need to be overcome to encourage use of renewable and efficient technologies?

What do you have to work with?
Energy Factor: People and Organizations

Before starting your assessment, here's how the residential task force in the hypothetical town of Jarlsberg began their assessment of people and organizations.

Assets

- We have a municipally-owned utility that says they want to offer the best service possible.
- The Jarlsberg Bank emphasizes service to the community.
- There's a local family that built a passive solar house back in the 70's and they pay practically nothing for heating, even in the winter.
- There are several architects in town that are interested in energy-efficient building design.
- There's a local solar hot water business that's been quietly doing business for the last 4 years.
- There's a group of students at the high school that have been doing some neat environmental projects.

Opportunities

- A developer is currently developing plans to build a subdivision on the outskirts of town.
- One of the service organizations in town (that many business people belong to) is interested in finding a project that helps the environment.
- The state energy office has just started a program to increase use of energy-efficient mortgages.
- A coalition of community groups is developing a proposal to build a Community Center.

Barriers

- Tenants have no incentive to invest their own money in efficiency measures when utilities are included in rent.
- Landlords don't have any obvious incentives to invest in efficiency when tenants pay their own utility bills.
- Developers aren't aware of the benefits of including energy-smart measures when they develop their budget to build.
- Developers and architects have no incentive to take the operating costs of buildings into account when new buildings are designed.
- Builders and contractors think it's too expensive to build with solar and energy-efficient design.
- Realtors don't understand energy efficiency issues enough to talk about them with their clients, or to promote energy-efficient mortgages.
- People might be interested in lower energy bills but they don't have the time to research what they should do and they don't have the upfront money to invest in improvements.

What do you have to work with?
Energy Factor: People and Organizations

Assets

Opportunities

Barriers

What do you have to work with?
Energy Factor: Financing

Assets

Opportunities

Barriers

What do you have to work with?
Energy Factor: Government

Assets

Opportunities

Barriers

Residential Task Force

Questions for the factor assessment worksheets

As you assess each factor, consider the following questions. These questions are intended to help stimulate your thinking and don't need to be answered in full detail.

People and Organizations

- ➤ Are homeowners, landlords, and renters aware of the economic benefits created by energy efficiency investments?
- ➤ Are organizations taking advantage of the resources available through Energy Partnerships for a Strong Economy? (see page 253)
- ➤ What businesses in your community offer energy-efficient technologies, renewable energy, or related services?
- ➤ Do people know where they can purchase simple devices such as energy-efficient light bulbs and efficient shower heads?
- ➤ Does your utility see energy efficiency as a power supply option? Is the utility looking for ways to provide energy services to customers at the lowest total cost?
- ➤ Who makes decisions at your utility about whether to offer energy efficiency programs? Who influences what decisions get made at your utility?
- ➤ How is your energy effort connected to the hot topics and concerns of your community?
- ➤ Are there any local or state organizations or agencies currently working on energy efficiency for residences? What are they doing? How can your task force work complement these efforts?
- ➤ Are local architects designing homes that take full advantage of cost-effective, energy efficiency measures? Are they aware of green building techniques? Are clients demanding them?
- ➤ Are home buyers aware of the operating costs of potential properties? Do real estate brokers present energy costs to clients?
- ➤ Are there any local residences that can serve as an example of energy efficiency?
- ➤ How aware of energy-efficient practices are contractors, builders, electricians, and others involved in the building industry?

Financing

- ➤ What low-cost/no-cost measures can save residential energy?
- ➤ How aware are home buyers and lenders of energy-efficient mortgages (EEMs)?
- ➤ What kinds of programs does your utility offer to help residents

invest in energy efficiency measures?

➤ How aware are developers that homes can be cost-effectively designed to consume half the energy of a typical home?

➤ Do local energy users have easy access to information on the cost-effectiveness of residential energy efficiency measures?

➤ What kinds of experiences have local residential energy users had in trying to get financing for energy improvements?

➤ Are local financial institutions aware of the low-risk nature of financing efficiency investments? Would they grant efficiency improvement loans for residential energy improvements?

➤ Are there any upcoming events that might offer opportunities for funding for energy improvements?

➤ Are there any homes currently being designed or considered that members of your task force could use to demonstrate the cost effectiveness of sustainable design?

➤ Is there a local community development corporation that could help finance residential energy improvements?

➤ Is affordable housing designed to have affordable utility bills?

➤ What residents are hit hardest by utility expenses? Are there programs that will help them cut these expenses?

Government

➤ If you have a municipal utility are local elected officials aware of what other municipal utilities are doing to promote energy efficiency? Are elected officials encouraging the municipal utility to promote energy efficiency and renewables?

➤ What existing local energy-wise policies will foster energy efficiency in the residential sector?

➤ What policies have been tried? What limited their success?

➤ Is there an energy office to implement a community energy plan?

➤ What, if anything, ensures that publicly funded affordable housing projects are energy efficient?

➤ Are government buildings energy efficient? Do they serve as an example to residents?

➤ Is government working with local utilities to create financial incentives for efficiency?

➤ Is energy efficiency a factor in building new public facilities? Are local officials aware of the budgetary incentives to incorporating efficiency measures into building designs from the very start?

➤ Does local government offer technical assistance to designers and architects to increase building design efficiency?

➤ How do local building codes encourage sustainable design? Do builders understand and take full advantage of energy standards?

Commercial/Industrial Task Force

Questions for the factor assessment worksheets

As you assess each factor, consider the following questions. These questions are intended to help stimulate your thinking and don't need to be answered in full detail.

People and Organizations

➤ Are businesses and trade associations aware of the economic opportunities created by energy efficiency investments?

➤ What businesses offer energy-efficient or renewable energy technologies, or related services?

➤ What incentives do local building designers (including architects, developers, contractors, building engineers, and electricians) have to make buildings as efficient as possible?

➤ Does your utility see energy efficiency as a power supply option? Is the utility looking for ways to provide energy services to customers at the lowest total cost?

➤ Are local businesses and organizations taking advantage of the resources available through Energy Partnerships for a Strong Economy? (see page 253)

➤ Are local businesses participating in the Environmental Protection Agency's Green Lights program?

➤ Are there any local or state organizations or agencies currently working on energy efficiency for business and industry? What are they doing? How can your task force work complement what is already being done?

➤ Are local architects and building engineers designing buildings that take full advantage of cost-effective energy efficiency measures? Are they aware of sustainable building techniques? Are clients demanding them?

➤ Are building buyers aware of the operating costs of potential properties? Do real estate brokers present properties' energy costs to clients?

➤ Are there any local businesses that have invested in energy efficiency that other commercial energy users could learn from?

➤ Are businesses aware that pollution prevention techniques also cut production costs?

Financing

➤ What kind of programs does your utility offer to help business and industry invest in energy efficiency measures?

➤ Do developers know that buildings can be cost-effectively built to consume 50% less energy than conventional designs?

➤ Does your state have an Energy Bank program (such as the Iowa Energy Bank) or any other financing assistance for public buildings and nonprofits?

➤ Do local energy users have easy access to information on the cost-effectiveness of commercial/industrial energy-efficiency measures?

➤ What kinds of experiences have local commercial/industrial energy users had in trying to get financing for energy improvements?

➤ Are local businesses participating in the Green Lights Program?

➤ Are local financial institutions aware of the low-risk nature of financing efficiency investments? Would they grant efficiency improvement loans to local energy users?

➤ Are there any upcoming events that might offer opportunities for funding for energy improvements?

➤ Are there any proposed building projects that could be used to demonstrate the cost-effectiveness of green design?

Government

➤ If the utility is publicly owned, are local elected officials aware of what other municipal utilities (such as Osage, Iowa's) are doing to promote energy efficiency? Are elected officials working to make the municipal utility promote energy efficiency?

➤ What existing local energy-wise policies will foster energy efficiency in the residential sector?

➤ What policies have been tried? What limited their success?

➤ Is there an energy office that can help implement a community energy plan?

➤ Are government buildings energy efficient? Do they serve as an example to residents?

➤ Is government working with local utilities to create financial incentives for efficiency?

➤ Is energy efficiency a factor in building new public facilities? Are local officials aware of the budgetary incentives to incorporating efficiency measures into building designs from the very start?

➤ Does local government offer technical assistance to designers and architects to increase building design efficiency?

➤ How does your local building code encourage sustainable design? How old is the code? Do local builders understand and take full advantage of energy standards?

➤ Are local businesses aware of all the resources the U.S. Department of Energy and Environmental Protection Agency provide to increase businesses' profitability through energy efficiency?

Transportation Task Force

Questions for the factor assessment worksheets

As you assess each factor, consider the following questions. These questions are intended to help stimulate your thinking and don't need to be answered in full detail.

People and Organizations

➤ Who makes transportation decisions in your community, county and state? What are the upcoming transportation decisions that should include energy-efficient alternatives?

➤ What kind of public participation process is being used in making these decisions?

➤ What are the main ways residents get to work, school, and shopping? What is the average number of vehicle trips per day in various neighborhoods of your community?

➤ Are transportation decision-makers taking full advantage of the opportunities for alternative modes provided by the Intermodal Surface Transportation Efficiency Act (ISTEA)?

➤ Are transportation decision-makers currently allowing different modes of transportation to fairly compete against each other? How do they evaluate and compare different modes?

➤ If your community has a public transit system, who uses it? How could ridership be increased? Are people rewarded for making an effort to use transit?

➤ Do local businesses offer employees incentives for reducing automobile use?

➤ Are developers in your community seriously considering how to make their developments pedestrian friendly? Are they aware of examples of transit-oriented development? Do developers believe that the community prefers developments that make it easy to get around without relying on a car?

➤ Are developers currently required to provide a minimum amount of parking for new offices? Are there ways to encourage developers to incorporate incentives for alternatives in new projects?

➤ Do employers provide free parking for employees? Do these employers provide comparable support for those who bike, walk, or use transit to get to work?

Financing

➤ What low-cost/no-cost measures can make your local transportation system more energy efficient?

➤ Are local transportation decision-makers taking advantage of the funding opportunities available for alternative modes through ISTEA?

➤ Is an inefficient transportation system currently creating an economic drain on workers and businesses? How?

➤ What's the average percentage of income that households must spend on transportation needs, including all costs?

➤ What's the local budget for street improvements? Sidewalk improvements? Bike ways?

➤ Could developers easily find buyers for property in transit-oriented projects in your community?

➤ Are local businesses taking advantage of tax credits to encourage employees to use public transit passes?

➤ Are there any upcoming funding decisions that offer an opportunity for financing for more efficient transportation modes?

➤ Is your state currently considering feebates or pay at the pump insurance? (See Transportation Task Force Packet.)

➤ Who is responsible for making transportation funding decisions at the state level? How are they determining which projects receive funding? Are they using the ISTEA criteria of increased energy efficiency and community economic enhancement?

➤ Are local drivers aware of the full cost of solo driving? Do they know how these costs compare to other transportation alternatives?

➤ Are transportation costs of new developments fully considered in new development proposals?

➤ What portion of total costs of driving are actually paid by user fees such as gas taxes? What portion of the total cost is subsidized by the public through general revenues?

Government

➤ Do local land use regulations promote development that is friendly to a variety of different transportation modes? Are land use decisions creating a community that makes it easy for people to get access to work, school, and shopping without needing a car?

➤ What's the average miles per gallon of your local government's fleet of vehicles? Is fuel efficiency one of the criteria used in purchasing public vehicles?

➤ Does local government assist developers in making projects that do not increase car dependence for future inhabitants and users?

➤ Do local planning staff weigh transportation impacts when considering whether to approve new developments? How are impacts measured? How are innovative transit-oriented projects encouraged during this approval process?

➤ Does your community and county government encourage employees to use efficient modes of transportation?

➤ Does your local government have demonstration vehicles, alternative transportation campaigns, or other innovative transportation projects?

➤ Which government departments and staff have the biggest roles in determining transportation patterns in your community? How are they involving pedestrians and cyclists in their transportation planning?

➤ Is your community in touch with the state bike/pedestrian coordinator? (ISTEA mandates that each state hire a coordinator who, among other duties, assists communities with developing pedestrian/bike plans.)

➤ What role do transportation demand management measures play in local transportation decision making? Is transportation demand management fully integrated into transportation planning?

➤ What kind of public resources are committed to providing free parking? Are equal amounts of resources committed to accommodating alternative modes of transportation?

Discovering Opportunities

Workshop Goal: To make the most of local resources, participants seek connections among assets, opportunities, and barriers. Then participants find how other communities' successes relate to local conditions.

WORKSHOP B AGENDA

1 Review the last meeting and preview the workshop agenda

2 Break into subgroups and look for connections between local assets, opportunities, and barriers

3 Share connections with the entire task force

4 Discuss the homework worksheet: What's worked in other places?

5 Wrap up and preview the next workshop: Creating Energy Plan project ideas

Facilitator Agenda

Twenty minutes

1. Review the last meeting and preview the workshop agenda

Briefly review Workshop A findings. Ask participants if they can answer any unresolved questions from the last workshop.

To make the most of local resources, participants will examine Workshop A findings to see how assets and opportunities can address identified barriers. Participants will also begin to find out how other communities have developed innovative approaches and overcome barriers. By discovering what's worked in other places, task forces can put proven projects to work locally and develop ideas of their own.

One hour

2. Break into subgroups and look for connections

Introduce the next step by referring to Workshop A findings and providing sample connections between relevant assets, opportunities, and barriers. Divide the group into subgroups and hand out a summary of Workshop A findings to each group.

Participants look for connections and related issues, circling and connecting them with markers. Each subgroup's recorder notes these connections on a large sheet of paper.

Twenty-five minutes

3. Share connections with entire task force

Each subgroup shares results with the entire task force. If subgroup ideas overlap, each group can briefly acknowledge repeated ideas and focus on ones that haven't yet been presented to the task force.

Ten minutes

4. What's worked in other places?

Distribute the "What's Worked in Other Places" homework worksheet. Before the next meeting, participants look at task force packets and any other available resources to see how others have addressed barriers and improved energy use.

Five minutes

5. Wrap up and preview the next workshop

Thank task force members for participating and set the next meeting date. At the next workshop, participants will briefly present examples of what's worked in other places and then brainstorm project ideas.

Facilitator Directions

This workshop encourages participants to examine Workshop A findings and to begin to think of ways to make the most of local assets and opportunities. The workshop also begins to examine what has worked in other places.

Making connections worksheet

1) Before the workshop, go through Workshop A findings and identify several assets that might be used to help overcome barriers. Use these examples to start the discussion. The example Connections Worksheet on page 138 shows how the commercial/industrial task force in the hypothetical town of Jarlsberg found connections between Workshop A findings.

2) Small groups (5 to 7 people) will make it easier for participants to review earlier information and find connections. Each small group will need a copy of the Connections Worksheet filled in with Workshop A findings (see notes to the right).

3) You may ask each subgroup to focus on either assets, barriers, or opportunities. Each subgroup should start with their particular column and draw connections to the others. The group handling barriers, for example, will look for possible solutions in the assets and opportunities columns.

4) As participants look for connections, the discussion can jump ahead into specific project ideas. Record these ideas on a flip chart, but remind the task force that they are still assessing what they have to work with and should resist the temptation to develop project proposals at this point

5) If participants run out of connections, check to see if they have tried to link every barrier on the list to an asset or opportunity. This step will help conclude the workshop and lead into the homework.

Meeting Materials, cont.

Find a way to provide participants with an easy view of Workshop A findings. This could either be:

- **A large version of the Connections Worksheet made from 8 1/2" x 11" sheets of paper taped together as needed. Each subgroup can share this version and write their comments directly on it. You can consolidate and edit Workshop A results to make them fit.**
- **A wall-size version of the Connections Worksheet made out of easel sheets of paper, using as much wall space as needed.**

What's worked in other places worksheet

This step will encourage participants to find out what other communities have done to increase energy efficiency and begin to relate these success stories to local conditions.

If participants are unable to find applicable examples, they can refer to additional task force packet sources and research these items before the next meeting. Tell participants it is not necessary to do extensive research and that basic information is all the task force needs for now.

Making connections worksheet

Here's an example of how members of the commercial/ industrial task force
in the hypothetical town of Jarlsberg looked for connections between assets,
opportunities and barriers.

Assets

People and Organizations

- The building supply store is willing to stock new products if demand exists.
- There's a high school student group that's concerned about the environment and looking for projects.
- The downtown association is interested in finding ways to help local businesses.
- The community college facilities manager has implemented many successful energy projects over the years.
- Our utility is eligible for a peer match and technical assistance from the regional federal power administration.

Government

- The extension service has a booklet on energy-efficiency measures for small businesses.
- EPA's Green Lights program provides assistance for commercial lighting retrofits.
- We have a municipally-owned utility.
- The state energy office offers a technical assistance program to help small businesses and public institutions make energy improvements.

Financing

- The Limburger Lodge has seen dramatic energy bill savings after doing a shower head retrofit.
- Several local banks have stressed that they want to be of service to the community.
- There are all kinds of financing resources listed within the Green Lights program.
- Many energy improvements will pay for themselves in less than a year. If businesses are aware of the assured early savings, they can see it makes sense to invest in the improvements.

Opportunities

- The school board is calling for proposals for remodeling and expanding the old Pecorino High School.
- Our utility is required to develop an integrated resource plan within the next few years.
- A developer is considering building a downtown office building.
- The director of the local utility has said he'd like to do more demand-side management programs but doesn't see how his utility can afford it.
- The Daily Jarlsbergian has announced it is looking for people willing to write regular columns.

- City Hall is going to be remodeled next spring.
- Other municipally-owned utilities have efficiency programs that are both economically beneficial for themselves and help their customers.
- The building department's new director wants to update the city's decade-old building code.
- Local government is worried about tight budgets and the impact of a new tax limitation initiative.

- Our area utilities must spend millions per year buying power from producers outside our area. They are currently buying power at a rate that efficiency programs could compete with.
- The state energy office is considering setting up an Energy Bank program that would offer 0% interest loans for public and nonprofit building retrofits.
- The local energy bill for all school and government buildings is almost half a million dollars. That's a lot of money that could be put to better use.

Barriers

- Many architects don't think efficiency measures work.
- Energy costs are often part of fixed rent rates — there's no direct incentive for building users to invest in improvements, and landlords don't see reducing operating costs as a means to financial rewards.
- Businesses are too busy to think about how to save on their energy bills - they don't know where to start.
- Buildings aren't designed using common sense. For example, cooling and heating engineers don't have any input in basic design features like windows and building orientation.

- Building codes are too rigid and do not encourage energy-smart design.
- Government bidding procedures favor proposals that have the lowest upfront building costs, without consideration for life-cycle operating costs of the building over time.
- City council doesn't consider energy issues important enough to develop any energy-wise policies.
- Local utility staff are skeptical that DSM can be a dependable and cost-effective supply resource.

- Building designers are financially rewarded for the size of the heating and cooling systems of buildings, rather than for the end result of building comfort.
- The upfront costs of energy improvements make it hard for building managers to make them a priority.
- Many underused financing programs sound good but require extensive paperwork.
- Businesses make decisions based on low upfront costs, and not on life-cycle costs.

Making connections worksheet

	Assets
People and Organizations	
Government	
Financing	

Opportunities

Barriers

What's worked in other places
homework worksheet

Using the task force packet information and any other available resources, examine other communities' successes. Do any of these other communities' successes address barriers or opporunties identified in Workshop A?

Barriers

Successes from other communities that address these barriers

Assets and Opportunities

What have other communities done to tap similar conditions?

What's worked in other places
homework worksheet

Using the task force packet, identify resources offered by organizations or state
and federal government that may help your efforts. Which of these resources
can help you address barriers or opportunities identified in Workshop A?

Barriers	Resources that could help address these barriers

Assets and Opportunities	Resources that could help tap these opportunities?

Creating Project Ideas

Workshop Goal: Take what you know about your local situation and what's worked in other places to brainstorm project ideas. Then, consider how to turn your ideas into reality and identify desired project results.

WORKSHOP C AGENDA

1 Review the last meeting and preview the workshop agenda

2 Report back on "What's worked in other places?"

3 Brainstorm project ideas

4 Discuss the homework worksheet: Exploring project requirements and results

5 Wrap up and preview next workshop: Selecting projects

Facilitator Agenda

Fifteen minutes

1. Review the last meeting and preview the workshop agenda

Post the Workshop A findings and Workshop B connections around the room. Explain that participants will refer to results from previous workshops and the descriptions of what's worked in other places to create their energy project ideas. Task force members will then explore their project ideas by using the homework worksheet.

Forty-five minutes

2. Report back on "What's worked in other places?"

Participants report on energy successes from other communities. If reports repeat the same successes concentrate on projects which the task force hasn't yet heard.

Forty-five minutes

3. Brainstorm project ideas

Participants begin brainstorming project ideas. When participants run low on ideas, refer to Workshop A findings and see if project ideas have missed important points. Check off the issues that are addressed by project ideas.

Ten minutes

4. Exploring project requirements and results

Explain that in order to select priority projects task force members will need to briefly consider the broad requirements and desired results of project ideas. Divide project ideas among individuals or subgroups, depending on whether the group wants to examine ideas individually or collectively. Preview the worksheet to see if there are any questions. Make arrangements for task force members to deliver their sheets to facilitators before the next workshop.

Five minutes

5. Wrap up and preview the next workshop

At the next workshop, participants will evaluate projects and select the proposals they want to pursue.

Facilitator Directions

If your task force members are like most, they've been eagerly awaiting a chance to bring their ideas together and talk about actual projects. This workshop brings participants to that point. Here's a few pointers on each of the workshop steps to keep the meeting moving.

Report back on "What's worked in other places?"

Subgroups may have made similar discoveries. Rather than listen to them repeat the same findings, have each stress their own unique ideas and briefly summarize any information that overlaps with others.

Brainstorming project ideas

Participants brainstorm project ideas, drawing from Workshop B connections and examples from other places. Post a large version of the connections that everyone can see. Have two recorders if needed.

The tips on page 256 will also help you conduct a successful brainstorming session. To make sure you are addressing all relevant concerns, go through your previous lists of barriers to improved energy use and see if the projects you have proposed will address them.

"Exploring project Ideas" worksheet

This worksheet will help participants examine what project ideas will require to become a reality and what each project will achieve. Once participants consider these basic project characteristics, they can more easily weigh alternatives in the next workshop.

It's easy for participants to get bogged down discussing the details of each project. Point out that the thinking stimulated by this exercise is more important than the answers it creates. Stress that participants need only brief responses and shouldn't spend too much time tracking answers. They can fully examine questions when selected projects are being implemented.

Participants can break into small groups and collectively explore project ideas, or they can sign up individually for ideas. Check off each idea until all ideas are assigned.

Although this exercise is intended as homework, your group can begin this step during the workshop. Participants will need to complete and deliver the "Exploring Project Ideas" worksheet to the facilitator before the next workshop. The facilitator will need to make enough copies of each completed worksheet so that participants can refer to them in the next workshop. To make it easier for participants to use worksheet results in the next workshop, you may want to condense all the returned worksheets into a master list of projects and their central characteristics.

Exploring project ideas
homework worksheet

To understand the possible benefits and drawbacks of each project idea, briefly answer the following questions. You should not need to do any extensive research to find the answers.

Project idea _____

1 What would the project achieve?
What barriers would it overcome?

_____

_____

2 Who would the project serve?

_____

3 Who would the project affect?

_____

4 What will it take to make the project a reality?
Consider needs such as the following:
- technical assistance
- funding
- time
- political support
- equipment and materials
- skills and expertise
- partnerships / joint efforts
- rough guess of level of investment:
  - no cost / low cost
  - large investment / long-term pay back
  - minor investment / quick pay back
  - no idea

_____

5 Energy results
How will this project improve the energy picture?
Will it:
- directly save energy?
- create conditions to make it easier to save energy?
- replace a fossil fuel energy use with a renewable energy source?

_____

_____

6 Economic results
How will this project help the economy? Will it:
- free up money previously spent on energy?
- stimulate demand for energy-saving products and services?
- keep more money in the local economy?
- create new jobs?

_____

_____

7 Will the results of this project be seen in the:
circle one
short term (less than 1 year)
mid-term (2 - 3 years)
longer term (more than 4-5 years)

Project idea _____

1 What would the project achieve?

What barriers would it overcome?

_____

_____

2 Who would the project serve?

_____

3 Who would the project affect?

_____

4 What will it take to make the project a reality?

Consider needs such as the following:

• technical assistance

• funding

• time

• political support

• equipment and materials

• skills and expertise

• partnerships / joint efforts

• rough guess of level of investment:

   • no cost / low cost

   • large investment / long-term pay back

   • minor investment / quick pay back

   • no idea

_____

_____

5 Energy results

How will this project improve the energy picture?
Will it:

• directly save energy?

• create conditions to make it easier to save energy?

• replace a fossil fuel energy use with a renewable
  energy source?

_____

_____

6 Economic results

How will this project help the economy? Will it:

• free up money previously spent on energy?

• stimulate demand for energy-saving products and
  services?

• keep more money in the local economy?

• create new jobs?

_____

_____

7 Will the results of this project be seen in the:

circle one

short term (less than 1 year)

mid-term (2 - 3 years)

longer term (more than 4-5 years)

Selecting Energy Plan Projects

Workshop Goal: Your task force will evaluate project proposals and select the strongest projects for the community energy action plan.

Facilitator Agenda

Ten minutes

1. Review the last meeting and preview the workshop agenda

Post or distribute the list of brainstormed projects and ask for any additional project ideas. Pass out the background information that has been developed for each project idea. In this workshop, participants will conduct the following three steps to evaluate and select priority projects.

➤ Weigh the strengths and weaknesses of project ideas.

➤ Create a menu of the strongest ideas.

➤ Select a complementary mix of priority projects.

One hour or more depending on number of projects

2. Weigh strengths and weaknesses of project ideas

Distribute scorecards and a copy of the project criteria. Ask participants if they think these are useful criteria and see if they have any to add. As a group, use the scorecard and criteria to evaulate a sample project idea.

Participants score all the projects listed. The average score for each project is tallied and all projects and scores are posted.

Ten minutes

3. Create a menu of the strongest project ideas

Using the "Project Menu" worksheet, list the ideas that did well in the first step and fill in those projects' characteristics. This step gives task force members an overview of all potential project goals, time frames, participants and methods.

Thirty minutes

4. Select projects for the Energy Action Plan

Through group discussion, or the point system described on page 155, participants choose priorities for the energy action plan.

Five minutes

5. Wrap up and preview the next workshop

In the next meeting, your task force will present the selected priority projects to the other groups. Before the next meeting, a subgroup may want to prepare a timeline of projects for the presentation.

Facilitator Directions

Narrowing a list of attractive ideas down to the ones you want to pursue can be a challenging task. Some task force members may feel uncomfortable attempting to evaluate project ideas with incomplete information. More complete information may be necessary at a later time for determining the details of various project ideas. But for now, task forces can use what they know to identify essential strengths and weaknesses and choose between various project concepts. If it's essential that your group resolve questions about a proposal, make addressing these concerns a project to pursue. Avoid getting caught up in the belief that all action can come only after lengthy analysis.

To ease the group decision-making process, this workshop offers three steps to help participants create a manageable list of projects for the energy action plan.

➤ Weigh project strengths and weaknesses using a set of energy project criteria and a scorecard.

➤ Generate a menu of the strongest proposals resulting from step one to create an overview of potential projects.

➤ Select a combination of the strongest projects to create an effective strategy for improving the energy picture.

This selection method offers a way for the task force to scrutinize individual projects and see how they relate to one another. This process will help participants select a mix of strong projects that make the most of local resources to improve the energy picture. Here are more detailed instructions for conducting these three steps.

Weigh project strengths and weaknesses using a set of energy project criteria and a scorecard.

First, participants will need to understand the energy project criteria they will use to examine their ideas. Review the criteria using the handout from page 156 and provide examples to illustrate each point. Ask if anyone has any other criteria they would like to add.

Next, by using the scorecard (page 160), each participant has an opportunity to decide how well each project performs on each item. Here are the steps for using the evaluation scorecard.

1) Hand out project idea lists and the results of "Project Requirements and Desired Results" worksheet filled out for each project idea.

2) Provide each participant with enough scorecards to evaluate every project idea.

3) As a group, evaluate a sample project with the scorecard.

4) Ask participants to fill out a scorecard for each project idea. Explain that scoring projects is a preliminary step for identifying their strengths and weaknesses. It is not necessary to know the exact answers to the scorecard questions. Participants can explore "maybes" and "don't knows" later. They don't need to take more than a few minutes to score each project idea. (In fact, if they do take more than a few minutes for each scoring this step can last quite a long time!)

5) Collect scorecards as participants complete them.

6) Add up the scores and the number of yes, no, and maybe responses for each project.

7) After all the projects have been scored, post the results.

8) As a task force, review the list of projects and the results. Emphasize that the scores are simply a starting point to indicate project strengths and weaknesses. Explain that the group now needs to create a menu of the strongest project ideas.

Generate a menu of the strongest proposals for an overview of potential projects.

This step will help participants create a list of the strongest projects, along with a listing of important characteristics. Refer to "Completing the Project Menu" on page 158.

1) Distribute Project Menu worksheets to each participant, along with a copy of directions for completing the menu.

2) Post a large version of the Project Menu on a wall or easel.

3) List the projects that scored well in the previous step. Ask participants if there are any projects that may not have had the highest scores but should still be considered.

4) As a group, fill in the characteristics of all the projects listed on the menu.

Select a combination of the strongest projects to create an effective strategy for improving the energy picture.

Before the selection process begins, point out that the Energy Action Plan will be most effective if it contains a variety of project approaches and a mix of projects that work well together. With this goal in mind, participants develop a list of the final projects they want to see in the Energy Action Plan.

Before the workshop, the facilitator should choose one of the following methods for selecting priority projects:

➤ Option A
Choose top priorities through informal group discussion:

Review the project ideas listed on the Menu. Discuss which projects should be the highest priority, and which combination of ideas will comprise an effective mix.

➤ Option B

Choose top priorities through a point system:

Give each participant three dot stickers of different colors. Assign a value of three to one color, two to the next, and one to the remaining color. On the wall-sized version of the Project Menu, participants post dots beside project ideas of their choice. They may affix all their dots to one item if they want to give it as many points as possible. The facilitator adds up point totals and lists the highest scoring projects. If you have many competing ideas, or haven't had any clear priorities emerge from the workshops, this method will help you make these selections. This method is especially useful if your task force has more than 10 members.

Develop a final list with timelines

To prepare to present your task force's plan to the other task forces, a volunteer may want to create a large listing of the proposed projects, along with a timeline and any other helpful means to communicate results.

Workshop variation: Hold two sessions

It may not be feasible to comfortably complete all three of these steps in one session. If you have many project ideas and a large group you may want to divide the workshop into two sessions. Ending the first session of the workshop at the completion of the project scoring provides a convenient interval to summarize the scorecard results. The next session can then start with the project scores listed and participants developing a menu.

Weighing Project Ideas

Your task force has developed a list of promising ideas. Given limited time and resources, it may be difficult to implement all of them. You will need to select a mix of top projects to create an effective strategy for improving the energy picture. Scoring each project by considering the following questions offers a way to examine project strengths and weaknesses. This will be a first step in deciding which proposals to consider for the action plan.

PROJECT CRITERIA

How easy is it to successfully implement the project?

Early successes build confidence and momentum for tackling harder projects. At the same time, some projects with the greatest potential for change may be harder to start. Whether a project succeeds depends on such questions as: Are the necessary resources and leadership available to carry out projects? Will the community support or oppose the proposal?

Is the project cost-effective?

Is the project a good investment? How quickly will the energy savings pay for the initial project cost? You probably won't know exact payback times, but if you have even a very rough idea of paybacks, you can compare the cost-effectiveness of one project to another. For instance, a shower head retrofit easily pays for itself in less than a year. A solar panel installation on a downtown building may take over five years to pay for itself in reduced energy bills. If it's done badly, it may never pay for itself.

Some projects will produce benefits not measured in cash. Deciding if these projects are a good investment requires knowing if the non-monetary benefits outweigh the cash costs. For example, education or demonstration projects may produce no direct energy or monetary savings. Yet they may result in increased awareness, which may lead to later economic benefits.

Will the project address identified barriers?

While early successes are important to build momentum, making significant, long-term improvements will require that some projects eventually address the barriers the task force identified. Ideally, priority projects will be a mix of those that produce immediate savings and ones that make it easier to pursue many efficiency measures for long-term savings.

Is the project fair?

Does the project unfairly burden certain people? Who pays for it? Who benefits, and who is harmed? While fairness issues are hard to assess, the above questions can help eliminate blatantly unfair projects and address proposal weaknesses.

Does the project have acceptable environmental impacts?

Some might think it unnecessary to examine the environmental impacts of projects promoting efficient and renewable energy. But because all activity affects the environment, you will want to consider hidden negative impacts of projects.

Some ways to find hidden costs include asking the following questions: What will the project change about the environment, and is that change acceptable to your community? What are the long-term effects of the project? What are the cumulative effects of the project? If the project involves manufactured products, what is used to make them? What wastes are produced in the manufacturing process, and where will they end up? What will happen to the product when it's discarded?

These questions will not result in final answers, but are a starting point to better identify a project's environmental shortcomings.

Will this project result in significant energy savings?

Given limited resources, you will want to compare each project's potential for saving energy over the short- and long-term. While you will not have exact numbers on savings, your group can make an educated guess on which projects will result in the most energy savings, based on what you have learned from task force packets.

While assessing projects, consider long- and short-term potential for energy savings. Some projects, such as a local government retrofit program, may immediately result in large energy savings. Others, like a state-of-the art building code, could improve energy use over the long haul.

How does the project improve the economy?

Some projects may immediately create new jobs. Others may help small businesses, while another might generate more disposable income. Given what you know, assess the project's potential economic benefits. Can the project be designed to have even greater local economic benefits?

> **Knowing enough to decide**
>
> How do you know enough about projects to predict their results and decide which should be priorities? How can you tell if it will result in significant energy savings, or have greater economic benefits than another project?
>
> While you may not know the answers to these questions, the criteria listed here will help focus discussion of project strengths and weaknesses. Through this discussion, some proposals will emerge with clear advantages over others. If it's critical to resolve questions about a proposal, make addressing these concerns a priority project.

Completing the Project Menu

Listing the strongest projects and their essential characteristics makes it easier to select a complementary mix of priority projects for the action plan. Fill in the Menu columns, page 161, by answering the questions below.

Timing of results: How quickly will the project produce results?
- ➤ Three months or less
- ➤ Three to six months
- ➤ Six months to a year
- ➤ Year or more
- ➤ 2-3 years

Projects producing results in three months or less, such as an energy fair, are simple ways to build momentum for future projects to improve the energy picture. Longer term projects, such as a financing program, will give you the chance to develop effective programs for overcoming essential barriers.

Difficulty: How difficult is the project to successfully implement?
- ➤ Easy
- ➤ More difficult
- ➤ Challenging

The number of decisions, participants involved, and the level of political activity required are some of the factors which determine project difficulty. Developing a short "Where-to-get-it" guide is an easy project, while a demonstration retrofit may be more difficult. Establishing a local government energy office may be quite challenging.

Leadership: Who takes the leadership role in the project?
- ➤ The private sector
- ➤ Government
- ➤ Citizens' group
- ➤ Nonprofit organization
- ➤ Utility
- ➤ Educational institutions

Approach: What approach does the project take to improve the energy picture?

➤ Education/demonstration/promotion
➤ Technical assistance
➤ Financing
➤ Incentives/disincentives
➤ Policy/ordinances
➤ Creating an organization

Barriers addressed: What barriers does the project work to overcome?

Consider your list of barriers from Workshop A. Which of these barriers does this project address?

Efficiency or renewables: Does the project match the end-use to the best, least-cost solution?

Does the project emphasize matching the energy demand, or end-use, with the best, least-cost measure to perform that task? Does it put renewable sources to work? Reducing energy demand should be the first step, but tapping local renewable resources is the long-term solution to plugging energy leaks.

Economic benefits: How does the project help the local economy?

Which of the following strategies does the project support?

➤ Plugs the leaks. The project reduces the amount of money spent on energy, freeing it up for other priorities.
➤ Supports existing businesses. The project reduces business operating costs or creates new local markets.
➤ Creates new local enterprise. The project builds an environment that encourages business start-ups.

Project scorecard

Circle the number that best corresponds to your view of the project.	Project Idea _____ strongly disagree strongly agree	Project Idea _____ strongly disagree strongly agree
This project:		
1 Will be easy to successfully implement.	1 2 3 4 5 don't know	1 2 3 4 5 don't know
2 Appears to be cost-effective.	1 2 3 4 5 don't know	1 2 3 4 5 don't know
3 Will address barriers to better energy practices.	1 2 3 4 5 don't know	1 2 3 4 5 don't know
4 Is fair: will not unfairly burden or benefit anyone.	1 2 3 4 5 don't know	1 2 3 4 5 don't know
5 Has acceptable environmental impacts.	1 2 3 4 5 don't know	1 2 3 4 5 don't know
6 Has a high energy savings potential.	1 2 3 4 5 don't know	1 2 3 4 5 don't know
7 Will benefit the local economy.	1 2 3 4 5 don't know	1 2 3 4 5 don't know
If you circled "don't know" on several items, but still think the overall project idea sounds good, exploring these unanswered items could become an action plan project.	Add up the numbers you circled for your total score: _____ Would you consider the project as a potential part of the Energy Action Plan? Yes ☐ No ☐ Maybe ☐	Add up the numbers you circled for your total score: _____ Would you consider the project as a potential part of the Energy Action Plan? Yes ☐ No ☐ Maybe ☐

Project menu

Project	Timing of Results	Difficulty	Leadership	Approach	Barriers Addressed	Efficiency or Renewables	Economic Benefits

Bringing It All Together

Meeting Goal: Task forces present their plans, identify complementary or conflicting projects, then combine findings to draft a local energy plan and establish steps for turning the plan into action.

AGENDA

1 **Introductions and preview the meeting goal**

2 **Task force reports**

3 **Bringing It All Together discussion**

4 **What's next:**
Discussion of first steps to turn the plan into action

5 **Wrap up and break for celebration**

Facilitator Agenda

Ten minutes

1. Introductions and preview the meeting goal

Welcome everyone, and if the group is not too large, conduct a round of introductions. Explain that the task forces will present their results and combine project ideas to form an overall action plan. Participants should look for projects that work together or conflict with each other. Before the meeting ends, identify initial steps needed to launch projects and ask for participants' help in turning the plan into action.

Each participant should receive a "Bringing It All Together" Worksheet to record their reactions to the task force presentations. Their responses will help determine how well the project ideas can work together.

Fifteen minutes each

2. Task force reports

Using a poster of the Energy Action Plan, a representative of each task force should present their group's project ideas. Presentations need not go into great detail. As in other presentations, speakers should only briefly discuss projects mentioned in other reports and concentrate on their unique ideas.

Twenty minutes

3. Bringing It All Together discussion

Participants discuss the "Bringing It All Together" responses and other suggestions and concerns about the draft energy plan. Summarize the results or assign a recorder to take notes on task force presentations.

Twenty minutes

4. What's Next: Discussion of first steps to turn the plan into action

Participants determine the first steps needed to turn the plan into action. They can also form subgroups to take responsibility for specific projects and schedule meetings to get started.

Five minutes

5. Wrap up and break for reception or potluck

Summarize meeting results and thank participants. While the community has learned much about energy, and created innovative ideas to improve the energy picture, the most important work lies ahead. Success will be measured by how well the community improves the energy picture. If a special event is planned, invite participants to stay and celebrate.

Meeting Materials

You will need:

- A large version of each task force Energy Action Plan
- Markers
- Copies of "Bringing It All Together" worksheets for each participant
- Door prizes and refreshments (optional)

Meeting Notes

This final meeting is a cause for celebration. Task forces have succeeded in taking the first steps to improve their local energy picture. At the same time, this meeting is the beginning of the most important part of the effort: Turning the plan into action.

Keeping the momentum going

Since the meeting is the culmination of much hard work, find ways to keep the momentum going:

1) Announce the meeting with a press release. Invite the media to cover the event. Also invite those who did not have time to participate in earlier meetings.
2) Hold the meeting in a large room that can accommodate all task force participants, other interested citizens, and the media.
3) After the meeting, mail summaries of the task force presentations and meeting results to all participants. Include a note on next steps and encourage people to join subcommittees to implement projects.

Preparing for the meeting

➤ Select a facilitator for the meeting. This person could be one of the original members of the energy committee or a task force facilitator.

➤ Find ways to make the event festive. You may want to:
  • Plan to conclude the evening with a reception or potluck.
  • Give door prizes of energy-saving products, such as efficient showerheads or compact fluorescent light bulbs. This incentive will liven up the evening.
  • Arrange for entertainment to conclude the evening.

Tips on using the "Bringing It All Together" worksheet

The introductory speaker should explain that this worksheet will help participants to take note of projects that complement and conflict with each other. As task force representatives present their projects, participants should also note what immediate steps can be taken to turn the energy plan into reality.

Bringing It All Together worksheet

Which projects complement each other?

_____

_____

_____

_____

Which projects conflict with each other?

_____

_____

_____

_____

Which short-term projects can be started now?

_____

_____

_____

_____

Which projects will prepare the way for others?

_____

_____

_____

_____

What are the main ways to keep the plan alive and turn the projects into reality?

_____

_____

_____

_____

If you were your community's _energy czar_, which first steps would you take to implement the energy action plan?

_____

_____

_____

_____

Energy Action Plan Summary

You can use this form to summarize the projects selected for the energy action plan, record who will be in charge of implementing them and who will be helping.

In the next three months: **Project Coordinator** **Volunteers**

_____

_____

_____

_____

In the next six months: **Project Coordinator** **Volunteers**

_____

_____

_____

In the next year: **Project Coordinator** **Volunteers**

_____

In the next two years: **Project Coordinator** **Volunteers**

_____

_____

Turning the Plan into Action

All too often, great ideas for a community's future end up gathering dust on a shelf. This section offers approaches to ensure that all your hard work results in tangible energy and economic improvements.

STRATEGIES

1 Build momentum with early successes

2 Develop leadership to ensure continued progress

3 Keep the issue on the community agenda

4 Stay focused on efforts that will make a difference

5 Identify tangible ways to chart your progress and success

6 Anchor the action plan in a local organization

Turning the Energy Plan into Action

Many communities have developed innovative plans for the future. Often the hardest part is making sure these plans and good ideas get implemented. To reward all the time and hard work residents have contributed, the workshops must result in more than an impressive list of project ideas. The true measures of achievement are improvements in the local energy picture and the community economy. Keep the following strategies in mind to ensure your effort produces tangible community benefits:

1. Build momentum with early successes

Select one or two simple, short-term projects and complete them immediately. Early successes will build momentum for continued progress and encourage people to tackle more ambitious projects. Projects such as the following will be both easy to accomplish and help reduce common barriers to better energy practices.

➤ Prepare and distribute a consumer guide to locally available energy-smart products and services.

➤ Complete a small business demonstration retrofit.

➤ Perform a City Hall lighting retrofit.

➤ Hold a workshop on energy-efficient building techniques for the local building and design community.

➤ Form a team of students, educators, and maintenance personnel to create a retrofit proposal for a local school building.

➤ Aim for a biweekly column in the newspaper on energy efficiency opportunities and local, ongoing successes.

➤ Develop a hands-on display of energy-efficient technologies and information for use at community events.

➤ Organize a community-wide Alternative Transportation Day, with prizes, food, and entertainment.

2. Develop leadership to ensure continued progress

To ensure that your plan becomes a functioning blueprint for change and not a dust collector sitting on a shelf, it's vital to create a core of enthusiastic and capable citizens for seeing projects through.

➤ Designate point people for each project.

➤ Encourage point people to develop a team of people to help implement the project. Give people small tasks that they can easily accomplish and feel good about. Work to increase people's capabilities.

➤ Keep a continual record of progress made on projects. Have frequent updates on project progress. Don't just let ideas fade away.

➤ Find out how project coordinators are doing on their projects and make sure they have adequate resources to successfully implement projects.

3. Keep the issue on the community agenda

The steps you've taken to develop the energy plan have already built community support for improving energy use. It's important to keep this momentum alive to achieve ongoing progress. To keep the ball rolling:

➤ Send news releases on energy and economic successes to the local newspaper.

➤ Send updates to workshop participants and encourage them to take part in implementing ongoing projects.

➤ Track accomplishments by putting someone in charge to monitor progress of all projects.

➤ Keep community leaders informed about achievements, and find ways for them to stay involved.

4. Stay focused on efforts that will make a difference

It's easy to get immersed in projects that have short-term impact and forget to address some of the more challenging issues that are at the root of inefficient energy use. Although short-term, feel-good projects are very important for giving people a sense of accomplishment, be sure to also pursue projects that will set significant change in motion. Identify several of the significant barriers that prevent more efficient energy use in your community. Develop and implement projects that address these barriers at least in some way during the course of the first year. These barriers might include:

➤ Lack of access to upfront financing.

➤ Disincentives for your utility to actively promote energy efficiency.

➤ Inadequate availability of local expertise, products and services.

➤ Disincentives to better energy practices in the building industry.

5. Identify tangible ways to chart your progress and success

In one year, how will participants know whether any of their efforts made a difference? Select several realistic goals with specific deadlines. Excessively ambitious goals, with no intermediate, easy steps for achieving them, are an effective way to discourage people. Modest goals will more easily lead to success and build a solid foundation for continuing achievement. Find ways to monitor progress on goals and celebrate successes, no matter how modest. Here are a few ideas:

➤ Hold an Energy Town Meeting on a yearly basis after your first meeting. Report on and celebrate progress made over the past year.

➤ Track the number of energy retrofits made on a yearly basis. Set a target number of retrofits to be made over a year. Report these results to government, relevant groups and the media. Develop a way to convey these results to the community through thermometer-type displays like those used in fundraising drives.

➤ Publicize energy dollar savings that are the result of public building retrofits.

➤ Report on the local availability of energy-efficient products. Are more stores stocking these technologies? Has demand increased?

➤ Set a target number of commercial energy retrofits to be completed in a specific time period. Report on how energy savings have helped local businesses improve their bottom line.

➤ Provide community feedback on progress. Tracking energy improvements on a large thermometer placed in a visible public space can serve to publicize efforts and create a campaign spirit.

➤ If the utility had a demand-side management (DSM) program before the planning process, report on increased energy savings and any program additions or improvements. If the utility did not have a DSM program, what progress has been made toward starting one?

6. Anchor the action plan in a local organization

While your community can initiate energy improvements with volunteer task forces and committees, some kind of stable local organization is critical for mobilizing the necessary resources to fully tap the opportunities over the long term. Every community that is succeeding in making significant increases in energy efficiency on an ongoing basis has a strong organization leading the effort. These organizations include utilities, community development corporations, local government energy offices or divisions, energy service companies, and nonprofit groups.

While the structure of the organization can vary, the ones making a difference have several characteristics in common. These include:

➤ Effective and inspired leadership, hungry for change, constantly looking for new opportunities to tap.

➤ At least one staff person whose job it is to improve community energy use. Developing and coordinating energy efficiency programs isn't something this person works on in their free time: its their main job responsibility.

➤ An understanding that improving energy practices is as much (if not more) a people issue as a technical one. Much emphasis is placed on education, publicity, networking with a wide variety of organizations and people, and developing collaborative efforts.

> Every community that is succeeding in making significant increases in energy efficiency on an ongoing basis has a strong organization leading the effort.

➤ The ability to keep learning and trying new approaches.

➤ Access to technical expertise for energy efficiency, and the ability to put information in a format users can easily understand and apply.

➤ The ability to mobilize resources for implementing a wide variety of programs and projects.

➤ Credibility, respect, and broad support from the community and people who use the organization's services.

➤ Solid support from people at the top. Whatever its structure, the organization is popular and receives strong support from elected officials, administration, executives, and other community leaders.

➤ Ability to produce a track record of energy saving results. All the above characteristics must ultimately lead to reduced energy expenses and more sustainable community energy practices.

The Task Force Packets

These packets offer workshop participants an overview of sustainable energy opportunities and examples of what's worked in other places, along with a list of resources to find out more.

Residential Task Force Packet

U.S. residences consume about $115 billion worth of energy a year. With readily available technologies and measures, the national residential energy bill can be reduced by more than 50%, benefiting household budgets, boosting local commerce, and keeping more money in the local economy.

This packet starts with an introduction to residential sustainable energy opportunities. The rest of the packet is divided into examples covering the three energy factors of people and organizations, financing, and government. These examples are just a small sampling of what's worked in other places and how people have found ways to tap sustainable energy opportunities.

TASK FORCE PACKET CONTENTS

➤ **Sustainable energy opportunities**

➤ **The three energy factors:**
  Factor #1: People and Organizations
  Factor #2: Financing
  Factor #3: Government

Refer to page 243 to find a list of books, newsletters, and organizations that can provide even more information on specific ways for improving energy use. This list does not attempt to be a complete bibliography of the many resources available. The resources listed were chosen either because they provide a good initial overview of their topic, or they provide a helpful listing of additional resources. While this information was accurate at press time, some of these contacts may have moved on. If you find a contact has been changed we'd appreciate it if you would let Rocky Mountain Institute know. You can reach us at (970) 927-3851 or the address listed at the beginning of the book.

Sustainable Energy Opportunities

How to save billions in the residential sector

Energy is not an end in itself but only a means of providing such desired services as warm houses, hot showers, and cold beer. These services are known as end-uses.

By thinking first about the end-uses we want energy to deliver, and then finding the best tool and the most appropriate form of energy for the task, we can use far less energy than currently required. Using this method it is possible to cut the national residential energy bill by more than 50%.

How much can you save in residential end-uses?

Summary of residential end-uses	Savings Potential*
Comfortable Indoor Climates	
Heating	50 -100%
	(100% with proper design)
Cooling	80 - 100%
	(100% with proper design)
Hot Water	65%
	(100% with solar)
Appliances	65%
Refrigeration	35 - 75%
Lighting	75%

* These figures demonstrate what is technologically possible. Realizing these energy savings will require an upfront investment. Cost-effectiveness and length of paybacks will vary with different measures.

The following section gives a brief overview of some of the measures and alternative energy sources that can efficiently deliver desired end-uses. This overview simply introduces a framework for discovering energy saving opportunities. Through the workshops, you can develop projects and programs that put these technologies and measures to work so your community can reap the benefits.

End-use: Comfortable indoor climates

Creating a comfortable climate through heating and cooling is probably your home's largest energy expense. Forty-six percent of household energy goes toward this end-use. About $13 billion worth of energy nationally, or $150 per household annually, escapes through holes and cracks in residences in the form of heated or cooled air. Plugging these leaks while improving insulation and heating systems generates big energy savings. Here are a few least-cost climate control alternatives:

Caulking, weatherstripping, and expanding foams

An average U.S. house has five square feet of air leaks, which can account for about 25-45% of your heating and cooling bill. Many of these leaks are in attics, basements, and around chimneys, pipes, and attic hatches. It's most cost-effective to plug leaks in the top and bottom of a house before working on windows and doors. For larger cracks, expanding foam is best. Inexpensive and easy to apply, caulking and weatherstripping can reduce leaks around doors and windows. Both are available in hardware stores.

Weatherization and insulation

Perhaps the most lucrative energy-saving measure, insulation keeps buildings cool in summer and toasty in winter. You can increase your comfort and decrease energy bills by insulating walls, attics and under the ground floor.

Window coverings

Several coverings are available, including simple curtains, roman shades, pop-in insulation panels, interior shutters and storm windows. These measures are a quick and relatively inexpensive way to boost the insulating value of windows and reduce heat loss in a home.

Programmable thermostats

Also known as a set-back thermostat, these devices lower room temperatures at night and raise the temperature just before residents wake up. Set-back thermostats can also turn up the heat in homes before residents return from work. When residents program the devices for two eight-hour, 10-degree setbacks, energy savings of over 20% are possible.

High performance windows

Windows are great for views and daylight, but they are also often the weakest link in a building's thermal barrier. In summer they can allow too much solar heat to enter a building, resulting in increased work for the air conditioning system. In winter, they can allow too much heat to escape.

High performance windows, namely low-e (for emissivity) windows and superwindows, solve both of these problems at once. These windows insulate far better than single- or double-pane glass, and the best superwindows insulate up to nine times better than a single pane of glass. High performance windows are designed differently for use in hot and cold climates. Special coatings block heat, in the form of solar infrared radiation,

> **About $13 billion worth of energy nationally, or $150 per household annually, escapes through holes and cracks in residences in the form of heated or cooled air.**

from escaping or from entering the house, depending on whether the window is for use in a hot or cold climate.

Besides cutting energy bills, high performance windows create more comfortable, pleasant, and productive living and work spaces. When carefully integrated into state-of-the-art design, high performance windows enable you to downsize or entirely eliminate the need for a conventional heating and cooling system in your home.

Furnaces

You can improve furnace performance through periodic maintenance. Modifications, such as installing an electronic ignition on a gas unit, also reduce furnace operating costs. Better yet, efficient gas furnaces can further cut the environmental and economic costs of heating. These furnaces are at least 10% more fuel efficient than the average while the best ones are 20% more efficient.

Space cooling measures: Keeping hot air out

One of the best ways to keep a building cool is to prevent heat from coming inside. Caulk, insulation, window films, windows with low-emissivity coatings, and awnings can all reduce your air conditioner's workload. Some buildings also have overhangs designed to prevent the sun from overheating their interiors.

Another effective way to keep buildings cool is to reduce heat produced inside the structure. Incandescent lights and inefficient machinery can all force your air conditioner to work harder than necessary. More efficient lighting makes things easier for your cooling system. Consistent maintenance, and improving the efficiency of system ductwork also keep buildings cool. Caulk, insulation, and superinsulated windows can help reduce the demand on air conditioners by keeping hot air out and cool air inside. Closing curtains and shading your air conditioner, windows, and house will also cut cooling needs.

Air conditioners

New air conditioners are 50% to 70% more efficient than the average unit in use. You should buy one with a thermostat to prevent overcooling. Remember, turning the air conditioner's thermostat lower than the desired temperature doesn't cool the building any faster. Closing the curtains, cleaning the air conditioner filters often, and setting the air conditioner thermostat at 78 degrees will also help you cut energy use. Alternatives to the refrigerated air conditioner include evaporative coolers that cost half as much as an air conditioner and have operating costs up to 80% less. Simple ceiling or portable fans also cool inexpensively.

Energy-efficient building design

The best way to efficiently provide comfortable climates is to design buildings right in the first place. With currently available technology it is possible to construct buildings that are five to ten times more energy-efficient than conventional ones. A variety of simple design features will significantly reduce lighting, heating, and cooling costs, as well as create more comfortable indoor environments. Energy-efficient design considerations will determine how the building is oriented to optimize solar access for lighting, heating, and cooling. They will also determine amount and kind of windows, type of building shell, daylighting and electric lighting systems, and heating, ventilation, and cooling systems. Constructing these super-efficient buildings can actually be less expensive than conventional construction methods. Even better, the avoided lifecycle energy costs can be comparable to the overall capital costs of the building.

The best way to efficiently provide comfortable climates is to design buildings right in the first place.

End-use: Hot water

Water heating is often the second highest home energy expense, after heating. Using hot water more efficiently is one of the simplest and most profitable ways of saving energy. Every gallon of water saved also reduces municipal sewage treatment costs and keeps more water in rivers and wetlands. Depending on the application, you can save nearly 2/3 of the energy used to heat water.

Reducing water heater temperatures

Homeowners often set water heaters at an unnecessarily high temperature. Reducing the heater's setting to 120 degrees lets the unit use less energy to heat water and maintain its temperature. It also prevents children and others from scalding themselves.

Water efficiency measures

A comprehensive water efficiency retrofit cuts both water and energy expenses. Efficient faucetheads and showerheads reduce hot water use and water heating bills. Many homeowners have discovered that installation of water-saving devices have cut water consumption by at least a third.

High-efficiency faucetheads offer a better quality of service than traditional units, while saving water and energy. An unrestricted flow of water out of a tap is inefficient, and much of the water splashes off the object being rinsed. Efficient faucetheads (2.5 gallons per minute or less) use half the water and energy, with greater wetting abilities. These units are not to be confused with a faucet "aerator," since some of the best models don't actually aerate the water.

Efficient water-saving showerheads can deliver a hard-hitting spray while cutting both water and heating costs by 25% to 60%. Today's efficient shower heads only use 2.5 gallons per minute or less, as opposed to a conventional fixture's 3- to 8- gallon per minute spray. Large energy users such as hotels, schools, or gyms can recoup the investment of replacing all their showerheads in a few months. Consumers should take care to avoid flow restrictor showerheads that use a washer to reduce water flow and produce an unsatisfying spray.

While there are not hot water savings, efficient toilets can reduce water bills and are part of a comprehensive water retrofit. Design improvements make it possible for these efficient toilets to use only .8 to 1.5 gallons of water per flush instead of 5 to 7 gallons for a typical toilet.

Water heater system insulation

Thirty percent of the energy used by an uninsulated water heater is simply radiated to the outside, causing your water heater (and your air conditioners in the summer) to have to work harder. Fortunately, adequate insulation can prevent much of this waste. Doubling or tripling average heater insulation will greatly improve insulating value for little cost. Hot water pipes lose up to 20% of the energy in the heated water if they are not insulated with fiberglass and foam.

Solar water heaters

Technological improvements in solar hot water heating systems over the last ten years have greatly improved performance and reliability. In some states, solar hot water heating systems have been providing household hot water needs for the past twenty years. Depending on the climate, a solar water heating system can provide 50 - 100 percent of a household's annual hot water needs. If the solar-heated water is replacing electric-heated water, these savings can add up to hundreds of dollars per year. The upfront costs of a solar hot water system can range from $2,000 to $5,000. Savings from a solar hot water heater will depend on how much hot water is used, whether water-efficient fixtures are used throughout the house, the type and size of the system, the cost of the electricity or fuel the household normally uses for water heating, and climate.

End-use: Household tasks and conveniences

With so many choices of household appliances, consumers need to be able to distinguish between highly efficient appliances and energy hogs. Consulting Energy Guide ratings for major appliances and referring to the information below can help you make an informed and energy-efficient purchase.

Cooking

A pressure cooker or crock pot consumes less than a quarter of the energy required by an ordinary pan. Toaster ovens can also cut your heating costs by a third to a half if you only have a little food to cook. Similarly, a microwave oven uses one fifth to one half of the energy of a conventional oven.

Refrigerators

The most efficient refrigerators on the market use about 200 kilowatt-hours of electricity a year, resulting in a $17 a year power bill. In contrast, the average refrigerator uses 1,200 kilowatt-hours and around $100 worth of energy. Even if you don't have a super-efficient refrigerator you can still save energy through a few simple measures. These steps include covering foods, vacuuming condenser coils, cleaning door gaskets, and turning off ice makers. Many people also keep old refrigerators in the garage with no more than a case of beer inside. Often, these semi-retired refrigerators are expensive and inefficient electricity hogs.

Golden carrot refrigerators

Thanks to a $30 million design contest, Americans are reaping the benefits of a new energy-efficient refrigerator which will save hundreds of dollars of electricity over its lifetime. Whirlpool beat out several major appliance makers in making a refrigerator 35% more efficient than the 1993 standard for a side-by-side model. The winner is also free of ozone-layer destroying chlorofluorocarbons. Organized with the help of the EPA, the "Golden Carrot" contest was initiated by the Consortium for Energy Efficiency, a program involving national environmental organizations and utilities. Contributions from 24 utilities totaled $30 million, and the winning icebox will be available to their customers ahead of everybody else. Part of the award will be paid directly to Whirlpool for marketing and producing the refrigerator. The other portion will be given out as rebates to refrigerator purchasers so that the price of the efficient unit remains competitive.

Washers and dryers

Efficient horizontal-axis washing machines can save 50% to 60% of the energy costs of a normal washer. These machines, which tumble clothing in water rather than immerse them, also reduce your water consumption. Even if you don't have one of these washers, or a dryer with a moisture sensor (which automatically turns the machine off when your clothes reach a predetermined level of dryness), you can still take simple steps to save energy. Cleaning the lint filter after each load, drying full loads, and using the cool-down cycle are all efficient measures. Better yet, use a clothes line that prevents lint and is easier on your garments.

End-use: lighting

Five to ten percent of an average home's energy consumption goes toward lighting. Nationally, it takes over a hundred Chernobyl-sized power plants to provide the energy for all the lighting in the U.S. However, super-efficient lighting systems, which can cut lighting energy use by at least 60%, can drastically reduce the need for these plants. Here are some least-cost lighting alternatives:

Compact fluorescent light bulbs (CFLs)

CFLs are four times as efficient and last 9 to 13 times as long as traditional incandescent light bulbs. Fluorescent lamps with electronic ballasts reduce energy use and provide better quality light with improved color rendition. The lamps come in many shapes and sizes to fulfill a variety of lighting

> **Americans spend over $30 billion per year on electricity to run residential appliances.**

needs. Their efficiency and long life can save $45 per bulb in power costs over their lifetime, assuming a rate of 8 cents per kilowatt hour. CFLs make the most economic sense when used in applications that need light for over four hours a day. These lights also save money by making it unnecessary to buy as many replacement bulbs.

Occupancy sensors

Ultrasonic and infrared occupancy sensors are a simple way of making sure lights aren't on any longer than necessary. Sensors turn lights on when someone enters a room, and turns them off when everyone leaves. They cost as little as $25 dollars per unit and pay for themselves within a year. Dimmers, timers, and light-sensitive switches that turn off outdoor lighting after sunrise, or at a certain time, also cut costs.

Daylighting

Daylighting makes use of windows and walls to provide sunlight to light a home during the day. In most circumstances, natural illumination can provide just as much, if not more, light as electric lamps. For example, a 3' x 5' window in direct summer sun can let in more light than a hundred ordinary 60-watt light bulbs. Daylighting design features include large windows, walls that bounce light around a room, and reflective blinds.

Superwindows with advanced glazings are sometimes necessary for a daylighting system. The advanced coatings on these windows help to regulate the amount of heat coming into or escaping from a building to keep warm in winter and prevent overheating in summer.

Benefits of daylighting extend beyond reducing dependence on electricity, too. All too often, traditional lighting schemes suffer from overlighting and glare, while a good daylighting system is less prone to these problems.

CFLs are four times as efficient and last 9 to 13 times as long as traditional incandescent light bulbs.

Alternative energy sources for delivering energy end-uses

Once you have tapped efficiency measures to reduce your energy demand, there are many ways to use renewable energy sources to meet what demand remains. The sun, wind, and falling water are all sources of affordable and environmentally-friendly energy. Not only are an increasing number of individual homeowners tapping renewable energy sources, but more and more utilities are also using renewables as an important power supply option.

Solar energy falls on every community in the country and is a virtually untapped power source. Solar energy is especially cost-effective for such tasks as water or space heating that require only simple forms of energy. Using the sun can also reduce demand for residential lighting, heating and cooling.

Solar energy can supply household electricity needs too. Photovoltaics convert sunlight into electricity. These solar panels are especially popular with homeowners at remote sites who are looking for a cost-effective alternative to power lines. Small photovoltaic systems can also power outdoor lighting, thereby eliminating the need to extend electric lines to lighting fixtures.

Utilities are also considering photovoltaics as a new source of supply. Not only are utilities developing solar power stations, but they are also installing solar panels throughout communities, at homes and businesses.

Wind is another underutilized power source. At one time, over 6 million windmills across the U.S. supplied power for households, farms, and industry. Today's wind generators produce electricity for several major utilities. In California, 15,000 utility-operated wind machines provide enough power for about 300,000 households.

These examples are just the tip of the iceberg of the potential of renewable energy resources. Renewables currently provide 13% of the nation's energy needs. A report by five of the U.S. national laboratories demonstrated that an accelerated renewable energy research and development program could allow the country to cost-effectively generate half of current U.S. energy use from renewables by the year 2030.

An accelerated renewable energy research and development program could allow the country to cost-effectively generate half of current U.S. energy use from renewables by the year 2030.

Factor #1: People and Organizations

Resource-efficient homebuilders, vendors of efficient products, and installers of renewable technologies are just some of the people that take the concept of efficiency and turn it into an economic asset. While individuals and organizations can benefit directly from energy-related jobs and income, they also are the ones that make the overall energy savings happen. Here are just a few examples:

A utility director takes efficiency into his own hands

Wes Birdsall is living proof that a single spark can start a community-wide effort to improve energy efficiency. In 1974, Birdsall, former general manager of the Osage, Iowa, municipal utility, set out to make his town more energy-efficient. He started by taking aerial infrared pictures of heat loss from local buildings to vividly depict the tremendous amount of energy wasted by the community. Then he went door to door to encourage better insulation. Over the years, Birdsall's efficiency efforts have made Osage an internationally recognized model of energy efficiency and kept thousands of dollars in citizens' pockets. Osage residents currently use 25% less energy than the state average at a 37% lower utility rate.

Local nonprofits promote efficiency

Founded in 1978, Urban Options of East Lansing, Michigan, offers a variety of energy services to the community. Urban Options has provided energy visits to over 3000 households, offering an energy audit and the installation of up to eight energy and water efficiency improvements. Urban Options also sells high-quality energy and water-saving products at wholesale prices. A demonstration home, an education program, and a tool lending library round out their services.

Center for Neighborhood Technology mobilizes resources

The Center for Neighborhood Technology identified high energy costs as a chronic factor in Chicago's high rate of housing abandonment. Landlords were raising rents, or deferring maintenance to meet these bills, both of which threatened the supply of affordable housing. Through its policy advocacy efforts, the Center secured a $15 million commitment, $5 million from the City of Chicago and $10 million from the People's Gas Light and Coke Co., for the Chicago Energy Savers Fund, a one-stop residential energy conservation program. Then, the Center anchored a consortium of city-wide and community groups, which successfully bid to manage the program through a network of eight Community Energy Centers managed by the community groups. The program was responsible for the retrofit of 12,000 units of low- and moderate-income housing. The multi-family components of the program resulted in average energy savings of 24%, representing over $1.5 million per year.

Energy savings can be especially helpful to lower-income households, which are hit disproportionately hard by energy expenses. After food and rent, energy is often the greatest expense for low-income families. At the same time, low-income families and individuals are more likely to live in homes with poor insulation, drafty windows, and faulty heating systems.

Developers create a better place to live

Persistence and innovation paid off for Davis, California developers Michael and Judy Corbett. The Corbetts wanted to build a housing development that incorporated energy-efficient and passive solar housing design, efficient land use, urban agriculture, and pedestrian/bike ways. The development designs included narrow streets, alternative run-off systems that rely on a system of streams and ponds, and orchards and vineyards coexisting with housing. Instead of welcoming innovation in design, city officials and lending institutions balked at approving permits and funding for the Corbetts' unique project. Persistently countering objections and proving their ideas would work, the Corbetts made their 240-unit development idea a reality. Supportive city council members also helped change regulations that would have prohibited some of the innovations in the development project. Today, Village Homes is the most sought-after place to live in Davis, and a living example of how energy-conscious housing developments can incorporate design that enhances overall quality of life.

Chicago builder guarantees efficiency savings

Chicago builder Perry Bigelow has focused on building energy-efficient housing since 1985. Bigelow's homes stress above-average insulation, insulated windows and solar orientation. Bigelow, who has consistently won the *Chicago Sun-Times* award for most energy efficient builder, offers a guarantee that a homeowner's annual heating bills will not exceed $200. Bigelow homeowners can also enter a contest to see who has the lowest heating bills. Recently, one household won the contest with an annual bill of $24 in Chicago's blustery climate. The prize? A trip to the tropics.

Utilities sponsor energy information store

A cooperative effort between four Oregon public utilities and the Bonneville Power Administration resulted in the "Energy Outlet," a 1,500-square foot store in downtown Eugene, Oregon. The information store serves as a referral and resource center, demonstrating energy efficient appliances, weatherization measures, and efficient lighting techniques. Customers can find out which local retailers stock the efficient technologies

> **Today, Village Homes is the most sought-after place to live in Davis, and a living example of how energy-conscious housing developments can incorporate design that enhances overall quality of life.**

on display, and which appliances qualify for utility rebate programs. Through interactive computer programs, store visitors can learn how building design and site planning can affect energy savings. A library of videotapes, magazines, and books completes the information store's line of products. The outlet offers free, accessible information in an environment free of sales.

Architects design it right the first time

While a house can be retrofitted to produce significant energy savings, getting it right from the beginning is the way to ensure maximum energy efficiency. Gregory Franta, a Boulder, Colorado architect, has been demonstrating the potential of sustainable building design since the 1970s. By using techniques such as daylighting, high levels of insulation, super-insulated windows and doors, and passive solar orientation to take full advantage of natural heating and cooling mechanisms, Franta has designed buildings which are among the most energy-efficient in the world. One of Franta's home designs is a 7,000 square-foot Colorado home that has a winter heating bill of $60 to $70 a month. Another Colorado residence designed by Franta has average yearly heating bills of about $11 and is cooled entirely by natural means.

Other architects can now get assistance for designing buildings to be more energy-efficient. The American Institute of Architects, the major professional organization for architects, now publishes an Environmental Resource Guide (ERG). The guide consists of four issues a year and provides information on design practices that encourage efficient and renewable energy use, as well as tips on other ecological building issues.

Homeowners go renewable

Homeowners can choose from several renewable energy sources for residential power loads, including microhydro, wind, and solar technologies. Of the three sources listed, solar technologies are the most common, since wind and microhydro are site specific. Many homeowners have decided on their own to tap abundant renewable resources, while others are offered the option by a utility.

Vermonter David Palumbo wanted his remote homesite to be independent of the local utility, and found that a microhydro system fit the bill. Microhydro, the most site-specific alternative energy technology, requires adequate water flows year-round and hilly terrain. Under ideal conditions, microhydro systems pay back for themselves faster than any other alternative energy technology. Palumbo's three-building household receives all its power through a hybrid solar and microhydro system. Taking advantage of natural streams and the steepness of the Green Mountains, Palumbo says half of his energy needs are fulfilled by microhydro technology; the rest comes from photovoltaic panels that produce electricity from the sun. These alternative energy sources enable Palumbo to live "off-the-grid" in his rural home.

Students get real world efficiency education

Washington D.C. 5th and 6th graders are learning about energy efficiency and teaching their families simple and inexpensive ways to save energy and money in their homes. In the classroom, students use math and science skills to analyze their home energy use. Students learn how to install and use setback thermostats, storm devices, caulking and weatherstripping, and hot water efficiency measures. Future plans call for the students to analyze how much energy their families save by using efficient technologies.

In British Columbia, a student wanders through a house, changes inefficient light bulbs, fixes a leaky faucet and chases a cat. But unlike any other residence, this home only exists on a computer program developed by students and the B.C. Hydro electric utility. The program, known as the Power Smart Game, educates students about efficiency by helping them retrofit a house, complete with flushing toilets, talking friends, and more. With the help of the game, the utility encourages students to become energy managers for their home and encourages parents to put the resulting savings into college funds.

Dartmouth College undergraduates have started "Operation Insulation," a group that weatherizes low-income homes in the Upper Connecticut River Valley. A local community services center helps the group find candidates for weatherization while area contractors and energy professionals train the students. Besides weatherization services, the group plans workshops on insulation, a weatherization sourcebook, and a tool library.

Utilities tests the potential of efficiency

Several utilities in North America have conducted intensive community-based efficiency programs to determine maximum savings potential through cost-effective retrofit measures. Ontario Hydro launched the Espanola Power Savers Project in June 1991 to learn what energy savings are possible and what influences people to conserve. Espanola is a town of 5400 people in Northeastern Ontario, Canada.

From the very beginning the project relied for its success on intensive community involvement and outreach. A Community Advisory Committee, consisting of representatives from a variety of community groups, provided direct community feedback and encouraged participation from key groups in the community, and organized special events. The local media has played an important role in the Espanola project. The local newspaper runs articles on the projects, ranging from an "energy tip of the month" to interviews with pleased customers. An educational component of the project reaches 53 classrooms, grades one through six.

The utility offered, free to participants, compact fluorescent light bulbs and hot water heater tune ups. The cost of other efficiency improvements, such as more efficient heating systems, windows and doors, and better insulation, were split between the utility and the home owner. With this arrangement, 87% of all eligible residences have had energy improvements made. During the first year of the project Espanola saved 7,424 Megawatt-hours.

Ontario Hydro will be monitoring and evaluating the results of the project through 1995. Results tracked will include net benefits and costs of the project, extent of long-term shifts in attitudes and behaviors, and the overall economic benefits resulting from the energy savings and jobs created by the project.

Tribal governments put solar power to work

Over 30 homes get power from rooftop photovoltaic (PV) panels in the Hopi village of Hotevilla, Arizona. The solar panels generate enough power to run household lights, a TV, a VCR, power tools and appliances. The other village power source, a gas generator, has a life cycle cost five times more than the PV system. As a result of the PV's popularity, the village plans to build a subdivision completely powered by solar energy.

The Klagetoh Chapter of the Navajo Nation has installed what is believed to be the largest residential application of photovoltaic (PV) technology in history. Solar systems are powering lights in 150 homes, and these systems can be expanded to produce electricity for refrigeration, televisions and radios. According to a Navajo Nation official, the systems provide a safer and healthier power supply that enhances quality of life. The project also generates economic development since Chapter members are picking up the marketable skill of working with PVs.

The Klagetoh Chapter of the Navajo Nation has installed what is believed to be the largest residential application of photovoltaic (PV) technology in history, lighting 150 homes.

National parks become destinations of efficiency

Working with the National Renewable Energy Laboratory, the National Park Service has built efficient passive solar homes in two of its crown jewels: Yosemite and Grand Canyon National Parks. Both buildings are designed to meet the specific weather demands of their environment. The Yosemite house is designed to stay cool during hot summer afternoons. To this end, the Yosemite house is well-insulated and relies on cold evening air to cool the building's mass. The Grand Canyon house is designed to stay warm in winter, and includes an efficient heating system, superwindows, and a high level of insulation.

Residents rebuild efficiently

In the wake of the Oakland Hills fire, homeowners are rebuilding with energy efficiency improvements. Seventy-eight families living in the Hiller Highlands development banded together to plan a rebuilding strategy that made energy efficiency a high priority. Now, 75% of these homeowners are installing efficiency improvements, including superinsulated windows.

Affordable housing groups make living affordable

In North Philadelphia, 23 passive solar homes designed by architect Bob Thomas fill a block developed by the National Temple Non-Profit Corporation and the local housing authority. Thomas felt that both the houses and their energy costs should be affordable. A year and a half after the homes were built in 1985, the monthly heating bills were around $25. The bills of neighboring non-solar homes were three times as much. The energy saving design of these homes, says Thomas, did not increase construction costs. Since Philadelphia is laid out on a north-south axis, Thomas believes the potential for more solar projects in the city is excellent.

Entrepreneur finds a sunny source of jobs and income

For Dan Brandborg, doing business in alternative energy has paid off beyond his wildest expectations. Brandborg owns Sunelco, a Hamilton, Montana supplier of solar energy systems. When he first started, he had no idea his sales would reach just under $1 million a year. Sales have continued to rise, and Brandborg has had to hire more employees.

Effective education enhances weatherization results

While most weatherization programs have traditionally focused only on installing energy-efficient devices, many utilities are now recognizing the importance of education in producing top energy-saving results. If energy advice accompanies installation of energy-saving technologies, the additional energy savings can be as high as 20 percent more.

Some organizations and utilities have decided to put this to the test. One test, conducted by the Alliance to Save Energy, and Niagara Mohawk Power Corporation (NMPC), showed that combining education with a weatherization program creates a greater increase in energy savings than running the same program without an educational component. NMPC added three education sessions and a low-cost financing plan to their weatherization assistance program. Customers who participated in the hardware-only weatherization program education visits had an average energy reduction of 16%, while those who took advantage of the educational component had an average energy reduction of 26%.

What should the educational component of weatherization programs consist of? Program evaluators have found that information alone will not

> **While most weatherization programs have traditionally focused only on installing energy-efficient devices, many utilities are now recognizing the importance of education in producing top energy-saving results.**

significantly increase consumer energy savings. Here are strategies that researchers have identified as promoting greater changes in energy users' behavior:

➤ Energy information should be individualized and tailored to unique circumstances in each residence.

➤ Feedback on the benefits of energy-saving efforts will motivate energy users to continue.

➤ Recognizing people who get results, and spotlighting their successes, reinforces their efforts and motivates others as well.

➤ Asking energy users for a written commitment to install efficiency measures of their choice.

Factor #2: Financing

Although upfront costs can be an obstacle to improved energy use, many communities have developed innovative financing solutions by pooling collective resources. Financing programs across the country have been designed to improve the efficiency of existing homes, promote the purchase and construction of energy efficient homes, and encourage residents to invest in cost-effective renewable technologies. The main sources for these financing programs are:

➤ Utilities
➤ Banks
➤ Nonprofit community development organizations
➤ Other community resources

Utilities

Utilities are one of the most logical financing sources for energy efficiency and alternative power sources. Unlike individual ratepayers, utilities routinely make investments with payback periods lasting decades. Utilities also have access to large amounts of capital. Many utilities spend millions of dollars annually to purchase their power supply. Spending that same capital on efficiency is like buying a source of power, a source that is less expensive than building a new power plant. The most progressive utility efficiency programs have budgets equalling four to five percent of their cost of power. Utility financing programs come in a variety of forms: rebates, 0% or low-interest loans, equipment leasing, and giveaways.

ZILCH: Zero interest loans for conservation help

The Fort Collins, Colorado, municipal utility makes zero-interest home energy improvement loans of up to $2000 to residents. Initially started with a Community Development Block Grant, the utility buys down the interest rates on the loans. Zilch loans have financed installation of insulation, solar water heaters, and other measures. The loan program approves financing for home energy improvements recommended by audits using "Energy Score," the city's Home Energy Rating System (HERS). Program administrators say the program's success lies in linking financing with a consistent means for assessing what improvements to make. The city also uses Energy Score ratings to help residents secure energy efficient mortgages. See below for more information on energy-efficient mortgages.

Solar municipal utilities

The Santa Clara, California, municipal utility runs a lease program that designs, installs and maintains solar water heaters. In a year's time, a solar water heater can cut a family of four's power bill by $300 or more. So far, over 260 residential units and a 70-unit motel have installed the heaters. Under the program, the city pays the upfront cost of the heater, and is eventually repaid by the property owner.

Similarly, the Sacramento, California, Municipal Utility District is aiming to replace 47,000 electric water heaters with solar units over a six-year period. As an incentive, the utility offers rebates and financing that gives customers a positive cash flow in the first month after installation.

Rebates for efficiency

The Super Good Cents Rebate Program, sponsored by the Northwest's Bonneville Power Administration, offers homeowners $800 rebates for installing solar water heaters. Coupled with state tax credits, these rebates make this technology attractive to homeowners on a budget.

Southern California Edison's "Welcome Home" Program encourages both large developers and owner/builders to construct energy-efficient homes. If their homes exceed state efficiency requirements, builders are eligible for rebates and marketing allowances. Edison would like to see the "Welcome Home" seal recognized as a guarantee of efficient construction.

Another Southern California Edison program finances efficiency modifications to existing homes. The Resident Energy Management Program offers rebates to homeowners who install efficient heating and cooling systems and refrigerators. The program, in conjunction with local water utilities, also offers incentives for installing water and energy-saving washing machines. Hundreds of thousands of participants have taken advantage of this retrofit financing program and its accompanying savings.

Banks

While banks routinely finance homes and cars, potential borrowers may run into barriers when it comes to getting loans for residential energy improvements. Usually, home energy improvement loans are too small to interest a bank. Moreover, some loan officers are unfamiliar with the financial benefits of energy-efficient investments. However, some communities and states are working with financial institutions to increase awareness of the profitability of sustainable energy investments and create financing alternatives. Here are a few examples.

The Neworld Green Loan Program

To encourage home owners to invest in environmentally related home improvements, Neworld Bank has created the Green Loan program. Interest rates for the Green Loan are one percent below the bank's standard fixed-rate home equity loan. Loan terms range from one to eight years, with loan amounts ranging from $3,000 to $25,000. To qualify, at least 50% of the loan must go toward environmentally related home improvements to an owner-occupied residence in Massachusetts. Bankable projects include energy-efficient window installation, caulking and weatherstripping, the

> SMUD aims to replace 47,000 electric water heaters with solar units over a six-year period. As an incentive, the utility offers rebates and financing that gives customers a positive cash flow in the first month after installation.

installation or upgrade of insulation, solar heating and hot water systems, and efficient appliances.

Nebraska dollar and energy saving loan program

Nebraskans can go to 343 financial institutions in 631 locations across the state to obtain low-interest loans to finance home energy improvements. The Nebraska State Energy Office used oil overcharge funds to capitalize their state-wide Dollar and Energy Saving Loan Program. The State Energy Office invited financial institutions across the state to participate so that every Nebraskan had easy access to financing, and so lenders could do what they do best. Since the loan program began in 1990 over 6,100 loans have been made.

Promoting energy efficient mortgages - "EEMs"

Since an energy-efficient home has lower utility bills, its owners have more income to spend on mortgage payments. Unlike a regular mortgage, an energy-efficient mortgage (EEM) factors in this additional cashflow and makes it easier to qualify for a mortgage when buying an energy-efficient home.

EEMs may also finance energy improvements to existing homes. Even though national secondary mortgage institutions (FHA, Fannie Mae, Freddie Mac) offer EEMs, few lenders and mortgage applicants know about them. Out of 60,000,000 loans eligible for EEM programs, only 16,000 used these incentives. But programs in Alaska, Colorado, and Texas are encouraging use of EEMs by publicizing their availability with the help of energy offices and builder associations, promoting them along with Home Energy Rating Systems (HERSs) and working with lenders. HERS, such as the one developed by Energy Rated Homes of America™, provide a standardized method for determining home energy efficiency based on factors such as insulation, windows and energy leaks. Increasingly, HERSs help banks determine home financing based on efficiency.

Nonprofit community development organizations

When financing has not been available from utilities and traditional financing sources, some communities have formed nonprofit entities to do the job. Community development corporations and cooperatives are two examples of these alternative financing organizations.

Community energy development corporations

As private, non-profit entities, community energy development corporations are in a unique position to forge partnerships among local developers, lenders, businesses, foundations, community groups and government.

CEDCs can also deliver a variety of energy services. The Vermont Energy Investment Corporation, for example, offers many energy financing services, including the Home Energy/Improvement Loan Program. This program provides technical assistance, energy audits and energy

> **Over 100,000 Danish families have invested in cooperatively owned and operated wind turbines scattered across the country. Thanks to these cooperatives, wind energy has blossomed in Denmark.**

improvement financing to low and middle income Vermonters. So far, the program has loaned over $500,000 to homeowners. VEIC also runs the Energy Investment Analysis and Energy Improvement Service, which provides consulting on energy efficiency measures for public housing authorities, nonprofit developers, owners of low-income housing, and individual property owners.

Cooperatives: From wind in Denmark...

Over 100,000 Danish families have invested in cooperatively owned and operated wind turbines scattered across the country. Groups of families establish wind power cooperatives by collectively buying one or more turbines. Each family pays for its share of the project, which is often financed by bank loans. Since there are about 3,000 wind turbines operating in Denmark, these loans are relatively easy to obtain. The collective buying power of several families allows them to buy efficient and cost-effective turbines, as well as sell excess electricity back to their utility. Thanks to these cooperatives, wind energy has blossomed in Denmark.

...to weatherization in western Massachusetts

For years, thrifty New Englanders have saved money with fuel cooperatives. Many of these organizations also offer weatherization materials and energy-efficient products at prices slightly above wholesale. Using members' combined purchasing power, Western Massachusetts's Center for Ecological Technology offers basic weatherization supplies at rock-bottom prices. Members can buy caulking, pipe-insulation, weatherstripping, programmable thermostats, vinyl storm windows, water conservation devices, insulating window shades and more, all at a significant savings.

Factor #3: Government

Because local governments have the power to set building standards, shape land use policies, and mobilize resources, they can be an important tool to institutionalize better energy practices for years to come. Here's a summary of some basic strategies that local governments can employ to improve the residential energy picture:

Lead by example:
➤ Perform energy efficiency retrofits on city buildings, and use them as demonstration sites.
➤ Draw on state-of-the-art renewable resources and energy-efficient design for new buildings.
➤ Use energy-efficient practices in all aspects of city operations.

Help remove barriers to energy-wise practices:
➤ Analyze what specific barriers exist in your town. Decide what can be done to overcome these barriers, and publicize findings.
➤ Provide technical and financing assistance to residents for home energy improvements.
➤ Increase awareness of energy alternatives among lenders, builders, contractors, and developers.
➤ Hold homeowner workshops on energy efficiency and renewable energy.
➤ Distribute consumer guides on energy efficiency such as a "Where to get it guide" to efficient goods and services.
➤ Offer technical assistance to builders, vendors, and contractors.
➤ Develop or promote standardized ways for assessing homes' energy efficiency.
➤ Promote existing financing opportunities, such as energy-efficient mortgages.

Serve as a catalyst for change
➤ Create incentives or requirements for passive solar and super-efficient home construction.
➤ Enact energy-smart land use codes.
➤ Initiate ongoing, community-wide, energy efficiency campaigns.
➤ Encourage demand-side management programs at local utilities.

Energy offices implement comprehensive programs

Several cities around the country have energy offices which serve as coordinating entities for community-wide energy programs. As the result of a comprehensive energy conservation policy adopted in 1979, Portland, Oregon, established an Energy Office and an Energy Commission. The office coordinates programs dealing with energy efficiency, transportation, land use planning, and water conservation. The office developed the city's Carbon Dioxide Strategy, which aims to reduce CO_2 emissions 20% below 1988 levels by the year 2010. Office staff coordinate joint energy efficiency ventures between utilities, state energy agencies, and service providers. One of the office's programs, the Block-by-Block Weatherization Program, has provided hundreds of households with free audits and weatherization. The program also includes neighborhood energy fairs and energy education.

The Energy Office director is funded by the City of Portland, with 5 other staff funded by grants and contracts. The office uses an especially innovative method to cover the salary for a city facilities energy management coordinator. A one percent "fee" on all city government energy bills raises about $70,000 per year. The coordinator in turn helps city departments reduce their energy bills. The potential energy savings identified the first year totaled more than $250,000.

Taking an integrated approach to energy efficiency

While many energy efficiency programs target only retrofits of existing buildings, some communities are using a more comprehensive and integrated approach to resource conservation issues. One of the best examples is the town of Ashland, Oregon (population 17,000). Ashland established an energy conservation division in 1982 within the city's department of community development. With an office right next to the city building and planning departments, the conservation division ensures that energy issues are considered in all stages of planning and building decisions. The city reviews building and development plans in the very earliest stages, while there is still time to make modifications. Energy issues are also considered in land use planning, with emphasis placed on encouraging vehicle-free transport.

The conservation division also offers water-heater wrapping, commercial building auditing, Energy Smart Design assistance, efficient street and area lighting, and residential weatherization. Some of these programs are co-sponsored by Bonneville Power Administration, the federal power marketing administration that sells electricity to Ashland electric municipal utility. All these programs play an important role in providing for Ashland's power supply needs: the annual savings are estimated at 8 million kilowatt-hours.

With an office right next to the city building and planning departments, Ashland's conservation division ensures that energy issues are considered in all stages of planning and building decisions.

> The city helped local businesses get in the act by developing a local currency to keep efficiency investments in the local economy.

Local government sparks community energy campaign

Lester Prairie, Minnesota went all out to spark interest in energy efficiency by launching a community campaign. The local city sponsored energy commission promoted efficiency with newspaper articles on energy, presentations to senior citizen groups, raffles for energy audit participants, door-to-door publicity of energy audits, and an energy fair. In a town of approximately 1200, these efforts resulted in 200 Home Energy Checkups and 30 commercial audits. The city helped local businesses get in the act by developing a local currency to keep efficiency investments in the local economy. After participating in the energy audit, residents and businesses received "Prairie Buck" discount coupons good for energy-efficient light bulbs at local hardware stores. The stores anticipated local demand and started carrying several energy-saving light bulbs. Lester Prairie soon had a better retail supply of efficient light bulbs than all of Chicago's stores combined. Not only did the program cut energy costs, but it also kept money in the community by meeting demand for energy-saving products locally.

Efficient homebuilding codes

According to the Alliance to Save Energy, if the 1991 model residential energy code developed by the US Department of Energy were adopted, it would save the average household $150 a year on bills. Codes are an effective tool for reducing energy costs throughout the community because they set minimum energy efficiency standards for efficient materials and construction techniques. Given ongoing improvements in efficient building technologies, your community may want to revise your building code if it dates back to 1980 or before. The Council of American Building Officials (CABO) publishes a model energy code that is a useful reference for developing an efficient code for your community.

A municipal utility can also develop standards to improve local residential efficiency. For example, the Osage, Iowa, municipal utility has set insulation standards that exceed state specifications for commercial and residential buildings. If potential customers fail to meet the standards for both new construction and retrofits, they do not receive utility service. Since 1984 all new construction in Osage has exceeded the utility's standards.

Encouraging solar design

Although it's practical to build comfortable and affordable houses that rely on passive solar heating, few builders take advantage of this technology. Some towns have encouraged technological innovation by developing incentives and policies that foster builder interest in solar construction.

For example, the city of Tucson is collaborating with the Arizona Home Builders Association, and other government agencies to develop the Tucson Solar Village. In addition to energy efficient technologies, the

Village homes will have passive solar design and solar water heaters. These features will help save residents 75 percent of energy normally used.

Other municipalities are encouraging passive solar design by requiring developers to lay out more east-west streets to capture south-facing solar access. If the project's layout is "solar friendly," developers can build at greater densities and win design approval points for passive solar features.

Developing a measure of home efficiency

How do potential home buyers know if one house is more efficient than another? An increasing number of states and municipalities are addressing this issue by developing and promoting Home Energy Rating Systems (HERS). For example, in Austin, Texas, the city government rates the efficiency of new homes with its Energy Star Program. The program's ratings compare a new home's energy costs to one built to minimum code standards. Ratings range from one star (a 7% savings from the baseline home) to three star (a 28% savings). Since 1985, the program has rated thousands of homes. Homeowners can then use these ratings as a selling point for their houses, as well as have access to financing mechanisms such as energy-efficient mortgages. Alabama, Arkansas, Iowa, Rhode Island, Vermont, and Virginia all have HERS programs; other states are joining them.

Retrofit ordinances up the efficiency of existing buildings

Some communities see the sale of a building as a perfect opportunity to upgrade the building's efficiency. Residential retrofit ordinances require home sellers to upgrade efficiency with increased insulation, water heater blankets and weatherstripping. San Francisco's retrofit ordinance led to the weatherization of 160,000 residential units and $6 million in savings.

Other communities have upgraded rental property efficiency. Landlords often have little incentive to invest in efficient technologies if renters pay energy bills. To overcome this barrier, Ann Arbor passed an ordinance requiring landlords to weatherize and install attic insulation in properties for which renters pay the utility bills.

City provides energy workshops for homeowners

The City of Fort Collins, Colorado, conducts an annual environmental program series that includes workshops on energy-efficiency aimed at homeowners. Session titles include "Controlling Energy Costs in All-Electric Homes" and "Home Energy Improvements-From the Foundation Up," are free to the public and last about two hours. Topics covered in the sessions include rate options, efficiency measures, and city conservation programs. The workshops also include a field trip to see a blower-door test to determine a building's air leaks. Participants in the workshops are also eligible for door prizes and free refreshments.

> San Francisco's retrofit ordinance led to the weatherization of 160,000 residential units and $6 million in savings.

Commercial/Industrial Task Force Packet

U.S. commercial and industrial energy users consume about $180 billion worth of energy a year. This bill could be cost-effectively reduced by more than 50% with readily available technologies and measures, directly benefiting businesses, boosting local commerce, and strengthening the economy.

This packet starts with an introduction to commercial/industrial sustainable energy opportunities. The rest of the packet is divided into examples covering the three energy factors of people and organizations, financing, and government. These examples are just a small sampling of how people have found ways to tap sustainable energy opportunities.

TASK FORCE PACKET CONTENTS
➤ **Sustainable energy opportunities**
➤ **The three energy factors:** Factor #1: People and Organizations Factor #2: Financing Factor #3: Government

Refer to page 243, to find a list of books, newsletters, and organizations that can provide even more information on specific ways for improving energy use. This list does not attempt to be a complete bibliography of the many resources available. The resources listed were chosen either because they provide a good initial overview of their topic, or they provide a helpful listing of additional resources. While this information was accurate at press time, some of these contacts may have moved on. If you find a contact has been changed we'd appreciate it if you would let Rocky Mountain Institute know. You can reach us at (970) 927-3851 or the address listed at the beginning of the book.

Sustainable Energy Opportunities

How to save energy worth billions

Energy is not an end in itself, but only a means of providing such desired services as lighting, comfortable buildings, manufacturing productivity, hot water, and office tasks. These services are known as end-uses.

By thinking first about what we want, and then finding the best tool and the most appropriate form of energy for the task, we can use far less energy than currently required. Using this method, it is possible to cut the national commercial/industrial energy bill by more than 50%.

How much can you save in commercial/industrial end-uses?

Summary of commercial/industrial end-uses	Savings Potential*
Comfortable Indoor Climates	
Space Heating	50 - 100%
(100% with proper architectural design)	
Space Cooling	80 - 100%
(100% with proper architectural design)	
Lighting	70 - 90%
Hot Water	50 - 100%
Motors	50%
Office Equipment	up to 95%
Refrigeration	25 - 45%
Cooking	10 - 30%
Process Heat	50%

* These figures demonstrate what is technologically possible. Energy improvements will require a financial investment. Cost-effectiveness and length of paybacks will vary with different measures.

The following section gives a very brief overview of some of the measures and alternative energy sources that can achieve desired end-uses more efficiently. There are volumes worth of information on all the technologies available for delivering these end-use services more efficiently. This overview simply introduces the framework for discovering energy saving opportunities. Through the workshops, you can develop projects and programs that put these technologies and measures to work so your community can reap the benefits.

Asking the right questions

Conventional approaches to energy planning have focused on increasing supply to meet growing demand. The emphasis has been on acquiring energy of any kind, from any source, at any price. This approach suggests that people want big gooey barrels of oil, lumps of coal, and raw kilowatt hours. What people really want are things like hot showers, cold beer, and comfortable buildings. So instead of trying to get more and more energy at whatever the cost, the more economical approach is to ask the following questions: What do we need energy to do? What's the least expensive way to accomplish these tasks, counting all costs? Asking these questions will help us provide the services we want from energy at the lowest cost to ourselves and society.

End-use: Lighting

Lighting accounts for more than half of all the electricity consumed in a typical U.S. commercial building. More than 30% of this electrical demand is consumed directly by cooling equipment that must compensate for the unwanted heat emitted by the lighting. According to Lawrence Berkeley Laboratory, converting to today's best hardware in lighting and lighting fixture technology could save as much as 80-90% of the electricity used for lighting and reduce other associated energy costs as well. Here are a few examples of some ways to get light more efficiently.

Compact fluorescent light bulbs (CFLs)

CFLs are four times as efficient and last 9 to 13 times as long as traditional incandescent light bulbs. Improved fluorescent lamps with electronic ballasts reduce energy use and provide better quality light with improved color rendition. They come in many shapes and sizes to fulfill a variety of lighting needs. CFL efficiency and long life means that they more than pay back their initial purchase price of $12 to $30. These bulbs make the most economic sense when used in applications that need light over four hours a day. These lights also save money by making it unnecessary to buy as many replacement bulbs. Labor costs drop too, because workers now have to make only one-tenth as many trips up the ladder to replace burned out bulbs. These savings can often pay for the cost of the bulbs.

Another way to reduce lighting bills is to provide more task lighting rather than ambient light. For example, instead of hanging several overhead fixtures high above a cluster of desks, use individual work lamps at each desk. This measure allows workers more control over the lighting at their desk and fosters more efficient energy use.

Occupancy sensors

Ultrasonic and infrared occupancy sensors are a simple way of making sure lights aren't on any longer than necessary. Sensors turn lights on when someone enters a room, and turns them off when everyone leaves. They cost as little as $25 dollars per unit and pay for themselves within a year. Dimmers, timers, and light-sensitive switches that turn off outdoor lighting after sunrise or at a certain time also cut costs.

Daylighting

Daylighting makes use of sunlight to light a building. In most circumstances, natural illumination can provide just as much, if not more, light as electric lamps. For example, a 3' x 5' window in direct summer sun can let in more light than a hundred ordinary 60-watt light bulbs. Daylighting design features include large windows, white walls that bounce light around a room, and reflective blinds.

Superwindows with advanced glazings are sometimes necessary for a daylighting system. The advanced coatings on these windows help to regulate the amount of heat coming into a building to prevent excessive

> **Lighting accounts for more than half of all the electricity consumed in a typical U.S. commercial building.**

cooling in winter and overheating in summer. Until recently, most office buildings did not use daylighting, because traditional windows caused interior overheating. However, new superwindows solve this problem.

Benefits of daylighting extend beyond reducing dependence on electricity, too. All too often, traditional lighting schemes suffer from overlighting and glare, factors that hinder worker productivity. A good daylighting system is less prone to these problems and creates a more comfortable workplace.

Efficient streetlights

High pressure sodium (HPS) and low pressure sodium (LPS) streetlights use half the electricity of conventional metal halide lamps and are well suited for outdoor and security lighting in commercial applications. While LPS lamps are more efficient, HPS lamps provide better color rendition. Some towns have installed a mix of LPS and HPS lamps, reserving the HPS lamps for downtown retail districts. San Jose, California, began converting to HPS lamps in 1983 and cut their streetlight power bill by 35%. By 1987, the program had a total cost of $5.5 million and had saved $9.7 million.

End-use: Hot water

Providing and using hot water more efficiently leads to some of the quickest and most profitable ways to generate energy saving opportunities. Every gallon of water saved also reduces sewage-treatment costs and keeps more water in rivers and wetlands. Depending on the application, you can save nearly 2/3 of the energy used to heat water.

Improved efficiency for gas heaters

Commercial energy users often set water heaters, like those found in restaurants and hotels, at an unnecessarily high temperature. Reducing the heater's setting to 120 degrees lets the unit use less energy to heat water and maintain its temperature. It also prevents children, employees, and customers from scalding themselves. Installing an automatic temperature setback device and other improvements costs about $50 and pays for itself in a few weeks if you use 2,000 gallons of hot water a day.

Water heater system insulation

Thirty percent of the energy used by an uninsulated water heater is simply lost to the room, causing any air conditioners to have to work harder. Fortunately, adequate insulation can prevent much of this waste. Doubling or tripling average heater insulation will greatly improve insulating value for little cost. Hot water pipes lose up to 20% of the energy in the heated water if they are not insulated with fiberglass and foam.

Water and energy efficiency measures

A comprehensive water efficiency retrofit cuts both the costs of water and energy. Faucetheads and showerheads reduce hot water use and heating bills. While efficient toilets don't reduce your energy costs, they do cut

> San Jose, California, began converting to HPS lamps in 1983 and cut their streetlight power bill by 35%. By 1987, the program had a total cost of $5.5 million and had saved $9.7 million.

water bills and are part of a comprehensive water retrofit. Hotels and other institutions have discovered that installation of water-efficiency devices cut water consumption by at least a third.

High-efficiency faucetheads offer a better flow of water than traditional units, while saving water and energy. An unrestricted flow of water out of a tap is inefficient, and much of the water splashes off the object being rinsed. Efficient faucetheads (2.5 gallons per minute or less) use half the water and energy.

Efficient water-saving showerheads can deliver a hard-hitting spray while cutting both water and heating costs by 25% to 60%. Today's efficient showerheads only use 2.5 gallons per minute or less as opposed to a conventional fixture's 3 to 8 gallon spray. Large energy users such as hotels, schools, or gyms can recoup the investment of replacing all their showerheads in a few months.

Energy-efficient dishwashers

Besides labor, energy is one of the main costs of washing dishes. Efficient commercial washing machines with gas booster heaters can save thousands of dollars a year. These water heaters cost 2 1/2 times more than an electric one, but they pay back the cost difference in under a year. A dishwasher with separate booster heaters enables users to keep their water heater set at 120 degrees instead of 180 degrees, for additional energy savings.

Solar water heaters

Using the sun to heat water can save a business 50% to 100% on their water heating bill. Businesses that use large amounts of hot water, such as car washes, laundromats, and hotels, can recover the upfront cost of installing a solar water system in the first several years of operation. Pools are also an ideal application of solar hot water heating opportunities. After the installation costs are recovered a business obtains its hot water at no cost.

End-use: Comfortable indoor climates

For the past forty years, heating and cooling buildings has been among the largest uses of energy in the country. In the summer, cooling is the largest component of peak summer demand for electricity, comprising 43% of the entire U.S. peak power load. During the winter, space heating is one of the largest end-uses. Improving building envelopes through insulation, sealing of air leaks, and better windows can reduce heating loads dramatically.

High performance windows

Windows are great for views and daylight, but they are also the weakest link in a building's thermal barrier. In summer they can allow too much solar heat to enter a building, resulting in increased work for the air conditioning system. In winter, they can allow too much heat to escape. High performance windows, namely low-e (for emissivity) windows and

> Businesses that use large amounts of hot water, such as car washes, laundromats, and hotels, can recover the upfront cost of installing a solar water system in the first several years of operation.

superwindows, solve both of these problems at once. These windows insulate far better than single- or double-pane glass, and the best superwindows insulate up to nine times better than a single pane of glass. High performance windows are designed differently for use in hot and cold climates. Special coatings block heat, in the form of solar infrared radiation, from escaping or from entering the house, depending on whether the window is for use in a hot or cold climate.

Besides cutting energy bills, high performance windows create more comfortable, pleasant, and productive work spaces. When carefully integrated into state-of-the-art design, high performance windows allow one to downsize, or entirely eliminate, the need for a conventional heating and cooling system in commercial office buildings.

Weatherization and insulation

Perhaps the most lucrative energy-saving measure, insulation keeps buildings cool in summer and toasty in winter. You can increase your comfort and decrease energy bills by insulating walls, attics and under the ground floor. Sealing air leaks with caulk and expanding foam is a cost-effective energy saver. Similarly, weather-stripping can reduce leaks around doors and windows.

Furnaces

You can improve a building's furnace performance through periodic maintenance. Modifications, such as installing an electronic ignition on a gas unit, also reduce furnace operating costs. Better yet, efficient gas furnaces can further cut the environmental and economic costs of heating by up to 20 percent.

Thermostats with timers

Also known as set-back thermostats, these devices lower building temperatures at night, when no one is around, and raise them just in time for comfortable day time temperatures. Set-back thermostats are also used in hotels to reduce the temperature in guest rooms when most guests are gone during the day. When the devices are programmed to set temperatures back ten degrees while the building is unoccupied, energy savings of over 20% are possible.

Air conditioners

New air conditioners are 50% to 70% more efficient than the average unit in use. Buying one with an adjustable thermostat will prevent overcooling and save additional energy. Closing shades (unless you have window glazings that prevent overheating), cleaning air conditioner filters often, and setting the air conditioner thermostat at 78 degrees will also help cut energy use. Alternatives to refrigerated air conditioners include evaporative coolers that cost half as much, and have operating costs up to 80% less. Simple ceiling or portable fans also cool inexpensively.

Typical industrial motors use 10 to 20 times their purchase price each year in electricity. This energy consumption is comparable to buying a $1,000 car and needing more than $10,000 worth of gas a year to run it.

Space cooling measures

One of the best ways to keep a building cool is to prevent heat from coming inside. Caulk, insulation, window films, high-performance windows, awnings and overhangs can all reduce heat gain and reduce the work your air conditioner has to do.

Another effective way to keep buildings cool is to reduce heat produced inside the structure. Incandescent lights and inefficient office equipment can all force your air conditioner to work harder than necessary. More efficient lighting and office equipment makes it easier for your cooling system to do its job. Measures such as improving the efficiency of system ductwork and maintenance also keep buildings cool.

Energy-efficient building design

The best way to efficiently provide comfortable climates is to design buildings right in the first place. With currently available technology it is possible to construct buildings that are five to ten times more energy-efficient than conventional ones. A variety of simple design features will significantly reduce lighting, heating, and cooling costs, as well as create more comfortable indoor environments. Energy-efficient design considerations will determine how the building is positioned, amount and kind of windows, type of building shell, daylighting and electric lighting systems, and heating, ventilation, and cooling systems. Constructing these super-efficient buildings can actually be less expensive than conventional construction methods. Even better, the avoided life-cycle energy costs can be comparable to the overall capital costs of the building.

End-use: Manufacturing and industrial processes

Motors play an important role in almost all manufacturing and industrial process systems. They also are costing the U.S. roughly $90 billion a year to run, and use more than half of all electricity produced. Typical industrial motors use 10 to 20 times their purchase price each year in electricity. This energy consumption is comparable to buying a $1,000 car and needing more than $10,000 worth of gas a year to run it. The good news is that, because motors have such high operating costs, replacing older motors with more efficient models will save large amounts of energy, often repaying upfront costs of replacement in 6 to 36 months. Enormous savings can be created by installing high-efficiency, appropriately sized motors with adjustable speed drives and power factor controllers. Wide use of these efficiency improvements could save up to 60 percent of the electricity spent on running U.S. motors.

End-use: Office tasks

It takes at least a dozen 1000 Megawatt power plants to power all the commercial sector office equipment in the country. Computers, copiers, and other office equipment consume about 6 percent of electricity in the commercial energy sector, and an even greater portion of office building electricity. With the popularity of these technologies, and the ever-increasing varieties and improvements, office equipment is one of the fastest growing electricity loads. The U.S. Environmental Protection Agency predicts that computers alone may account for 10 percent of all commercial electrical consumption by the year 2000.

One of the simplest ways to generate large energy savings in office equipment is to turn off idle machines or put them into standby or "sleep" mode. About 30-40% of U.S. microcomputers are left on all night and weekend. Shutting these machines down can cut computer energy use by up to 70%. U.S. businesses waste some $4 billion worth of electricity each year by leaving unnecessary lights and office equipment on when not in use.

Most new computers are far more efficient than their predecessors of even a few years ago. The latest inkjet printers, laptops, and notebook computers currently lead the pack in computer energy efficiency. The U.S. Environmental Protection Agency's Energy Star rating program can help you identify the best efficient computer buys.

End-use: Refrigeration

Refrigeration accounts for 8% of all commercial energy use. Grocery store refrigerated display cases make up 85% of this figure. Typically, over half of a grocery store's energy bill is for refrigeration. With efficient technologies, one can save almost half of this energy.

Minor design improvements, including single fans, redesigned cases, and improved airflow can cut energy loads in display case refrigerators by 15%. Replacing an open case refrigerator with one that has advanced display window coatings and door frames can reduce energy loads by over 50%. Efficient compressors and motors will add at least a 10% energy savings.

End-use: Cooking

Cooking consumes 5% of all commercial sector energy, and is the major energy end-use in restaurants and related institutions. The potential for savings, particularly in kitchens serving many meals a day, is great. Electric fryers, duplex griddles (which have a top and bottom cooking surface), and convection ovens all cut cooking times and save energy and money. Finally, simple steps like putting tops on pots when necessary and careful use of utensils, can reduce burner energy costs. Solid state controls and efficient ceramic burner technology are other ways to cut energy use.

> **U.S. businesses waste some $4 billion worth of electricity each year by leaving unnecessary lights and office equipment on when not in use.**

End-use: Laundry

Both energy and water savings are possible with efficient laundry technologies. In areas where water is expensive, these measures can have payback times of less than a year, and generate thousands of dollars in savings.

Moisture sensors, water recycling systems, heat recovery systems, and horizontal-axis machines are representative of these efficient technologies. Solar water heating systems, as described above, are cost-effective measures for commercial and industrial laundry systems.

The cost of washing linens and dishes can be greatly reduced for hotels, restaurants and other institutions. Many hotels have cut labor and energy costs by simply asking guests if they'd like to have their linens changed less frequently than once a day.

Alternative energy sources for fulfilling energy end-uses

Once you have fully tapped efficiency measures to reduce your energy demand, there are many ways to develop renewable energy sources to provide the energy to deliver end-uses. The sun, wind, and falling water are all sources of affordable and environmentally friendly energy. Individual businesses, institutions, and industries can tap renewable technologies such as solar water heating and solar electric power systems. They can also join together and encourage local utilities to invest in renewables to fulfill overall power supply needs.

Solar energy falls on every community and, compared to its full potential, is virtually untapped. Solar is especially cost-effective for such tasks as water or space heating. Designing buildings properly will also reduce demand for energy for lighting, heating and cooling.

Solar energy can also provide electricity directly for a business. Photovoltaics, or solar panels, convert sunlight into electricity. Solar panels are especially popular with enterprises located at remote sites that are looking for a cost-effective alternative to power lines. Solar power is especially useful for such outdoor energy needs as emergency call boxes, security lighting, traffic hazard signs, and street lighting. Small photovoltaic systems can also power outdoor lighting, thereby eliminating the need to extend electric lines to lighting fixtures.

Utilities are also considering photovoltaics as a new source of supply. Not only are utilities developing solar power stations, but they are also installing solar panels on businesses dispersed throughout a community

If you live in an area with enough of it, wind can be both a reliable and economical source of electricity. At one time, over 6 million windmills across the U.S. supplied power for households, farms, and industry. Wind technology has come of age and there are a wide variety of advanced, rugged wind machines. Wind machines can either be used to provide electricity directly at a business site, such as for pumping water, or can be linked to the utility and sell power to them. Currently there are more wind machines feeding power into utility grids than are used for any other application. Utilities are also investing in wind farms as an alternative power supply. In California, 15,000 utility-operated wind machines provide enough power for about 300,000 households.

Cogeneration has become an increasingly popular alternative energy source for commercial and industrial end-uses. Cogeneration takes waste heat from industrial processes and uses it to generate electricity for other purposes such as heating. Cogeneration works best in larger commercial and institutional settings. The most common type of cogeneration systems take steam from an existing boiler to turn a turbine to produce electricity. Others use natural gas to run an electricity-producing generator. The water that cools the generator is then used to provide heat and hot water. Another system uses a gas engine to power a water chiller. The waste heat from the engine produces hot water. Cogeneration is most appropriate for buildings or industries that need both hot water (for space heating or industrial process heat) and electricity. Federal regulations also allow cogenerators to sell their electricity back to utilities, so some companies use their cogeneration system as a separate source of cash.

These examples are just the tip of the iceberg of alternative and renewable energy's potential. Renewables currently provide only 13% of the nation's energy needs. A report by five of the national laboratories demonstrated that an accelerated research and development program in renewables could allow the country to cost-effectively generate half of current U.S. energy use by the year 2030 from renewables.

> In California, 15,000 utility-operated wind machines provide enough power for about 300,000 households.

Factor #1: People and Organizations

Although the knowledge and technology exists to improve energy efficiency by more than 50%, we've barely scratched the surface of efficiency opportunities. Your community can charge ahead by involving a wide variety of people in implementing energy cost-cutting alternatives. Business owners, retailers, facilities managers, architects, and entrepreneurs are just some of the people that can help turn energy efficiency into an economic asset. Here are just a few examples of how a variety of people and organizations are playing a role.

Local retailers bring products to market

The Iowa Association of Municipal Utilities works with member utilities to develop energy efficiency programs that strengthen the economies of Iowa towns. The program emphasizes cooperating with local retailers in each participating town to get energy-efficient products on the market. First, with the help of the OPTIONS computer program, the municipal utility and a citizens energy committee determine which efficiency measures make sense in their town. Local retailers are then asked if they carry the desired products, and if they do not, they are asked if they can get them. Based on the retail price of the products, the local utility determines what kind of incentives they can offer to encourage residents to purchase the products. The retailers then begin to stock the recommended efficient furnaces, lighting systems, and showerheads. To make things more convenient for the purchaser, the retailers remove large, old equipment and install the new. The arrangement benefits everyone: residents and businesses cut energy costs with the more efficient technologies, since products are now conveniently available, and retailers benefit from more sales.

A radio station owner makes renewables hum

Thanks to station owner Malcolm Brown, the studios of Jeffersonville, New York's public radio station, are unlike any other in the nation. With his own money, former philosophy professor Brown built a microhydro plant that uses flowing water to produce electricity that powers the studio. In the plant's first four years of operation, it produced an average 20 kilowatts of output, enough to power 29 homes. A passive solar heating system also helps heat the studios.

Rural entrepreneur branches out into energy

While Chums, Ltd. is best known for its outdoor gear, this small, innovative company found that making efficient manufacturing equipment is another market opportunity. Based in rural Hurricane, Utah, a town of 4,200, Chums has 70 full-time employees. Six employees work for Chums' energy division, which builds efficient manufacturing machinery for regional clients. These include a local precision machine shop and a mountaineering goods manufacturer. This division also has helped increase the efficiency of the company's main product line, sunglass retainers. The company has also been experimenting with rotary expanders (devices such as turbines that harness gases and put them to work) that can be used for geothermal, solar thermal, and solar-generated steam applications.

Business managers cut costs

Many managers think of business-related energy costs as a standard operating expense over which they have no control. However, many business operators are finding that energy use can be an area of significant savings opportunities.

Replacing 2,000 incandescent light bulbs with compact fluorescent fixtures has paid off in more ways than one for the Sheraton Tacoma Hotel. A customer survey had shown that patrons wanted more light in the rooms. But upgrading the brightness of the incandescent bulbs would have increased the hotel's energy use. A decision was made to go to CFLs. With the fluorescents, not only did the hotel please its guests by increasing its illumination levels, but it also cut its electric bill for lighting by two-thirds. Generally, lighting costs in most commercial establishments can be cut up to 75 percent while providing better illumination equal to or better than current levels. These systems pay back for themselves within two to five years.

A Hecla, South Dakota grocery found it was overheating in the summer and burning 2,500 gallons of fuel oil in winter. These conditions were caused by poor insulation and by refrigeration compressors that created waste heat. But an electrician/refrigeration service person came up with a solution. The store's ceiling was lowered and insulated while vents and blowers allowed the waste heat to warm the store in winter. When the improvements were complete, the store was spending $500 per year on fuel rather than $2,500.

Houses of worship congregate for better energy use

Houses of worship often provide a variety of community services, ranging from childcare to housing development. Enterprising religious organizations have started to see energy efficiency as a way to free up more money for these services, and set an example of good stewardship at the same time. The Interfaith Coalition on Energy (ICE) has helped religious congregations in the Philadelphia area reduce their energy use since 1980. Serving a variety of faiths, ICE publishes a newsletter with tips on energy-efficient measures, where to find products, and how to cover upfront costs of improvements. ICE also helps distribute energy-efficient technologies, and sponsors workshops to help congregations make their buildings more resource efficient.

Financial institution banks on innovative headquarters

As part of a campaign to shed its stodgy image, and to create a better environment for its employees, the Nederlandsche Middenstandsbank (NMB) built a new, energy-efficient bank headquarters. The building includes a hot water storage system that obtains its heat from an onsite cogeneration facility. The structure itself stores heat from passive solar design and waste heat. Daylighting techniques provide a significant amount of the building's light. The cost of building the headquarters was comparable to building other office buildings in Holland. Not only does the building have reduced energy costs, but the energy savings have helped the bank meet its other design goals. Absenteeism has dropped because of the bank's attractive indoor work environment, and the new building has also helped build the institution's reputation as progressive and creative.

Architects prove good design means efficient

The Croxton Collaborative, an architectural firm headed by Randolph Croxton, specializes in resource-efficient building design. The Collaborative's projects have included creating an office for the Audubon Society by renovating what was once a Manhattan 1890s department store into one of the most resource-efficient spaces in the country. Croxton's design work for the Audubon Building stressed goals of healthy indoor air quality, low embodied energy (the energy required to produce building materials), and resource-efficient operation. Designing with these goals in mind has paid off. The structure uses 61% less energy than a conventional building. In addition, the efficient headquarters recycles 80% of wastes and reduces acid rain and greenhouse-causing emissions.

Completed in 1993, the Audubon headquarters is considered to be among the most desirable pieces of real estate in Manhattan. A leasing agent says space in the building is in high demand due to low energy bills, a non-toxic building environment, and a pleasant, day-lit work environment.

For Croxton, creating resource-efficient buildings isn't a specialized form of architecture. The collaborative views environmentally friendly buildings as simply taking principles of good design to their logical conclusion: All architects interested in good design will want their buildings to operate as efficiently as possible.

Stadium makes a home run for efficiency

Pittsburgh Steelers and Pirates fans will be treated to a show of efficient energy use at home games. After hearing of a lighting retrofit at San Diego's

> **The Audubon headquarters will use 61% less energy than a conventional building. In addition, the efficient headquarters recycles 80% of wastes and reduces acid rain and greenhouse-causing emissions.**

Jack Murphy Stadium, the chairman and the capital projects coordinator of Three Rivers stadium decided their stadium could use a few lighting improvements as well. The $234,000 retrofit has cut the stadium's power bills by $113,000 a year and will pay back for itself in about two years. After that, the stadium will be adding that amount each year to the bottom line. Now that's a grand slam.

An energy action coordinator cuts college's costs

New York's Hamilton College has learned a lucrative lesson on the profitability of energy efficiency. Under the leadership of an Energy Action Coordinator hired by the college, the school has cut electricity consumption by 15% and campus utility bills by $200,000. Replacing incandescent light bulbs with compact fluorescents was one of the first steps the school pursued. Now the new lamps are saving $4,000 a month, which is a 211% annual return when coupled with a utility rebate for each bulb. Put that one in the textbooks. Other college campuses, have also realized significant savings. Columbia University cut energy bills by $2.8 million, yet at no net cost.

Manufacturer sews up profits with utility help

Under the leadership of Wes Birdsall, the Osage, Iowa, Municipal Utility has been on the cutting edge of energy efficiency in both the residential and commercial sectors. Since 1974, utility director Birdsall has initiated several programs to make local businesses more efficient, including free energy checks for industrial customers. The utility also offered to pay businesses two year's interest on the cost of installing energy efficiency measures. One sock factory cut the cost of knitting a dozen socks from $.48 to $.34 and has increased its production 295% and workforce 290% since 1984. Birdsall's efficiency efforts save local residents $1.2 million in energy costs each year and have added a hundred new jobs to the community economy. As a result, the town has experienced an economic renaissance.

Farmers cut energy costs through water efficiency

Concerned about burdening farmers in their service territory with rising electric rates, the Umatilla Electric Cooperative Association found a way for customers to reduce energy costs. This Pacific Northwest electric co-op initiated an Agribusiness Task Force of farmers, food processors, and other agricultural interests. Because irrigation is a major farm energy use, the task force recommended that the utility hire an irrigation specialist to develop programs to help farmers save energy. The utility's programs include a computer/phone irrigation scheduling network that provides irrigation recommendations. Overall, the co-op's energy and water efficiency programs have resulted in 20%-25% water and energy savings for the farmers.

> Under the leadership of an Energy Action Coordinator, Hamilton College has cut electricity consumption by 15% and campus utility bills by $200,000.

Factor #2: Financing

Cost-cutting improvements such as installing energy-efficient lights, improving a building's heating system, and installing more efficient motors will often require upfront financing. While many businesses and institutions might not have the available cash to invest in these improvements there are a variety of sources that can be tapped or created. Here are several sources of energy-efficiency investment funds for the commercial and industrial sector.

Utilities

Utilities are one of the most logical financing sources for energy efficiency and alternative power sources. Unlike individual ratepayers, utilities routinely make investments with payback periods lasting decades. Utilities also have access to large amounts of capital. Many utilities spend millions of dollars annually to purchase their power supply. Spending that same capital on efficiency is like buying a source of power, a source that is less expensive than building a new power plant. The most progressive utility efficiency programs have budgets equalling four to five percent of their cost of power. Utility financing programs come in a variety of forms: rebates, 0% or low-interest loans, equipment leasing, and giveaways. Here are a few examples of utility financing tools:

Power authority HELP for lighting

New York businesses are finding it much easier to change to more efficient lighting thanks to the New York Power Authority's High Efficiency Lighting Program. HELP provides lighting audits, retrofits and financing. The utility has set up a Conservation Loan Bank to finance the retrofits. Loan payments are charged to a customer's utility bills. The utility, which is actively involved in each part of the program, also guarantees a three-year payback on each project.

Utility rebates for agricultural energy savings

Pacific Gas and Electric provides financial incentives to help farmers increase energy efficiency within their operations. The utility provides free energy audits, pump tests, and irrigation system analyses. Farmers can then take advantage of utility energy-saving recommendations through the utility's rebate program. Rebates of up to $450 are available for energy- and water-saving equipment. Financial assistance is also available for switching to more efficient irrigation techniques. While the program is aimed at helping farmers save energy, it also result, in substantial water savings.

> **Spending capital on efficiency is like buying a source of power, a source that is less expensive than building a new power plant.**

Incentives encourage motor and speed drive efficiency

Since 1986, Northern States Power, which serves the Northern Midwest, has provided rebates to commercial and industrial customers to encourage motor and adjustable speed drive efficiency. In the first eight months of 1993, NSP paid out nearly $655,000 in rebates. Customers who install efficient motors and drives in new applications, or retrofit existing systems, are eligible for this incentive program. NSP also offers free motor testing to help demonstrate the benefits of efficient units. Sellers of efficient equipment, a group the utility regards as important trade allies, are also eligible for incentives.

Energy Service Companies

Energy Service Companies provide a one-stop shopping approach to energy efficiency. ESCOs perform energy audits, provide financing, select and install energy saving measures, and monitor, measure, and verify energy savings. Often, ESCOs pay the upfront cost of the retrofit, billing the customer in installment payments, which depend on the extent of the energy savings. These payments are often guaranteed to be less than what the customer would normally be paying for monthly energy bills.

Contracting for efficiency

Equipment contracts provide access to efficient equipment without the upfront purchasing cost. The equipment can range from compact fluorescent light bulbs to heavy manufacturing machinery. Instead of borrowing cash to buy equipment, the interested party borrows the equipment itself. There is no down payment, and the monthly lease payments are less than loan payments for buying the equipment. The resulting savings exceed the equipment lease.

Financial institutions

While banks and other financing institutions routinely finance business expansion and start-ups, potential borrowers often run into barriers when it comes to getting loans for commercial energy improvements. Usually, energy improvement loans are too small to catch a bank's interest. Moreover, most loan officers are unfamiliar with the financial benefits of energy efficient investments. While we wait for banks to catch up, here are two examples of alternative financing resources that have been created.

Revolving loan funds foot the bill

Revolving loan funds (RLFs) make loans available for businesses and organizations at low interest rates. As borrowers repay their debt, the fund makes new loans. Existing organizations, such as merchants' associations, service clubs, banks, utilities, and chambers of commerce, may create a RLF by pooling resources.

> **Revolving loan funds make loans available for businesses and organizations at low interest rates. As borrowers repay their debt, the fund makes new loans.**

Three banks in Cortez, Colorado each lent $26,000 to a revolving loan fund to finance energy improvements in area small businesses. The state energy office matched the local banks' money to buy down interest rates. Participating businesses are able to pay loans back with the resulting energy savings in less than three years.

A CATALYST for financing

The Catalyst Group, located in Brattleboro, Vermont, is an investment banking and financial services company, with a difference. Catalyst arranges financing for energy efficiency in both the private and public sectors. Catalyst can also design financing programs which can assist a utility or community to meet its energy efficiency goals. For the commercial sector, Catalyst focuses on financing energy and lighting system leases. It also helps governments secure tax-exempt financing for efficiency projects.

Public entities

Government, at the local, state, and federal levels, offers a range of financing mechanisms and resources. These range from loans for the small business owner all the way up to million dollar bond issues to fund comprehensive retrofit programs.

Bonds for efficiency

Government entities, such as municipal utilities, have the authority to issue tax-exempt bonds. A bond is a type of IOU. Governments or businesses issue bonds to investors with a promise to repay the loan by a certain date, along with regular interest payments. While bonds are crucial for raising money to build public buildings, repair roads, and provide public services, they can also be used to finance energy-efficiency programs.

Eugene Water and Electric Board, Oregon's largest public utility, is financing its Energy Resource Management Plan with a $150 million bond issue. After a citizen-based resource planning effort, nearly 75% of Eugene voters approved the financing measure. The bond money will help the utility implement its resource plan, which calls for energy efficiency, direct application of renewables, cogeneration, and hydro.

Local governments can also issue bonds to finance energy improvements in public buildings. Ann Arbor, Michigan's Energy Efficiency Financing Project provided $1.4 million in municipal bonds for retrofits to 30 buildings. These retrofits included lighting, insulation, and heating improvements. Bond financing enabled the city to keep a greater portion of the resulting energy savings in-house.

State governments offer financing

Several states have organized a variety of financing programs, ranging from one-stop audit/financing services to low-interest loan programs. Check with your state energy office to see if your state offers programs such as the following.

> Eugene Water and Electric Board, Oregon's largest public utility, is financing its Energy Resource Management Plan with a $150 million bond issue.

The Iowa Energy Bank is a one-stop resource that helps municipalities, nonprofit organizations, and schools tap into energy savings without dipping into operating budgets. The Energy Bank links existing resources and expertise for energy audits, technical assistance, and zero-interest loans to improve energy efficiency around the state. The program has improved the efficiency of several hundred public buildings since its establishment in 1986.

Oregon's Small Scale Energy Loan Program (SELP) helps businesses, homeowners, and public agencies fund retrofits, and save millions of dollars statewide. The loans vary in size, and can be used in conjunction with state tax credits for energy-efficient technologies.

Small Business Administration offers energy loans

The U.S. Small Business Administration offers loans to assist small businesses to engineer, manufacture, distribute, market, install or service energy-saving measures. To apply for these loans, call your state U.S. Small Business Administration office and ask to speak to a loan officer about energy loans authorized in Section 7 (a) (12) of the Small Business Act.

Green Lights offers financing directory

The U.S. Environmental Protection Agency's Green Lights Program has a computerized database of financing resources for energy-efficient lighting and other building efficiency improvements. The database includes utility and other third-party financing sources. Call the Green Lights hotline at (202) 775-6650 to request a Financing Directory diskette, or for more information on Green Lights.

Factor #3: Government

Because local governments have the power to set building standards, shape land-use policies, and mobilize resources, they can be an important tool for setting a sustainable energy course for years to come. Here's a summary of basic strategies local governments can employ to improve the commercial/industrial energy picture:

Lead by example:
- ➤ Install cost-effective energy efficiency measures in public buildings.
- ➤ Install renewable energy and cogeneration systems where practical.
- ➤ Implement procurement practices that fully consider operating and life-cycle costs.
- ➤ Require all new public buildings to be constructed using sustainable building design principles.
- ➤ Track resource costs in government operations and give staff incentives to find ways to reduce them.

Help remove barriers to energy-wise practices:
- ➤ Offer technical assistance to commercial and industrial energy users.
- ➤ Offer citizens the information to make more informed decisions.
- ➤ Develop financing partnerships between lending institutions, businesses, and other funding sources.
- ➤ Put energy efficiency at the top of the community agenda.
- ➤ Demonstrate how energy efficiency benefits the local economy.

Serve as a catalyst for change:
- ➤ If utilities or other energy organizations are not promoting a sustainable energy future, create an energy office to lead the effort.
- ➤ Fully consider energy consumption in development proposals.
- ➤ Create incentives for exemplary energy practices and recognize efforts.
- ➤ Create energy codes that require efficiency measures in new buildings as well as those offered for sale.
- ➤ Establish hook-up feebates that require builders to pay a fee for inefficient buildings while giving rebates to those who are efficient.
- ➤ Encourage gas and electric utilities to implement demand-side management programs.

Here are a few examples of how government has put some of these approaches into practice:

Setting an example at city hall

When Petaluma, California officials received an energy audit that said the municipal government could cut energy costs by 23%, they jumped at the chance to save money. Retaining a contractor, the city retrofitted such municipal buildings as City Hall with compact fluorescent lights and a computerized heating and cooling system. Over the first year of the program, the city hopes to reduce its $197,700 energy bill by $45,800. In ten years, Petaluma anticipates it will come out ahead by more than $422,000. Petaluma officials also hope to make energy improvements to their wastewater treatment plant, the city's largest single electricity user.

School board builds solar school

North Carolina's Johnston County School Board wanted something that made sense for the long term. Recognizing that North Carolina schools spend more on energy and maintenance over a building's lifetime than on constructing the building itself, the board decided to build the passive solar Four Oaks Elementary School. This building consumes half the energy of a typical school and has low maintenance costs. The school was also built within budget and was completed ahead of schedule.

Library checks out efficiency

In Mt. Airy, North Carolina, local government has built a library that deserves a spot in the record books. The Mt. Airy Library uses 53% less energy than the same size building would using conventional design practices thanks to a blend of passive solar design, daylighting, insulation, air locks and heat pumps. This building also uses 80% less energy than the City Hall, a similar-sized building. In terms of building cost, the library was competitive with other structures built with advanced design features. The U.S. Department of Energy financed part of the building's cost, as it considered the library to be a demonstration site.

PVs power remote airport

Visitors flying into southeastern Utah to visit such attractions as Lake Powell now arrive at the country's first solar-powered aviation facility, the Cal Black Memorial Airport. Spurred by the project's engineering firm and the Utah Division of Energy, the San Juan County government decided to use solar electricity to fulfill energy needs at the airport, which is located beyond the reach of power lines.

The airport draws on its photovoltaic system to power airstrip lights, interior lighting and other operations. The PV system is quiet, nonpollut-

> Petaluma anticipates it will come out ahead by more than $422,000.

ing and inexpensive to run and maintain. Initial estimates indicate that the system will pay back for itself in less than five years.

Buying the right thing

When municipalities buy such equipment as light bulbs, they are often legally bound to buy the bulb that has the lowest initial price, without regard for operating costs. Unfortunately, this procurement method may prevent government from buying the most efficient technologies, even if they will be less expensive to operate in the long run. However, cities like Seattle and San Jose have explored basing purchases on life cycle costs, which are the total costs of buying and operating a piece of equipment. By looking at life cycle costs, these towns have passed over such technologies as incandescent light bulbs in favor of compact fluorescents, which are the best buy for the long term.

City government gives builders efficiency IDEAS

Barriers in the building and design industry have made it difficult for architects and contractors to build as efficiently as possible. Recognizing these barriers, San Jose, California runs the IDEAS (Innovative Design and Energy Analysis Service) program to encourage energy efficiency in new commercial and industrial buildings. This free service provides energy-saving design and planning help to developers, architects, and engineers.

IDEAS works with builders in the early stages of project development and provides general information on efficient building technologies. The service is also a clearinghouse of successful construction case studies and energy consultant referrals.

City lights the way to savings

Seattle, Washington converted many of its street lights to efficient, high pressure sodium (HPS) units. Starting in 1983, the city replaced over 80,000 street lights, saving over 26 million kilowatt-hours. As an added bonus, the streets are now lit 12% more brightly than before.

Efficient building codes

Given ongoing improvements in efficient building technologies, your community may want to revise your building code if it dates back to 1980 or before. The Council of American Building Officials (CABO) publishes a model energy code that is a useful reference for developing an efficient code for your community.

Similarly, Osage, Iowa's municipal utility has set minimum insulation standards for commercial and residential buildings. If potential customers fail to meet the standards, which apply to both new construction and retrofits, they will not receive new utility service. As a result, all new

> **By looking at life cycle costs, Seattle and San Jose have passed over such technologies as incandescent light bulbs in favor of compact fluorescents, which are the best buy for the long term.**

construction for the past several years has exceeded the utility's standards. Other towns have set a sliding scale for utility hook-up fees based on building efficiency.

City establishes a one-stop-shop for energy savings

The City of Berkeley established a Community Energy Services Corporation to provide a "one-stop shop" that offers a complete range of energy services to commercial, public, and residential properties. A nonprofit corporation, the Community Energy Services Corporation provides energy audits and project management. It also helps clients find energy services financing.

Flood-stricken village rises again with solar

After years of flooding from the Kickapoo River, including a 1978 disaster that devastated Main Street, the village of Soldiers Grove, Wisconsin, relocated in its entirety to higher ground. Concerned with its increasing dependence on heating oil, the village (population 564) required that new buildings be several times more energy efficient than required by state construction codes. The community also mandated that half of each new building's energy needed to come from the sun. Today, villagers enjoy several daylit and passive solar-heated establishments, including the Solar Town Pharmacy on Passive Sun Drive, the Kickapoo Valley Medical Clinic on Sunset Avenue, and the Fire Station on Sunbeam Boulevard, East.

EPA promotes efficient lighting and buildings

Green Lights, Energy Star Buildings, and Energy Star Computers are extremely successful voluntary programs sponsored by the U.S. Environmental Protection Agency. They have encouraged many U.S. businesses, organizations, and governments to install energy-efficient technologies.

Over 1,000 organizations and businesses have already joined Green Lights, EPA's flagship Energy Star Program. Participating organizations agree to survey their facilities and install energy-efficient lighting systems wherever it is profitable and does not compromise lighting quality. In return, EPA provides technical support and public recognition. Green Lights participants realize considerable savings, improved lighting quality, and public recognition of their environmental actions.

The Energy Star Buildings program follows the same principle as Green Lights. It seeks to help companies limit the pollution their buildings cause, and save money in the process. It also includes broader opportunities for profitable commercial building investments in efficient heating, ventilation, and air conditioning.

The Energy Star Computers program also helps reduce commercial energy use by increasing computer efficiency. This increase in turn reduces

> **Concerned with its increasing dependence on heating oil, Soldiers Grove required that new buildings be several times more energy efficient than required by state construction codes.**

cooling and electric loads. Participating companies, representing about 60% of U.S. sales of desktop computers and 80% of the laser printer market, have signed agreements with EPA and are introducing products that power down when not being used and cut energy use by 50-75%. Products that qualify are identified by the EPA Energy Star logo.

EPA estimates that these three Energy Star programs, Green Lights, Energy Star Buildings, and Energy Star Computers can save participants approximately 40% of the operating costs associated with buildings, with a return on investment exceeding 20 percent.

In addition to cutting electricity bills, the program also reduces pollution. According to the EPA, if the U.S. converted to efficient lighting wherever profitable, it would prevent the emission of 232 million tons of CO_2, 1.7 million tons SO_2 and 900,000 tons of NO_x.

Climate Change Action Plan promotes industrial efficiency

Through the federal Climate Change Action Plan a variety of DOE and EPA programs have been developed or expanded to encourage energy efficiency in U.S. industries. DOE Energy Analysis and Diagnostic Centers provide energy efficiency audits for small and medium-sized manufacturing plants. The average EADC audit recommends annual energy savings of approximately $40,000 per year. Since its inception in 1976 the program has completed 5100 assessments generating energy savings of approximately $517 million. DOE also offers the Motor Challenge Program, through which industries can sign up as partners to receive resources to increase motor efficiency. Resources offered include education and training materials, workshops, decision tools, and direct technical assistance. Both of these programs are part of Energy Partnerships for a Strong Economy, a collection of initiatives offered by DOE's office of Energy Efficiency and Renewable Energy. To find out more about these programs and others, and how to take advantage of them, see page 253.

Transportation Task Force Packet

Transportation fuel can account for more than half of all energy used in some communities. At the national level, America's transportation fuel bill is draining the economy at a rate of over $170 billion a year. And that's just a fraction of the total costs of the nation's transportation system. Other costs include building and maintaining roads, buying and repairing vehicles, purchasing insurance, and accidents. Indirect transportation costs not measured in dollars include air pollution, congestion, reduced free time, loss of open space, and communities centered around cars rather than people. Finding ways to reduce your local transportation bill through better policies and efficient technologies not only boosts the local economy, but also enhances quality of life.

This packet is an introduction to transportation energy-saving opportunities, and gives examples in the three energy factor areas. Your task force can refer to these examples as you develop measures that will work for your community.

> ## TASK FORCE PACKET CONTENTS
>
> ➤ **Sustainable energy opportunities**
>
> ➤ **The three energy factors:**
> Factor #1: People and Organizations
> Factor #2: Financing
> Factor #3: Government

Refer to page 243 to find a list of books, newsletters, and organizations that can provide even more information on specific ways for improving energy use. This list does not attempt to be a complete bibliography of the many resources available. The resources listed were chosen either because they provide a good initial overview of their topic, or they provide a helpful listing of additional resources. While this information was accurate at press time, some of these contacts may have moved on. If you find a contact has been changed we'd appreciate it if you would let Rocky Mountain Institute know. You can reach us at (970) 927-3851 or the address listed at the beginning of the book.

Sustainable Energy Opportunities

Your community is a rare one if it doesn't experience the costs of our current transportation system: pollution, congestion, energy waste, frustration, sprawl ... the list goes on and on. These problems are largely due to two major flaws in the way we have approached transportation planning for the past several decades.

First, we've been asking the wrong question. The main question underlying the current approach to transportation planning has been "How do we help more cars move more quickly?" Unfortunately, this question ignores the main purpose of transportation. The question should be "How do we help people get access to work, play, shopping, and other places more efficiently?" By not asking this fundamental question, we've severely limited the range of transportation answers.

Second, when solutions other than laying more pavement are proposed, current transportation decision-making does not give them a chance to compete fairly. Because we do not currently count and weigh the total costs of all possible solutions, the standard approach to solving transportation problems appears most cost-effective. Some of the many uncounted costs include pollution, energy costs, costs absorbed by individual users, insurance, and maintenance.

Transportation planning will result in solutions that are far more energy efficient, and that preserve the livability of our communities when two fundamental changes are made in our thinking about transportation. First, solutions must be rooted in an awareness that the end use of transportation is convenient, safe, and efficient access, rather than simply moving more cars. At the same time, transportation planning must evaluate and respond to the true costs of varying solutions.

Transportation energy use and its associated costs are a significant part of the currently uncounted costs in comparing transportation alternatives. The following section introduces some of the energy-efficient alternatives for moving people and goods. As you read through them, think of which methods your community currently uses in transportation planning. In the workshops, you can focus on developing projects and programs that put these opportunities to work.

ISTEA: A new approach

With passage of ISTEA, the Intermodal Surface Transportation Efficiency Act, Congress created a transportation planning framework that can help communities create access at the lowest total cost. The intent of ISTEA is to develop a transportation system that better serves the goals of protecting environmental and community quality, and promoting energy efficiency and economic development. The challenge will be how to make the intent of ISTEA a reality. ISTEA will be referred to throughout this section, with its implications for funding, citizen involvement, and planning.

There are three main approaches for reducing the transportation fuel bill:
➤ Increasing fuel efficiency
➤ Promoting the efficient use of vehicles
➤ Reducing demand for travel

This summary starts with some of the simplest ways individuals and businesses can reduce their transportation fuel bill. However, as you will see as you read through the examples, effectively addressing our ever-increasing transportation fuel tab and its accompanying costs will ultimately require finding ways to reduce demand for vehicular travel.

Increasing fuel efficiency

A range of measures, from simple oil changes to the latest high-tech, high-mileage supercars, can increase fuel efficiency.

Efficient Cars

If the U.S. were to increase the average mileage of its car fleet from 19 miles per gallon to 22 mpg, it would eliminate the need for the amount of oil we used to import from Kuwait and Iraq. Adding another nine miles per gallon nationally would reduce the need for us to import any oil from the Persian Gulf. Given that both foreign and domestic automakers offer safe and peppy cars that get well over forty miles per gallon, achieving improved gas mileage should not be too hard.

Efficient fleets

Many governments and private companies own fleets of cars. More efficient fleets can significantly reduce fuel costs. A few miles per gallon increase in mileage can create an annual savings of hundreds of dollars per car.

Even though it may not be economically feasible to convert a fleet all at once to more efficient cars, regular maintenance, such as routinely changing motor oil, aligning wheels, and maintaining proper tire pressure, can help fleets cut fuel costs. Other measures, such as installing radial tires, reduce environmental costs, such as additional pollution.

Super-efficient supercars

While a four-passenger car that gets over three hundred miles per gallon sounds like something out of science fiction, don't be surprised to see these cars on the road within a decade. Not only will these vehicles get tremendous gas mileage, but they will also offer better performance and safety than existing autos. These "supercars" will be made of extremely light and strong materials, like carbon fiber composites commonly found in Indy cars and aircraft. Rather than relying on a traditional gas-powered engine or an electric battery system for power, supercars will use a mix of both. Supercars will be powered by a small and extremely efficient gas engine that drives an

> Addressing our ever-increasing transportation fuel tab and its accompanying costs will ultimately require finding ways to reduce demand for vehicular travel.

electric generator, which provides power to the wheels and a small battery. This system combines the most efficient aspects of gas and electric drive technologies.

Efficient use of vehicles

The biggest gains in vehicle efficiency result from increases in the number of riders in a vehicle rather than increases in mpg. For instance, a five mile per gallon bus carrying 14 passengers will get 70 person miles per gallon mpg. On the other hand, a single occupancy vehicle that gets 20 mpg will get only 20 passenger miles per gallon.

Sharing rides

A nine-passenger vanpool can cut energy use by nearly 83% compared to the cost of nine people driving themselves to work. On a more modest scale, a three-person carpool reduces fuel use by two-thirds. These programs also help to reduce parking and vehicle maintenance costs. In many cases, car and vanpooling is less expensive than using mass transit systems.

Promoting higher PMPG with high occupancy vehicle lanes

High Occupancy Vehicle (HOV) lanes encourage commuters to carpool. To drive in an HOV lane, a car must contain a minimum number of passengers (typically three). These special lanes generally have less traffic, and cars on HOV lanes on toll roads and bridges often travel for free. Ideally, the development of HOV lanes stresses converting existing lanes rather than building new ones.

Traffic lights in sync

Synchronizing traffic lights can improve transportation efficiency and reduce pollution. Depending on the system, local governments can cut travel time by up to 25%, fuel use by 13% and air emissions by 10% through computerized timing. These improvements are also cost-effective as demonstrated by one study that found for every project dollar spent, motorists save 25 gallons of gas.

Buses

Since an average bus gets at least 5 mpg, it only needs to carry four passengers for it to be more fuel-efficient than the average American car. When a commuter takes a bus instead of driving, the amount of polluting hydrocarbon emissions are reduced by nearly 90%, and carbon monoxide emissions are cut by over 75%. Bus systems are also incorporating features that make them more convenient for passengers, including elevated bus stops that speed loading, and electronic systems that indicate to waiting passengers how long before the next bus comes by.

Trains

In more ways than one, rail travel is more efficient than cars or trucks for transporting people and goods. Rail passengers can travel with one sixth or less the energy used by a single-occupancy vehicle. Trains can move

> Since an average bus gets at least 5 mpg, it only needs to carry four passengers for it to be more fuel-efficient than the average American car.

freight with one-eighth the energy required by trucks. Rail also uses land efficiently. For example, two railroad tracks can carry as many people per hour as a 16-lane highway. In addition, passenger rail is nearly 18 times as safe as travel with the private automobile. Despite these advantages to rail travel, between 1958 and 1989 federal government support for highways was more than $213 billion, while support for rail came to only $23 billion.

Reducing demand for motorized travel

Although today's transportation vehicles are 37% more efficient than they were 20 years ago, we're actually logging 89% more miles on the road. Unless we reduce demand for motorized travel, we will keep using more fuel, despite fuel efficiency increases, simply because we have more people driving more miles. High mileage cars are only part of the solution. While they may keep us from running out of fuel or clean air, they won't keep us from running out of roads, open space, and patience. Here are a few measures for reducing demand for vehicle travel.

Home offices and telecommuting

While working at home is nothing new, the availability of fax machines, modems, and multiline telephones make home offices an increasingly attractive choice. By staying home, workers eliminate the time spent commuting and save money, as they no longer need to buy gas or transit passes. Multi-use zoning permits residents to operate businesses out of their homes, currently an illegal act under many zoning regulations. A variation of the home/office concept is telecommuting, in which employees work for a company located elsewhere, but do their work at home, linked to the central office by phone and fax.

Promoting bicycle infrastructure

Other countries have developed a bicycle infrastructure that has helped cycle commuting become a way of life. Japan's 1980 census showed that 7.2 million commuters rode their bicycles to work or to commuter rail stations. Thirty-two percent of Denmark's workforce pedals to work, with another nine percent riding to commuter train stations. Other amenities that encourage cycling include bike ways, showers and lockers for cycle commuters at work and transit stations, and free bikes.

Beating parking spaces into transit passes

Another traffic-cutting measure involves reducing the number of parking spaces that planning agencies typically require of any new development. Rather than construct a parking space for an apartment or office, some European builders are instead offering tenants a perpetual mass transit pass. Paid for by an interest-bearing fund set aside by the developer, a perpetual transit pass costs less than building a parking space and allows the parking space to be used as a garden area or as an expansion of the building.

> Although today's transportation vehicles are 37% more efficient than they were twenty years ago, we're now logging 89% more miles on the road.

No matter where you want to go, there you are

Some communities are finding ways to make land-use decisions centered around people rather than cars. Most current community land-use policies require single-use zoning for either homes, offices, or shopping areas. These different community needs are then linked by miles of uninviting pavement and parking lots. On the other foot, pedestrian-based developments rely on a mix of stores, businesses, and homes, all within a five-minute walk of each other. Separate walk and bike ways link these different destinations so that bikers and walkers don't have to compete with cars. The result is a friendly, bustling environment with easy access to where residents want to be. Ultimately, the best mode of transportation is being there already.

> Ultimately, the best mode of transportation is being there already.

Factor #1: People and Organizations

Professional planners used to be the only ones developing transportation solutions. Now, with the critical need to find energy-efficient and more convenient ways to move people and goods to their chosen destination, a wide variety of groups need to play a role in developing and implementing alternatives. Here are some examples of how some of these groups have shared in making transportation decisions.

Citizens put bikes on the political agenda

Thanks to the foresight of several citizens back in 1966 bicycles are now a significant part of the transportation system in Davis, California. When increased urbanization began pushing bikes off the streets in the 60's, several Davis residents asked the City Council for dedicated bike ways. The Council scoffed at their request, maintaining that modern Americans don't want bicycles for transportation, and that bikeways on existing roadways would be unacceptably hazardous. The residents then circulated a petition asking that bike paths be established on principal travel routes through the community. In the next city council election, bikeways were the hottest issue, and the candidates committed to making bikes a part of transportation planning won by a landslide. In 1967, Davis established its first bike ways, the first developed in the U.S. since the turn of the century. Through the years, Davis has tapped researchers at the local university to make the bikeways system as safe and convenient as possible. Today, Davis has 50 miles of bike ways (compared to 100 miles of roads) and 25% of all trips taken in town are on bikes.

> Today, Davis has 50 miles of bike ways (compared to 100 miles of roads) and 25% of all trips taken in town are on bikes.

Enticing people to try new commutes

To get people out of their single-occupancy cars and onto bikes and buses, communities have begun organizing "Bike-to-Work" or "Alternative Commute" days. On these special-event days, cyclists, bus passengers, carpoolers and pedestrians receive incentives for using an alternative to driving alone. Incentives range from the edible (breakfasts, including cooked-to-order flapjacks and muffins) to the mechanical (bike tune-ups) to the simply enjoyable (prizes), all donated by local businesses. Other enticements include a corporate challenge that encourages local businesses to compete against each other to see which can have the highest percentage of employees taking a commute alternative to work. Sometimes these events are included in a week of alternative commute events, kicking off with an "Efficiency Grand Prix" consisting of all different kinds of transportation modes competing against a car.

Employers provide incentives for transportation alternatives

Palo Alto, California's impressive network of lighted bike paths, bridges and bicycle lockers aren't the only incentives for residents to pedal to work. For example, the Alza Corporation offers workers money each day they ride their bicycles to work. Xerox also offers special incentives to bicycle commuters, including a shower room complete with towel service. Other Silicon Valley companies have provided bike parking and employee shuttles with bike racks. In other communities, employers have offered commute incentives, including free mass transit passes, employer-financed car and vanpools, and special premiums, like free breakfasts, for using them.

Community revitalization group makes pedestrian link

Chatanooga, Tennessee recently converted a condemned automobile bridge into the world's longest pedestrian span, thanks to a local nonprofit committed to involving citizens in revitalizing their community. When the historic Walnut Street Bridge was in danger of being torn down, Chatanooga Venture formed a committee to look into other solutions. By asking citizens what they thought, Chatanooga Venture found that there was considerable support for saving the bridge.

Of the $4 million required to restore the bridge, both federal and local government pledged $3.5 million. Local citizens made up the difference by buying name plates to be posted on the bridge's planks from Chatanooga Venture.

The Walnut Street Bridge now provides an important link between downtown businesses and North Chatanooga. This improved access to downtown, and the pedestrian enhancements, have made North Chatanooga a more attractive location for employers, creating additional jobs and increased economic activity. On a good day, up to a thousand people cross the foot bridge to North Chatanooga. The bridge also provides a pedestrian link between the downtown and the park areas running along the Tennessee River, including a 60-mile bike and pedestrian path.

Citizens group makes the land use connection

In response to a proposed Portland area freeway, 1000 Friends of Oregon, a statewide citizens' group, launched the LUTRAQ (Making the Land Use, Transportation, Air Quality Connection) Program in 1990. The proposed $200 million freeway project was based on projected traffic increases generated by conventional developments that are required to have only a few residents per acre and keep residences separate from commercial and industrial sites.

The LUTRAQ program explored alternative development that makes biking, walking, and alternative transit convenient and feasible. The project wanted to see if this type of development could offset the projected traffic increases that were driving demand for the new freeway at a lower total cost.

LUTRAQ gathered data to compare the behavior of residents living in areas having varying degrees of pedestrian friendliness, measured by such factors as ease of street crossing and uninterrupted sidewalks. The LUTRAQ team found that mixing land uses and providing pedestrian amenities has a significant effect on auto ownership and choice of transportation mode. With these findings, LUTRAQ developed an alternative to the freeway that stressed land-use changes as well as a series of transit improvements, modest expansion of the local road system, improvements to local pedestrian and bicycle facilities, and disincentives to drive. The Oregon Department of Transportation will include the LUTRAQ alternative as one of five alternatives to be examined in the environmental impact statement for the freeway, the first time an alternative based on altered land-use patterns has been examined in an Environmental Impact Statement.

Most transportation planning models consider only automobile and public transit data to forecast future transportation demand. The LUTRAQ model incorporates information on biking, walking and land use patterns, and their role in the transportation picture. With assistance from several consulting firms, private foundations, and federal agencies, the LUTRAQ team will be publishing their information and offering a transportation planning framework that can be used in other parts of the country as well.

Citizens must ensure ISTEA goals are met

The Intermodal Surface Transportation Act (ISTEA) has created unprecedented opportunities for energy-efficient transportation solutions. However, whether ISTEA succeeds in creating energy-efficient transportation alternatives will depend on citizens and public officials who are aware of what ISTEA has to offer and who press for full implementation of the intent of ISTEA.

In the past, most transportation decisions have been made by professionals using a narrow range of criteria. Citizen participation was usually limited to public comment on fully-developed proposals. ISTEA opens up opportunities for increased and more meaningful citizen participation. ISTEA requires states to develop state-wide transportation plans and that the public be involved at all stages of transportation decision-making. What this involvement will look like, and how citizens can be assured a meaningful role, is still evolving. Citizens across the country have the opportunity to help define this new level of participation by contacting their local, regional, and state transportation planning agencies to get involved in upcoming transportation decisions. Rather than commenting on a limited range of alternatives after they have been developed, citizens can play a critical role in expanding the range of proposals from the very beginning.

> The **LUTRAQ** team found that mixing land uses and providing pedestrian amenities has a significant effect on auto ownership and choice of transportation mode.

One of the most important roles citizens can play is in ensuring that planning organizations fully evaluate the 15 factors that now must be considered when developing transportation plans. These factors include whether transportation proposals are consistent with federal, state, and local energy conservation programs, goals, and objectives; the effect of transportation decisions on long-term land use plans; and the overall social, economic, energy and environmental effects of transportation decisions. Meaningful ways of evaluating these factors, and ensuring that alternatives are then fairly considered, will require active and informed citizen participation.

Coalitions critical for effective change

Building a coalition of diverse local interests is a critical tool for improving the transportation system, whether the goal is getting more funds from the federal government or simply improving local bus service. Chambers of commerce, environmental groups, labor groups, neighborhood associations, and school boards are just some of the groups that have a stake in more efficient local transportation. Groups that are often at odds with each other can agree that a more efficient transportation system is in everybody's best interest. By joining forces groups can achieve far more than if they work alone toward better transportation solutions.

> One of the most important roles citizens can play to ensure ISTEA goals are met is in ensuring that planning organizations fully evaluate the 15 factors that now must be considered when developing transportation plans.

Factor #2: Financing

There are two roles that money can play in improving the transportation picture. Upfront capital is often necessary to make transportation efficiency improvements. At the same time, monetary incentives or disincentives can play an important role in communicating true costs and encouraging more efficient transportation practices. This section gives examples in both of these areas as well as listing innovative proposals that are waiting to be implemented.

Transportation policy creates new funding opportunities

The federal government currently collects 14.1 cents for every gallon of gas sold in the U.S, most of which goes toward a transportation projects fund that has been authorized to spend up to $155 billion from 1992 to 1997. In the past, almost all this federal money was dedicated to highway construction, eliminating the chance for other transportation choices to compete. Under the Intermodal Surface Transportation Efficiency Act (ISTEA) a wide range of transportation options are now eligible for federal funds. Some of these new options include bike and pedestrian facilities, traffic monitoring and control, acquisition of scenic easements, transportation planning, and transportation management systems. How federal money is spent will be determined by local and state planning organizations. These entities are required by ISTEA to get public input to ensure that a wide range of alternatives are fairly considered for funding.

Campaigning for bonds and sales/use taxes

Bonds and sales taxes, common ways to fund construction of public facilities and provide public services, can also be used to fund innovative transit alternatives. The rural Roaring Fork Valley of Western Colorado is tapping these public financing tools to address its car-related problems. These problems include urban-scale congestion, violation of clean air standards, hazardous rush hour traffic, and eroding community character.

Through a comprehensive community planning process, citizens and elected officials developed a transportation wish list to help cure the valley's transportation maladies. The list includes increased bus service, development of a light-rail system, and the purchase of an abandoned rail bed for future mass transit and trail use. The group examined a variety of ways to fund the measures, including property tax increases and user fees.

Out of this wide range of public finance options, planning participants decided that bonds and a sales and use tax were the best alternatives since they were both politically feasible and could raise enough capital to successfully fund the measures. County officials then put the issues on the

November ballot. In an election year charged with anti-tax sentiment, a coalition of both business and environmental interests succeeded in motivating voters to support a tax increase and bond issues. In addition to securing immediate financing for local transportation alternatives, the victory also positions the county to compete for federal Intermodal Surface Transportation Efficiency Act (ISTEA) matching funds down the road.

Making it pay to drive less

In Singapore, drivers who wish to travel in the central business district must buy a pass that allows them entry into this area. To prevent traffic problems from getting worse, congestion pricing systems collect tolls to use downtown roads, tunnels, bridges, and parking at times of peak use.

Publicizing the hidden incentives of efficiency

The savings from driving a more efficient vehicle creates a persuasive incentive for commuters to switch to a car with higher gas mileage. It's straightforward, for example, to replace a 20 mpg car with one that has a 40+ mpg rating. Assuming you drive 20,000 miles a year with a 20 mpg car, and gasoline averages $1.30 a gallon, you would pay $1300 a year for gas. With a 40 mpg car, you would spend only $650. A bicycle commuter can usually recoup the cost of their vehicle in a year's time while gaining health benefits. Making this information known more widely will encourage community savings.

Tax-free transit benefit encourages alternatives

Employers can now give workers a tax-free mass transit benefit. In the past, employers could take unlimited tax deductions for what they spent on employee parking. However, in an effort to encourage mass transit use, 1992 federal energy legislation now puts a cap of $155 per month on this deduction. More important, the legislation also offers a deduction for mass transit benefits of up to $60 monthly, which is often enough for an unlimited bus pass.

Alternative transportation rebates

California offers income tax credits and a sales tax exemption to individuals who convert their cars to electric power. Individuals who take advantage of the state's offer receive a tax credit of up to $1,000. These incentives may also include other kinds of zero or low emission vehicles as they become more readily available. The 1992 Federal Energy Act also offers a 10% rebate of up to $4,000 for electric vehicles and up to $2,000 for alternative fuel cars.

> **Under ISTEA a wide range of energy efficient transportation options are now eligible for federal funds. How this money is spent will be determined by local and state planning organizations.**

Developing vital mass transit hubs

Transportation hubs such as rail and bus stations linked to commercial spaces can boost the local economy. Washington D.C.'s Union Station is one such hub. Visitors can catch a train, go to a movie, get lunch, and go shopping, all under the same roof. Turning transportation centers into lively public places increases use of transit alternatives while creating economic benefits.

In other cities, light rail corridors have been lures for economic development. For example, Buffalo, New York's rail system has attracted $900 million worth of commercial and residential development clustered around train stations. Portland, Oregon and Atlanta, Georgia have experienced similar development patterns centered around their rail lines. On a smaller scale, some communities have developed hubs with the assistance of chambers of commerce and merchants. Like Union Station, these centers feature shops, cafes, and visitor information centers, and their proximity to mass transit reduces the need to use a car.

Walking into profit

Making towns more pedestrian-friendly and reducing car traffic is good for business. After developers created pedestrian zones in the U.S., U.K., and Germany, sales in the zones increased by as much as one-quarter. In Munich, an 85,000 square meter pedestrian zone owes its commercial success to increased foot traffic and easy access to public transportation. Many American communities that have converted downtown streets to pedestrian use have found that retail sales are highest in these pedestrian areas, and that these public spaces attract a rich cultural life.

Innovative options waiting to be implemented.

Pay or get paid with vehicle feebates

Feebates are perhaps the most powerful and promising means to encourage consumers to choose efficient cars over guzzlers. They're also very simple. When a consumer buys a new car, she receives a rebate if the car is a peppy, fuel-efficient car or pays a fee if her choice is a 10 mpg behemoth. The fees pay for the rebates, so the whole policy is revenue neutral. Already in use in Ontario, Canada, feebates require purchasers of guzzlers to pay a fee, while efficient car buyers receive a rebate of $100 Canadian. The California State Legislature passed a feebate bill in 1990, but it was not signed by the governor.

Maryland's feebate program, enacted in 1992, has been delayed by federal concerns that the program violates a law preventing states from setting up regulations regarding fuel economy standards. However, both the state and federal government are attempting to resolve these concerns.

> Buffalo, New York's rail system has attracted $900 million worth of commercial and residential development clustered around train stations.

Pay-at-the-pump insurance rewards driving less

Pay-at-the-pump insurance is another promising policy innovation. Instead of mailing in insurance payments every six months, your insurance costs are built into the price of every gallon of gas that you buy. The more you drive, the more insurance you buy, and the less you drive the less you have to buy. Since insured drivers would no longer have to subsidize uninsured ones, this measure would also lower insurance premiums. Pay-at-the-pump insurance kills not two, but three birds with one stone: insurance costs go down for everyone, all drivers are covered, and everyone has an incentive to drive less.

Commuting efficient mortgages

Similar to existing energy-efficient home mortgages, a commuting efficient mortgage would count the money that people save through lower energy bills when considering mortgage applications. Taking transportation expenses into account would allow homeowners with a shorter commute to get a bigger mortgage for their house because they have a lower transportation bill. Commuting-efficient mortgages would make urban housing a more affordable option.

Transit stipend for employees

Currently, if an employer provides free parking, their employees receive it as a tax-free benefit. Under a transit stipend program, employers offer a cash benefit, which employees can spend on a parking space or on a bicycle or transit passes. If employees don't spend all of their stipend, they can pocket any remaining money. Given that commuters who use an alternative to driving still bear its costs through higher taxes, insurance, etc. a stipend can help level the transportation playing field. Employers can also profit from less demand for parking spaces. A modest drop in parking demand allows employers to either lease, sell, or avoid building new spaces, which can be worth over $15,000 apiece.

> **Under a transit stipend program, employers offer a cash benefit in place of free parking, which employees can spend on a parking space or on a bicycle or transit passes, and pocket the remaining money.**

Factor #3: Government

Here's just a few ways local governments can help steer transportation choices in a more sustainable direction:

Promote least-cost and participatory approaches to transportation planning

➤ Provide accessible opportunities for public participation during each stage of developing transportation solutions.

➤ Develop ways to count all costs to evaluate and compare, and choose among all modes of transportation.

➤ Shift planning emphasis from moving cars to providing citizens better access to desired destinations with a wide array of means.

Lead by example

➤ Increase the average fuel efficiency of public fleets.

➤ Encourage and reward employees for using alternatives to the single occupancy vehicle.

➤ Encourage alternative access modes in day-to-day operations.

Create and promote efficient transportation alternatives throughout the community

➤ Work with the private sector to create incentives for using more efficient modes.

➤ Develop engaging alternative transportation campaigns.

➤ Provide staff support to develop transportation alternatives.

➤ Construct pedestrian and bicycle paths.

➤ Obtain demonstration alternative vehicles.

Develop energy-wise transportation policies

➤ Require all new developments to take innovative approaches to reduce automobile dependency.

➤ Promote housing in job-rich areas and employment opportunities in residential areas.

➤ Create disincentives to drive.

➤ Ensure that all development and road construction provides new or expanded bicycle paths and sidewalks. Involve pedestrians and cyclists in reviewing the practicality of proposed improvements.

➤ Change land use zoning laws to create a pedestrian, bicycling, and transit-friendly community.

➤ Change street-design requirements to encourage efficient use of energy and land.

Federal law provides an innovative planning framework

Through the Intermodal Surface Transportation Efficiency Act (ISTEA) the federal government is encouraging a new direction in transportation planning. Under ISTEA, transportation options must now be evaluated using such criteria as energy efficiency, air pollution, overall environmental quality, community character, traffic congestion, and economic development benefits. ISTEA, therefore, allows a wider variety of transportation alternatives to compete for federal support. Another federal policy, the 1990 Clean Air Act Amendments, work in conjunction with ISTEA to restrict construction of highway expansion projects unless the projects help meet clean air goals.

While ISTEA offers a powerful framework to expand the range of options on the transportation planning menu, many state and local officials do not yet fully understand its requirements or the opportunities it offers. The intent of ISTEA is to develop a transportation system that better serves the goals of environmental and community quality, energy efficiency, and economic development. However, since the means for applying these criteria are still being defined, these goals will only be realized with active citizen participation at the local and state level. While the federal policy provides a framework for integrated transportation planning, it is at the local level that alternatives must be envisioned and initated to define how ISTEA can move the country toward a more efficient transportation system.

Curitiba's comprehensive car cures

While this Brazilian metropolis of 1.5 million has seen its population triple over the last two decades, it has avoided many of the transportation problems afflicting cities a fraction of its size. Under the leadership of Mayor Jamie Lerner, a planner and an architect, the city has developed programs that reduce the need for commute trips.

Unable to afford a subway, Curitiba built an efficient and innovative bus system that cost 300 times less than a train. Inexpensive to ride, Curitiba buses offer unlimited transfers and express routes to key points in the city. Thanks to computerized traffic signals and bus-only lanes, the buses swiftly make their way around town. "Tube Stations," resembling a cross between an airport gate and a subway platform, expedite bus loading. Passengers pay their fares when they board the tube station, and when the bus arrives, they climb aboard without delay. The buses themselves were designed in collaboration with the local Volvo plant that manufactures the vehicles and sells them to the city at a discount. Construction materials for the tube stations also come from local suppliers.

Besides making it easier for people to get around, Curitiba is also exploring how citizens can minimize commuter trips and avoid the sprawl

> Curitiba's transit system has enhanced the local economy by creating markets for locally-made products and increasing job opportunities.

that afflicts cities like Los Angeles. Mixed-use zoning that places residences within easy walking distance of businesses and mass transit lessens the need for private cars. Auto-free business districts have become popular gathering spots. One of these districts is particularly popular, as it showcases restaurants, stores, and other businesses that are open 24 hours a day.

Curitiba's initiatives have paid off in more ways than one. Over a million passengers a day ride its buses. This sum is four times as many passengers as Rio's (a city six times the size of Curitiba) subway system carries. More important, the transit system has enhanced the local economy by creating markets for locally-made products (like the buses) and increasing job opportunities. Curitibans also have more disposable income since their transportation expenses are well below the national average.

Making government fleets more environmentally friendly

Oakland, California's East Bay Municipal Utility District (EBMUD) takes several steps to make its vehicle fleet more environmentally friendly. These steps include recycling motor oil and antifreeze, regular testing of light truck emissions, and prompt repair of any faulty vehicle emission systems. In addition to keeping vehicles as efficient as possible, EBMUD also uses environmentally-friendly cleaners, and recycles as much as it can.

Some states now have legislation setting mileage standards for government fleets. For example, Connecticut has passed a global warming act that requires state cars to have a minimum 29 mpg fuel economy. In 1997, this standard increases, and by 2000 cars must have a 45 mpg rating.

City government promotes employee bicycling

City employees in Glendale, Arizona have a unique incentive to cycle to work: free bicycles. Drawing on the police department's unclaimed property, the city government gives free bicycles to employees who pledge to ride to work at least three days a week. In Palo Alto, California, city government sponsors a monthly "Leave Your Car At Home Day" and pays its employees for work-related bicycle travel. Other local governments provide employee mass transit passes and carpool coordination.

Government agency creates ride alternatives

The Denver Regional Council of Governments offers the RideArrangers program that promotes alternatives to the single-occupancy vehicle as a commuting choice. RideArrangers offers information on public transit and helps set up vanpools, carpools, and corporate rideshare programs. For cyclists, RideArrangers has set up the Bike Buddy program that matches riders with others so that they can cycle to work with companions.

> Connecticut has passed a global warming act that requires state cars to have a minimum 29 mpg fuel economy. In 1997, this standard increases, and by 2000 cars must have a 45 mpg rating.

Using alternative vehicles to conduct business

One of America's most efficiency-minded utilities, the Sacramento Municipal Utility District (SMUD) relies on electric cars to carry out some of its operations. SMUD has built many electric vehicle recharging plants around town, including a solar powered one, which turns the cars into truly emission-free vehicles. The utility is also working with a local airport and military base to develop electric vehicle use at those locations.

Encouraging employees to telecommute

California's state government is a big booster of telecommuting. In 1988, a limited number of state employees, mostly located in Sacramento, started a two-year telecommuting pilot program. This effort led to an approximate 30% reduction in overall trips. Because the pilot program was so popular, the state began a permanent program in 1990, which now includes participants from 15 state agencies.

Working with the private sector to encourage alternative commuting

The city of Boulder, Colorado has started the Go (Great Options in Transportation) Boulder program which works closely with employers to encourage use of alternatives to single occupancy vehicles. One of Go Boulder's programs is the ECO Pass, an unlimited bus pass that allows passholders to receive a free cab ride in the event of a daytime emergency. Employers have been eager to offer the pass because it is a fully tax deductible benefit that saves them the high cost of constructing more parking spaces. Businesses can also be reimbursed by Go Boulder for up to a quarter of the cost of the passes. A local hospital and hundreds of businesses have taken advantage of this pass.

Other Go Boulder programs include a vanpool program that runs throughout the Denver/Boulder metro area. Partially funded by the Surface Transportation Program (STP) of the federal Intermodal Surface Transportation Efficiency Act, the program helps make mass transit more convenient for many citizens, including the elderly and the disabled. Go Boulder's other projects include an annual Bike Week, a pedestrian program, and participation in drafting the local transit master plan.

Swapping parking for alternatives

Parking offsets that allow developers to build fewer parking spaces in exchange for promoting alternative transportation has become a popular policy option. For example, Chicago allows builders a 10% reduction in the number of required parking spaces for buildings that have a direct connection to a subway station. Other reductions are linked to creating pedestrian walkways, bicycle facilities, and accessibility of transit passes.

> **The Go Boulder program works closely with employers to encourage use of alternatives to single occupancy vehicles.**

Creating incentives for carpooling and mass transit

City governments, including Portland, Oregon and Seattle, Washington, are using the incentive of preferred parking for van and carpools. High-occupancy vehicles can park all day in downtown locations and are exempted from paying parking fees. Agencies and private companies can also offer this incentive to carpoolers.

Thanks to a law passed by the California state legislature, Golden State employers receive tax credits if they subsidize worker transit passes. Legislation pending in other states could also provide tax incentives and subsidies for worker mass transit passes. Other proposed laws include a plan to cut rush hour tolls in half for cars with three passengers, charging nothing for vehicles carrying four or more.

Land-use policies link housing and work places

Portland officials decided to center development around the local rail and bus system, rather than roads. Specifically, the city encourages business and residential development in close proximity to mass transit. Portland hopes that joint development of rail stations with the private sector will make the light rail system entirely self-sustaining. Other steps to reduce citizen dependence on cars include restrictions on downtown parking and creating bus-only lanes.

Integrating better transit into existing community design

While existing cities may have been designed with only the car in mind, it's never too late to make a community friendlier to transportation alternatives. For example, Toronto, Canada has many policies that encourage developers to build housing and offices near existing mass transit lines and business districts. Spurred by a mix of zoning regulations and incentives, the majority of new apartments and offices are built within easy walking distance of the city's subway system. Due to these development patterns, 77% of downtown workers use public transit to get to work.

Bicycles and pedestrians now part of transportation planning

ISTEA requires that each state create a bicycle and pedestrian coordinator position within the state Department of Transportation. The federal government will fund 80% of this position, with a 20% state matching funds requirement. The resources available to local communities from this coordinator include assistance in the development of bicycle and pedestrian facility plans; information on current sources of funding for bike and pedestrian programs; and guidelines for developing comprehensive pedestrian/bicycle plans. North Carolina is already benefiting from a state bicycle office. Its Bike Office looks at every upcoming road building proposal and considers how to integrate bicycle improvements into the project. Past

> Spurred by a mix of zoning regulations and incentives, the majority of new apartments and offices in Toronto are built within easy walking distance of the city's subway system. 77% of downtown workers now use public transit to get to work.

improvements have included bike paths, signs, shoulders, and parking that have all made the state's roads more friendly to cyclists.

Bikes for everyone

Even if they don't own a bike, Copenhagen, Denmark residents can be cycle commuters. Recognizing the high economic and social costs of auto use, the city funds a fleet of 3000 bicycles. To use a bike, Copenhagenites insert coins into a specially designed rack to release one of the cycles. When they return it to a rack, their deposit is returned. Mechanics regularly maintain the bicycles, that are distinctly designed and painted a special shade of white to discourage theft.

Task Force Resources

Here's a list of on-line information services, hotlines, publications, newsletters, and organizations that you can tap for additional information on sustainable energy alternatives. These resources can also lead you to additional helpful sources. Also be sure to contact your state energy office, utilities and regional U.S. Department of Energy offices.

On-line information services

If you have access to Internet, these on-line information services can link you immediately to a vast amount of information on energy efficiency and renewable energy-related topics.

CREST Solstice

Operated by CREST, the Center for Renewable Energy & Sustainable Technology, Solstice is an on-line information service available via the Internet for energy professionals, policy makers, and anyone interested in expanding their knowledge about renewable energy, energy management, and energy policy.

Once connected to Solstice, you can choose from a wide variety of databases, including a directory of organizations that provide information on energy-efficient technologies; a guide to alternative energy resources; and a list of energy-efficient strategies for policymakers and educators. Solstice is constantly updated to make the most up-to-date information on energy alternatives accessible. Access is available 24 hours a day, and is free and open to all with Internet access.

How to access Solstice:
You can use FTP (the File Transfer Protocol) and Gopher (the information-gathering software rodent) to access CREST's archive of energy-related information, which includes multimedia presentations, newsletters from trade organizations, image collections, and more. To access with ftp, open "solstice.crest.org", log in as "anonymous", and give your email address as the password. Once connected, go to the "pub/" directory to find the CREST archive. With Gopher, simply direct your Gopher software to open "gopher.crest.org".

Accessing Solstice via the World Wide Web:
You can also experience Solstice via the World Wide Web. Combining images, sounds, and text, the Web is a collection of software tools that allows you to browse information on the Internet with a simple point-and-click interface. To take full advantage of CREST's Web site, you need a computer that is connected directly to the Internet, and Web browsing software such as NCSA Mosaic. The URL (Uniform Resource Locator) you will need to visit Solstice is http://solstice.crest.org/ For more information contact:
The Center for Renewable Energy and Sustainable Technology (CREST)
c/o Solar Energy Research and Education Foundation (SEREF)
777 North Capitol Street NE, Suite 805
Washington, DC 20002
(202) 408-0663

ECONET

The Institute for Global Communications maintains ECONET, a bulletin board for more than 10,000 individuals and organizations. ECONET has complete electronic mail services as well as an Internet gateway. It also maintains a variety of forums on climate change, energy, recycling, hazardous wastes and many other topics. ECONET is a subscription-based service which charges $12.50 per month. For more information, send an email message to: support@igc.apc.org. Or write or call:
Institute for Global Communications (IGC)
18 De Boom Street
San Francisco, CA 94107
(415) 442-0220
Fax (415) 546-1704

Energy Efficiency and Renewable Energy Network (EREN)

EREN is a U.S Department of Energy sponsored Internet gateway to worldwide information on energy efficiency and renewable energy technologies. Resources may be accessed by browsing through an alphabetical listing of Internet sites, broad subject divisions, types of services, or types of organizations providing a variety of resource materials. To access EREN use the Uniform Resource Locator (URL) http: / / www.eren. doe.gov

For more information, write, call, or email the Energy Efficiency and Renewable Energy Clearinghouse (EREC)
PO Box 3048
Merrifield, VA 22116
(800) 363-3732
email energyinfo@delphi.com

Energy Ideas Clearinghouse

The Energy Ideas Clearinghouse Bulletin Board Service (EICBBS) has over 5,000 users from a variety of energy professions that you can communicate with 24 hours a day. You can also take advantage of electronic mail services, access a wide variety of energy forums and discussion groups, and download software files and databases. There are also 400 postings in the Job/Resume data base as well as a current list of energy events in the Training Calendar.

To register and use the system immediately, set your communications software to 8 data bits, 1 stop bit, no parity and full duplex (no echo). Computers must be able to emulate an ANSI, ANSI-BBS, or VT100 terminal type. Once the software has been configured, EICBBS can be accessed by dialing (206) 586-6854. Once on-line, follow the menu system. For person-to-person assistance about the EICBBS, contact:
Energy Ideas Clearinghouse bulletin Board Service
Washington State Energy Office
PO Box 43165
Olympia, WA 98504-3165
(206) 956-2237

National Energy Information Center

The U.S. Department of Energy's Energy Information System maintains an electronic publishing system (EPUB). EPUB allows the general public to electronically access selected energy data from a variety of statistical reports and energy studies. While EREN deals specficially with energy efficiency and renewable energy, EPUB offers statistical information on energy use, supply, prices, and so forth. The system is a menu-driven, bulletin board type system with extensive on-line help. It can be accessed free of charge 24 hours a day using a computer with an asynchronous modem.

To use the system immediately, follow the same directions described for the Energy Ideas Clearinghouse above. Once the software has been configured, EPUB can be accessed by dialing (202) 586-2557. From that point, follow the menu system.

More information about EPUB, or about other publications and data about energy use and technologies within the United States can be accessed from:
National Energy Information Center
EI-231
Energy Information Administration
Forrestal Building, Room 1F-048
Washington, DC 20585
(202) 586-8800
email infoctr@eia.doe.gov.

Hotlines

Energy Efficiency and Renewable Energy Clearinghouse (EREC)

Funded by U.S. Department of Energy, the EREC hotline provides a wide variety of information on renewable energy and efficiency measures. EREC has technical experts on staff that can answer questions on a wide range of energy efficiency-related subjects including practical implementation advice and sources of products and services. They also have an inventory of more than 500 publications, fact sheets, resource and referral listing, and bibliographies. Call or write them to receive a comprehensive listing of the services they offer.

Energy Efficiency and Renewable Energy Clearinghouse (EREC)
PO Box 3048
Merrifield, VA 22116
(800) 363-3732

Technical Inquiry Service

U.S. Department of Energy
National Renewable Energy Laboratory (NREL)
NREL's Technical Inquiry Service provides access to information on community application of renewable technologies and how to assess renewable energy potential in your area.
(303) 275-4065 Steve Rubin
Fax (303) 275-4091
email rubin@tctlink.nrel.gov

Many state energy offices offer information hotlines as well.

Publications

Alternatives to the Automobile: Transport for Livable Cities

By Marcia D. Lowe

This report looks at community planning, mass transit and other ways of decreasing auto dependence. The book assesses both the financial and environmental costs of various transportation modes. Available for $5 from:
Worldwatch Institute
1776 Massachusetts Avenue NW
Washington, DC 20036
(202) 452-1999
Fax (202) 296-7365
email worldwatch@igc.apc.org
Ask for a list of Worldwatch publications for other useful information for your task force.

The Audubon House: Building the Environmentally Responsible, Energy-Efficient Office

by National Audubon Society and Croxton Collaborative, Architects
Audubon House tells the story of how a team of architects, environmentalists, engineers, interior designers, and contractors transformed a 19th-century structure in downtown Manhattan into the most energy-effi-

cient, environmentally-responsible office building ever designed. Available at bookstores for $24.95.

John Wiley & Sons, Inc.
The Wiley Series in Sustainable Design
Professional, Reference and Trade Group
605 Third Avenue
New York, NY 10158-0012

Building Sustainable Communities: An Environmental Guide for Local Government/Energy: Efficiency and Production

By Cheryl Sullivan and Vincent Robinson
This indispensable guide describes successful local government energy policies and programs from across the country, including more detailed descriptions of some of the examples cited in this workbook. The book also includes copies of ordinances and policies. Available for $20 for government, nonprofits, and individuals and $40 for businesses from:

The Global Cities Project™
2962 Fillmore Street
San Francisco, CA 94123
(415) 775-0791
Fax (415) 775-4159

The Car Book: An Indispensable Guide to the Safest, Most Economical New Cars

By Jack Gillis
A comprehensive guide to car safety, fuel economy, and maintenance, this book can help you find the most efficient cars on the market. The book's findings are based on federal government tests and studies sanctioned by the Center for Auto Safety, the leading automotive consumer group. Available for $11 plus $2.75 shipping and applicable tax from:

Harper Collins Publisher
PO Box 588
Dunmore, PA 18512
(800) 331-3761

Community Loan Programs

This handy 9-page publication outlines the steps to creating a community loan program, based on the Nebraska Energy Office's exten-sive experience in creating energy-efficient loan programs. Available from:

Nebraska Energy Office
PO Box 95085
Lincoln, NE 68509
(402) 471-2867
Fax (402) 471-3064

Consumer Guide to Home Energy Savings

By Alex Wilson and John Morrill
Containing chapters on insulation, lighting, heating systems and more, this book examines ways to make homes more energy efficient. The guide lists appliances by model and ranks their energy efficiency. Available for $6.95 plus applicable tax and $2 shipping from:

American Council for an Energy Efficient Economy (ACEEE)
2140 Shattuck Avenue, Suite 202
Berkeley, CA 94704
(510) 549-9984
ACEEE publishes numerous other useful publications, so ask for their entire publications list.

Cool Tools: State and Local Policy Options to Confront a Changing Climate

By Pamela Wexler and Susan Conbere
An excellent summary of local and state legislation regarding procurement, utility regulation, land use planning, energy taxes and transportation. The Center for Global Change is also developing a computerized database covering laws, bills and policy proposals that address state and locally regulated activities that produce greenhouse gases. Available for $6 from:

Center for Global Change
University of Maryland at College Park
The Executive Building, Suite 401
7100 Baltimore Avenue
College Park, MD 20740
(301) 403-4165
Fax (301) 403-4292

Economic Renewal Guide

Rocky Mountain Institute
By Michael Kinsley
For anyone who intends to get sustainable economic development moving in a commu-nity, this book details how to organize a community and conduct a series of collaborative town meetings that lead to practical economic development projects. The guide includes background on sustainable development and facilitation skills. Available from:

1739 Snowmass Creek Road
Snowmass, CO 81654-9199
(970) 927-3851
Fax (970) 927-4178

Energy-Aware Planning Guide

This comprehensive guide offers more than 40 different energy-conserving policy ideas and 270 implementation ideas for improving energy use through better land use, transportation and building practices. The guide describes over 115 local government programs, including contact information for each. Written for the State of California, the guide is a handy tools for communities in all 50 states. Available for $19.00 from:

California Energy Commission
Attn: Publications MS-13
1516 Ninth Street
PO Box 944295
Sacramento, CA 94244-2950
(916) 654-4287

Homemade Money: How to Save Energy and Dollars in Your Home

Rocky Mountain Institute
By Rick Heede and the Staff of RMI
The Homemade Money is a comprehensive guide to putting your home on an energy diet. The book outlines how to weatherize and insulate your home, upgrade and maintain heating and cooling systems, cost-effectively reduce window heat loss, buy new efficient appliances, lights, and water heaters, and use the sun's free energy. New cost-effective technologies and equipment are described, efficient home design and construction is discussed, numerous sources are listed. Available for $14.95 from:

1739 Snowmass Creek Road
Snowmass, CO 81654-9199
(970) 927-3851
Fax (970) 927-4178

Energy Solutions for Cities and Counties

An indispensable fact-sheet series that summarizes a variety of successful energy efficiency and renewable energy programs from around the country. Concise and very readable, these fact sheets will be a very useful addition to your planning effort. Each case study also includes addresses and phone numbers of where to get more information. Titles include: Energy Efficiency Strengthens Local Economies; Buildings that Save Money with Efficient Lighting; Energy Dollars Relieve Municipal Budgets. Fact sheets are free in quantities up to 10 from:

Cities and Counties Project
U.S. Department of Energy
National Renewable Energy Lab
1617 Cole Boulevard
Golden, CO 80401-9889
(303) 231-1234
Fax (303) 275-4053

Energywise Options for State and Local Governments

By Michael Totten and Nita Settina with Jack Gold, Thomas Gray, and Katherine Tammaro

Containing case studies of energy efficiency measures that have been implemented at the national, state, and local level, this book is an invaluable resource for task forces. Available for $15 from:

Center for Policy Alternatives
1875 Connecticut Avenue NW, Suite 710
Washington, DC 20009
(202) 387-6030

The Environmental Impact of the Car

Edited by Jim Beard et. al.

This volume presents the financial, social, and environmental costs of automobile use, looks at historical patterns of automobile use, and provides specific policy recommendations to promote alternatives. Available for $5 from:

Greenpeace
Public Information
1436 U Street NW
Washington, DC 20009
(202) 462-1177

Environmental Resource Guide

The American Institute of Architects publishes a comprehensive guide of key environmental issues for architects interested in practicing "green architecture." Topics include energy efficiency, land use, siting, natural resources, and recycling. The guide also contains references to additional helpful books, periodicals, and publications. The guide is updated three times a year and is available for $275 a year from:

AIA Orders
PO Box 60
Williston, VT 05495-0060
(800) 365-ARCH (2724)

The Going Rate: What It Really Costs to Drive

This handy report can help you examine the true costs of driving, including costs incurred by roadway building and maintenance, highway services, air pollution, imported oil, accidents, congestion, land loss, and more. Available from:

World Resources Institute
Suite 700
1709 New York Avenue NW
Washington, DC 20006
(202) 638-6300
Fax (202) 638-0036

Helping Consumers Save Energy
and
Guiding Principles for Low Income Consumer Energy Education

These two publications focus on the role that energy education plays in encouraging customers to change energy use behaviors, install inexpensive efficiency measures, and maintain new energy-efficient technologies. To receive the publications send a self-addressed, stamped envelope with $.52 postage to:

Dave Brook
Oregon State University Energy Extension Program
800 NE Oregon Street, Unit 10
Portland, OR 97232
(503) 731-4104
Fax (503) 731-4570

How to Reduce Your Energy Costs: The Energy Efficiency Guide for Small Business

By The Center for Information Sharing

A handy guide to help businesses learn about ways to save energy and money. This guide provides information for conducting a walk-through audit to look for efficiency opportunities throughout a business, as well as tables to calculate savings. Available for free from:

Elizabeth Hornbrook
U.S. Small Business Administration
Region VIII
633 17th Street
North Tower, 7th Floor
Denver, CO 80202-3607
(303) 294-7186
Fax (303) 294-7153

Lean and Clean Management: How to Boost Profits and Productivity by Reducing Pollution

by Joseph J. Romm
Published by Kodansha International:
New York

This book details how businesses can dramatically cut costs and increase productivity through adopting environmentally sound manufacturing and operating practices. Full of inspiring examples and strategies, this book is a must for your commercial/industrial energy task force. Available through book stores.

National Bike Month Organizers Kit

This kit provides step-by-step tips for organizing community cycling events, including sample press releases and letters to potential sponsors to hold "Bike-to-Work" events. Available for $8 from:

League of American Bicyclists
190 W Ostend Street, Suite 120
Baltimore, MD 21230-3755
(410) 539-3399
Fax (410) 539-4396
email bikeleague@aol.com

The New Solar Home Book

By Bruce Anderson with Michael Riordan

This book gives a thorough overview of putting the sun to work in your future or existing home. Includes sections on windows, photo-

voltaic panels, and solar hot water heating. Available for $16.95 from:
Brick House Publishing
4 Limbo Lane
PO Box 266
Amherst, NH 03031
(800) 639-8409
Fax (603) 673-6250

The Next American Metropolis: Ecology, Community, and the American Dream

By Peter Calthorpe

Calthorpe offers comprehensive guidelines for addressing the traffic, housing, and environmental problems of sprawl. Advocating a fundamental change in current patterns of community design, this book also provides the means and principles to promote the transformation of existing communities. Available for $24.95 plus postage from:
Princeton Architectural Press
37 East Seventh Street
New York, NY 10003
(800) 458-1131

Plugging People into Power: An Energy Participation Handbook

This is handy publication on how to shape utility energy plans and policies. Although it's written for a Northwest audience, the handbook is useful for people across the country interested in public involvement in power planning. Available from:
Brick House Publishing
Northwest Conservation Act Coalition
217 Pine Street, Suite 1020
Seattle, WA 98101
(206) 621-0094
Fax (206) 621-0097

A Primer on Sustainable Building

Rocky Mountain Institute
Dianna Lopez Barnett and William D. Browning

This is a handy guide for architects, developers, and anyone else interested in green building. The *Primer* gives tips on site selection, landscaping, energy-efficient building techniques, building ecology, and reasons for going green. Available for $16.95.
1739 Snowmass Creek Road

Snowmass, CO 81654-9199
(970) 927-3851
Fax (970) 927-4178

Real Goods Alternative Energy Sourcebook

By The Real Goods Staff

A 400-page comprehensive primer and encyclopedia of alternative energy technologies. Detailed articles help the layperson understand the benefits of many renewable technologies and what's involved in using them to power home energy needs. Available for $16 plus applicable tax and $3.50 shipping from:
Real Goods
966 Mazzoni Street
Ukiah, CA 95482-3471
(800) 762-7325
Fax (707) 468-9486

Recipe for an Effective Campus Energy Conservation Program

by Walter Simpson, Energy Officer of SUNY Buffalo

Written by the person who succeeded in saving millions of dollars on energy bills for the SUNY campus, this is an invaluable guide for anyone launching or running an energy efficiency program. Available from:
Union of Concerned Scientists
2 Brattle Square
Cambridge, MA 02238-9105
(617) 547-5552
Fax (617) 864-9405
email menu@ucs.usa.org

Renewables Are Ready Campaign Materials

The Renewables Are Ready campaign provides briefing papers and information sheets focused at key players who can influence and encourage the use of renewables in local communities. The campaign targets power producers, teachers, builders, elected officials, and investors. For more information or to obtain materials, contact:
The Union of Concerned Scientists
See above

The Role of Community-Based Organizations in Demand Side Management

This paper describes how electric and gas utilities can work with existing community organizations to deliver energy efficiency programs and become more active in local economic development. Available for $15 from:
Center for Neighborhood Technology
2125 West North Avenue
Chicago, IL 60647
(312) 278-4800

Running an Energy-Efficient Hotel

Aimed at lodging managers who wish to cut energy use, this publication helps managers assess their energy use and includes sections on cost accounting, energy audits and technologies. Available for free from:
California Energy Extension Service
1400 10th Street
Sacramento, CA 95814
(916) 323-4388

School Programs: Retrofitting Today's Schools & Educating Tomorrow's Energy Consumers

This publication provides the best one-stop summary of school energy efficiency and energy education programs, including a thorough listing of where to go for additional resources. Available for $15 from:
IRT Environment
PO Box 10990
Aspen, CO 81612-9689
(970) 927-3155

"Supercars: The Coming Light-Vehicle Revolution"

This paper discuss the technical aspects of ultralight supercars that can get 300 miles per gallon. In addition to describing hybrid electric/gasoline powerplants, the paper also assesses composite building materials and new manufacturing techniques. Available for $8 from:
Rocky Mountain Institute
1739 Snowmass Creek Road
Snowmass, CO 81654-9199
(970) 927-3851
Fax (970) 927-4178

Steering a New Course: Transportation, Energy and the Environment

By Deborah Gordon

This book explores efficient transportation technology and policy options. Chapters cover greenhouse gases and other air pollutants, alternative fuels, innovative transportation policies, and ultra-fuel efficient vehicles. Available for $19.95 plus shipping from:
Union of Concerned Scientists
See above

Sustainable Energy: A Local Government Planning Guide for a Sustainable Future

The three cities of San Jose, California, San Francisco, California, and Portland, Oregon developed this useful guide as part of the Sustainable Cities Project. The guide contains tips on building local government support and copies of the three cities' energy policies and lists of policy options. Publication number LG-10, available from:
Energy Efficiency and Renewable Energy Clearinghouse (EREC)
PO Box 3048
Merrifield, VA 22116
(800) 523-2929

Transportation for Sustainable Communities

A practical guide to tackling local transportation issues, this collection includes sections on building coalitions, developing an action agenda, and relating transportation issues to clean air and land use concerns. Available for $10 plus $2 shipping from:
The Center for Neighborhood Technology
2125 West North Avenue
Chicago, IL 60647
(312) 278-4800

What Works Report #1: Air Pollution Solutions

By Mark Malaspina, Kristin Schafer, and Richard Wiles

This report describes local policies, citizen campaigns and government and business programs that are useful in reducing transporta-

tion-related pollution. Available for $17 (includes postage and handling) from:
The Environmental Exchange
1930 18th Street NW, #24
Washington, DC 20009
(202) 387-2182

Newsletters and Periodicals

Conservation Monitor

A free monthly bulletin, Conservation Monitor reports on energy efficiency activities and issues in the Pacific Northwest. Although it has a regional focus, this publication is an invaluable resource for groups around the country interested in innovative utility and community efficiency programs. Available for free from:
Conservation Monitor
PO Box 900928
Seattle, WA 98109
(206) 285-4848

Energy Design Update

Directed at builders, contractors, and developers, this technical newsletter reports on new products, designs, and technologies. Available for $297 a year or $157 for small businesses, contractors, and weatherization programs from:
Cutter Information Group
37 Broadway
Arlington, MA 02174
(800) 964-5118
Fax (800) 888-1816

Energy User News: News for Building Managers & Engineers

Each issue details commercial and industrial efficiency project case studies. Issues have focused on HVAC systems, lighting and climate control. Available for $69.50 a year from:
Energy User News
PO Box 2165
Radnor, PA 19089
(800) 247-8080

Environmental Building News

Environmental Building News targets building professionals interested in reducing the

environmental impact of their buildings. This bimonthly examines building materials and the latest in efficient building techniques. Available for $60 a year for individuals and small businesses from:
Environmental Building News
RR 1, Box 161
Brattleboro, VT 05301
(802) 257-7300
Fax (802) 257-7304

Home Energy

This monthly magazine contains examples of how utilities, energy organizations, and businesses are implementing energy efficiency programs nationwide. Home Energy is an indispensable resource for keeping current with residential energy efficiency programs. Available for $49 a year from:
Home Energy
2124 Kittredge, #95
Berkeley, CA 94704
(510) 524-5404

Home Power

Home Power Magazine is one of the best sources on using renewable energy to power households. Each bimonthly issue contains examples and tips for using solar, wind, and other renewable technologies. Available for $15 a year from:
Karen & Richard Perez
PO Box 520
Ashland, OR 97520
(916) 475-0830
Fax (916) 475-3179
email richard.perez@homepower.org

In Business Magazine

To see many other examples of people making a living through resource-efficient or other environmental businesses, be sure to look up copies of In Business. This monthly magazine also contains additional resources for learning more about business opportunities in environmentally-friendly enterprises. Available for $23 a year from:
419 State Avenue
Emmaus, PA 18049
(215) 967-4135

The Neighborhood Works

Published by the Center for Neighborhood Technology, The Neighborhood Works is a bimonthly magazine examining community policy issues. The Center for Neighborhood Technology (CNT) is a Chicago-based organization that focuses on the role of energy use, job creation, housing development, food production, and material use in building better urban communities. The Neighborhood Works is available for $30 a year from:

Center for Neighborhood Technology
2125 West North Avenue
Chicago, IL 60647
(312) 278-4800
Fax (312) 278-3840

Organizations

The following organizations have publications and information that will be useful resources for the Energy Town Meeting and the energy planning workshops. Call or write them for their latest publications list and information on current energy-related projects. These organizations may also be able to refer you to additional resources. Also remember to contact the organizations that might be working on energy issues in your region, listed on pages 50 through 53.

Alliance to Save Energy

1725 K Street, Suite 509
Washington, DC 20006
(202) 857-0666
Fax (202) 331-9588
The Alliance to Save Energy works on a variety of energy policy issues and has an extensive publications list including titles on model building codes, energy education, updates on federal energy policy, and more.

Alternative Energy Resources Organizations (AERO)

25 South Ewing, Room 214
Helena, MT 59601
(406) 443-7272
Fax (406)442-9120
email paulreichert@desktop.org
A Montana nonprofit organization, AERO serves the needs of people working to promote renewable energy and conservation, sustainable agriculture and greater community self-reliance.

American Council for an Energy Efficient Economy (ACEEE)

1001 Connecticut Avenue NW, Suite 801
Washington, DC 20036
(202) 429-8873
Fax (202) 429-2248
email Liz burke%ccmail@pnl.gov
ACEEE conducts research on energy efficiency to stimulate the adoption of energy-conserving technologies and practices. ACEEE has an extensive list of publications, including titles on utility policy, energy efficiency in buildings, transportation and climate change, energy-efficient motor systems, and regulatory incentives for demand-side management. For policy-related questions, contact the DC office. Contact ACEEE for their publications list at their Berkeley office:
2140 Shattuck Avenue #202
Berkeley, CA 94704
(510) 549-9984.

American Public Transit Association (APTA)

1201 New York Avenue NW, Suite 400
Washington, DC 20005
(202) 898-4000
Fax (202) 898-4070
APTA publishes a packet of materials to help you organize a local transit coalition. The kit lists local transit coalition contacts, sample organizing materials, and fact sheets. APTA also offers Public Transit: The Benefits of Investment, a handy fact sheet collection covering public transit's role in economic stimulus, energy conservation, clean air, and more.

American Solar Energy Society (ASES)

2400 Central Avenue, Suite G-1
Boulder, CO 80301
(303) 443-3130
Fax (303) 443-3212
email ases@igc.apc.org
ASES promotes education in fields related to solar energy and publishes a variety of information on solar-related topics, including the monthly magazine Solar Today, issue papers on implementation of solar technologies, and sustainable development. Contact ASES for their catalog.

American Wind Energy Association (AWEA)

122 C Street NW, 4th Floor
Washington, DC 20001
(202) 383-2500
Fax (202) 383- 2505
AWEA offers more than 35 publications and education resources. Their free catalog lists publications on measuring your wind resource, the economics of wind energy systems, energy and regulatory policies affecting wind energy, and reference books on wind energy use. They also offer a monthly newsletter.

Bicycle Federation of America (BFA)

1506 21st Street NW #200
Washington, DC 20036
(202) 463-6622
Fax (202)463-6625
BFA is the only national organization devoted exclusively to advocating the needs of both bicyclists and pedestrians. BFA works with public agencies and national associations to ensure new transportation legislation, policies, and programs enhance and expand the opportunities for bicycling and walking. In addition to three major advocacy projects, BFA is a clearinghouse for information on all aspects of bicycling and pedestrian issues. BFA publishes Pro Bike News, a monthly newsletter, and Bicycle Forum, a quarterly journal.

Campaign for New Transportation Priorities

900 2nd Street NE, Suite 308
Washington, DC 20002
(202) 408-8362
Fax (202) 408-8287

CNTP develops transportation policies which address economic progress, safety, energy security, and environmental protection. CNTP also publishes a variety of transportation policy papers.

Campus Ecology Program

National Wildlife Federation
Campus Outreach Division
1400 16th Street NW
Washington, DC 20036
(800) 432-6564

Campus Ecology Program offers a variety of resources to help students, professors, and administrators develop environmental programs on campus. Campus Ecology resources include issue packets, one-on-one consultations, site visits, newsletters, organizing skills, and a book for performing a campus environmental audit.

Catalyst Leasing Group, Inc.

83 South Main Street
Brattleboro, Vermont 05301
(802) 254-3645

In addition to its own direct energy financing services (described on page 218), Catalyst has a network of resources which communities can tap to invest in energy improvements. Catalyst offers a half hour of free consultation to community energy advocates. Contact Hervey Scudder at the above number.

Center for Global Change

University of Maryland at College Park
The Executive Building, Suite 401
7100 Baltimore Avenue
College Park, MD 20740
(301) 403-4165
Fax (301) 403-4292
email asmiller@wam.umd.edu

The Center for Global Change seeks innovative solutions to global environmental problems and studies their relationships to energy use, economic development and equity. The Center evaluates and recommends policies, technologies and institutional reforms to promote sustainable development and reduce the risks of environmental degradation, particularly those posed by climate change and ozone depletion. Research results are disseminated through publications, seminars, training and other outreach activities.

Center for Policy Alternatives (CPA)

1875 Connecticut Avenue NW, Suite 710
Washington, DC 20009
(202) 387-6030
Fax (202) 986-2539

CPA is a non-partisan think tank that connects innovative people and ideas to build a sustainable economy. CPA develops public policies, drafts legislation, and serves as a clearinghouse for alternative policies and programs. CPA publishes regular *State Reports* with details of new legislation, and a monthly newsletter *Alternatives.*

Citizen Action

Suite 403
1730 Rhode Island Avenue NW
Washington, DC 20036
(202) 775-1580
Fax (202) 296-4054

Citizen Action is conducting energy campaigns in a number of states around the country relating to energy efficiency, renewables, transportation policy, and utility reform. Call to see if they are active in your state.

Concern Inc.

1794 Columbia Road NW
Washington, DC 20009
(202) 328-8160
Fax (202) 387-3378

CONCERN, Inc., a national, nonprofit environmental education organization provides environmental information for community action. It serves as a clearinghouse, catalyst, and facilitator for programs, policies and practices that are environmentally healthy, economically sound, and socially equitable. CONCERN publishes several handbooks relating to energy efficiency and renewable energy.

Consumer Energy Council of America Research Foundation (CECA/RF)

2000 L Street NW, Suite 802
Washington, DC 20036
(202) 659-0404
Fax (202) 659-0407

CECA/RF is a leading national resource for information, analysis and technical expertise on the social and economic impacts of a wide variety of energy and environmental policies. CECA has expertise in forging successful partnerships among public and private sector organizations, state and local groups, businesses, utilities, consumers, environmentalists, and government agencies on a wide variety of energy policy issues. Their monthly newsletter, The Quad Report, focuses on the linkage between demand-side management and energy efficiency and the environment.

Cooperative Development Foundation

1401 New York Avenue NW, Suite 1100
Washington, DC 20005
(202) 638-6222
Fax (202) 637-6222

CDF is a national foundation representing every sector of the cooperative movement. CDF works with other development groups to help fund and strengthen cooperative development projects in the U.S. and abroad.

Critical Mass Energy Project

215 Pennsylvania Avenue SE
Washington, DC 20003
(202) 546-4996
Fax (202) 547-7392
email cmep@essential.org

Critical Mass works to promote safe, economical, and environmentally sound energy alternatives and publishes a long list of excellent resources. Publication titles include: The Renewable Source: A National Directory of Resources, Contacts, and Companies (state by state listing of 2200 organizations working with renewable energy systems and policies); The Green Buyer's Car Guide: Environmental Ratings of 1994 Cars and Light Trucks; and A Sustainable Energy Blueprint and Budget. Contact Critical Mass for their publications list for additional resources and prices.

Energy Efficient Building Association

1829 Portland Avenue
Minneapolis, MN 55404
(612) 871-0413
Fax (612) 871-9441

EEBA develops and disseminates technical information on the design, construction, and maintenance of energy-efficient buildings. They sponsor annual international conferences, expositions, seminars and workshops. Write for their list of publications on energy-efficient house design and construction.

Energy Rated Homes™ of America (ERHA)

5401 JFK Boulevard Suite I
North Little Rock, AR 72116
(501) 374-7827
Fax (501) 771-1722

ERHA is a membership organization which provides uniform energy rating system (UERS) support to its members. ERHA assists states in starting up the UERS program, maintains a data bank of houses rated under the UERS, provides oversight, direction, and quality control of the program.

Environmental Defense Fund (EDF)

257 Park Avenue S
New York, NY 10010
(212) 505-2100
Fax (212) 505-2375

EDF works on a variety of energy policy issues, and offers a publication list containing titles on topics such as Climate Change, utility policy, auto fuel efficiency standards, America's Energy Choices, and renewables. Contact them for an information packet and free catalog.

Friends of the Earth (FOE)

1025 Vermont Avenue NW, Suite 300
Washington, DC 20005
(202) 783-7400
Fax (202) 783-0444

FOE works on a wide variety of energy and environmental issues, including environmental tax reform to increase investment and support for energy efficiency, and developing a comprehensive survey of federal funding for environmental and energy-related programs.

For more information on FOE's energy-related programs contact Gawain Kripke at the number listed above. FOE's "Earth Budget" report is available by calling Public Interest Publications at 1-800-537-9359.

Green Development Services Program

Rocky Mountain Institute
1739 Snowmass Creek Road
Snowmass, CO 81654-9199
(970) 927-3851
Fax (970) 927-4178

Rocky Mountain Institute offers technical and design consultation on environmentally responsible techniques and technologies of the design, construction, and management of residential and commercial real estate projects. The Green Development Program helps in exploring site considerations, opportunities for energy and water efficiency, and resource efficient and healthy building materials.

Greenpeace USA

Greenpeace–Public Information
1436 U Street NW
Washington, DC 20009
(202) 462-1177
For information on the Greenpeace
Energy Campaign, contact:
4649 Sunnyside Avenue North
Seattle, WA 98103
(206) 632-4326
Fax (206) 632-6122

The Greenpeace Energy Campaign works for a national energy policy that promotes energy efficiency and the development of sustainable renewable resources. Greenpeace has a variety of energy and climate change publications, including case studies of energy efficiency and renewable energy; a report on global warming; an extensive report on the causes of climate change, and a catalog of over 500 extreme weather events.

Institute for Transportation and Development Policy (ITDP)

611 Broadway, Room 616
New York, NY 10012
(212) 260-8144

ITDP offers an extensive publications list which includes readings on sustainable global

and North American transport strategies. Other topics include bicycles and other nonmotorized forms of transportation.

Interfaith Coalition on Energy (ICE)

7217 Oak Avenue
Melrose Park, PA 19027-3222
(215) 635-1122
Fax (215) 635-1903

Through newsletters, seminars, booklets, videotapes and on-site consultation ICE inspires and guides congregations to use measurably less energy to create money for community service while practicing environmental stewardship.

International Council for Local Environmental Initiatives (ICLEI)

City Hall, East Tower, 8th Floor
Toronto, Ontario
CANADA M5H 2N2
(416) 392-1462
Fax (416) 392-9111

ICLEI is an international association whose mission is to work with municipalities to solve environmental problems at the local level, and connect these issues to global environmental issues. ICLEI runs a "Cities for Climate Protection Campaign" which has the goal of recruiting 100 cities worldwide to make political commitments to reduce CO_2 and create jobs in the process. Contact ICLEI to find out how to join, or to get their list of essential publications such as "Saving the Climate, Saving the Cities" and "Financing Energy Efficiency".

LUTRAQ (Making the Land Use, Transportation, Air Quality Connection)

Keith Bartholomew
1000 Friends of Oregon
534 SW Third Avenue, Suite 300
Portland, OR 97204
(503) 497-1000
Fax (503) 223-0073
email kab@friends.org

LUTRAQ was started by 1000 Friends of Oregon, a statewide land-use watchdog group, to explore the connections between land use and transportation problems. LUTRAQ is developing a land use-based alternative to a proposed freeway, and can offer insights on their approach to other groups around the country.

National Association of Energy Service Companies (NAESCO)

1440 New York Avenue NW
Washington, DC 20005
(202) 371-7812
Fax (202) 393-5760

NAESCO is a national association for energy services companies, offering conferences and newsletters to its members. NAESCO also publishes a list of energy service companies bidders list, of member ESCOS.

National Association of Fleet Administrators, Inc.

120 Wood Avenue S, Suite 615
Iselin, NJ 08830-2709
(908) 494-8100
Fax (908) 494-6789

This association deals with fleet management issues and publishes Fleet Executive Magazine. Containing helpful information on how to increase fleet efficiency, a year 's subscription is $48.

National Audubon Society

700 Broadway
New York, NY 10003
(212) 979-3000
Fax (212) 979-3188

National Audubon Society offers a number of resources on energy efficiency and sustainable building practices. Their office "Audubon House" (described page 214) is an example of a green office building and tours are available on Fridays. They also have a video on the Audubon House (15 and 30 minute versions, $12.95 and $6.95); fact sheets, wind and biomass resources.

The National Design Assistance Center for Resourceful Building

PO Box 100
Missoula, MT 59806
(406) 549-7678
Fax (406) 549-4100

This organization offers practical advice to builders on constructing a more efficient and environmentally sound home. Builders can submit design ideas to this organization and receive recommendations on resource efficiency, building materials, creation of a healthy living environment, and elements of low-cost building. For more information on their consulting services contact:

Passive Solar Industries Council (PSIC)

1511 K Street NW, Suite 600
Washington, DC 20005
(202) 628-7400
Fax (202) 393-5043

PSIC is a national network for builders, architects, utilities, consumers, and industry organizations with an interest in affordable, sustainable, high-quality building practices. PSIC offers practical, useful information about passive, or "climate-responsive" design techniques. Call PSIC to find out about their Guidelines books for new construction and remodeling, as well as their user-friendly performance analysis software. PSIC also publishes a newsletter and offers design workshops.

Public Private Transportation Network

Suite 1100
8737 Colesville Road
Silver Spring, MD 20910-3921
(800) 522-7786

This free technical assistance program is aimed at the transportation industry, including managers and policymakers. PPTN helps identify financing methods for transit and develop new transportation systems.

Public Technology, Inc. (PTI) Urban Consortium Energy Task Force

1301 Pennsylvania Avenue NW
Washington, DC 20004-1793
(202) 626-2400
Fax (202) 626-2498

PTI is a nonprofit organization of more than 20,000 local government entities. PTI develops technology innovations for the public sector, and helps local governments maintain a balance between urban development and environmental responsibility. PTI's Urban Consortium Energy Task Force develops innovative yet practical approaches for local energy management and sustainability. Call PTI to obtain a list of PTI resources and energy efficiency funding opportunities offered through the Urban Consortium Energy Task Force.

Renew America

1400 16th Street NW, Suite 710
Washington, DC 20036
(202) 232-2252
Fax (202) 232-2617

Renew America seeks out and promotes exemplary environmental programs to inspire communities and businesses to meet environmental challenges. Through Renew America, organizations work together, exchanging ideas and expertise in an effort to renew the nation's community spirit through environmental and economic success. Renew America publishes the Environmental Success Index, which contains more that 1,600 effective environmental programs.

Safe Energy Communication Council (SECC)

Suite 805
1717 Massachusetts Avenue NW
Washington, DC 20036
(202) 483-8491
Fax (202) 234-9194

SECC is an environmental coalition of national energy, environmental and public interest media groups working to increase public awareness of the ability of energy efficient and renewable energy sources to meet an increasing share of our nation's energy needs, and of the serious economic and environmental liabilities of nuclear power.

Sierra Club

408 C Street NE
Washington, DC 20002
(202) 547-1141
Fax (202) 547-6009

Sierra Club provides policy information on a range of global warming and energy issues, as well as in-depth information on auto fuel economy standards and their benefits to the environment, human health, and the economy.

Solar Energy Industries Association (SEIA)

122 C Street NW, 4th Floor
Washington, DC 20001
(202) 383-2600
Fax (202) 383-2670

SEIA is the national network of solar energy businesses, offering conferences and workshops to its members to increase industry profitability and demand for products. SEIA offers a listing of members across the country.

Surface Transportation Policy Project (STPP)

1400 16th Street, NW
Washington, DC 20036
(202) 939-3470
Fax (202) 939-3475

STPP is a network of diverse organizations, coalitions and grassroots groups whose goal is to develop a national transportation policy that better serves the environmental, social and economic interests of the nation. STPP seeks to frame public debate about federal transportation policy and to help craft a new transportation program that focuses on moving people and goods, rather than vehicles, without favoring any single mode of transportation. Call STPP to receive their newsletter which is packed full of useful information for local transportation planning.

Transportation Alternatives

92 St. Mark's Place
New York, NY 10009
(212) 475-4600
Fax (212) 475-4551

Based in New York City, Transportation Alternatives works to promote bicycling by grassroots organizing, political lobbying and direct action. TA publishes City Cyclist, a newsletter containing information useful to bicycle advocates anywhere. A year's subscription is $20.

Union of Concerned Scientists (UCS)

2 Brattle Square
Cambridge, MA 02238-9105
(617) 547-5552
Fax (617) 864-9405
email menu@ucs.usa.org

The Union of Concerned Scientists offers a wide variety of important resources on energy efficiency and renewable energy. Publications include Powering the Midwest: Renewable Electricity for the Economy and the Environment, and Cool Energy: The Renewable Solution to Global Warming. See other titles listed above. Contact UCS for their entire publications list and other resources.

US Climate Action Network

1350 New York Avenue NW, Suite 300
Washington, DC 20005
(202) 624-9360
Fax (202) 783-5917
email uscan@igc.org

US Climate Action Network tracks climate change policies and what communities and organizations across the country are doing to address climate change issues. The Network also publishes a monthly newsletter.

US Public Interest Research Group (US PIRG)

218 D Street SE
Washington, DC 20003
(202) 546-9707
Fax (202) 546-2461

US PIRG is the national association of state PIRGs, representing over one million citizens. US PIRG and various state PIRGS work on a variety of energy issues, including stronger efficiency standards for cars and household appliances, transportation policy, and utility reform. You can call US PIRG to see if there is a PIRG in your state.

DOE and EPA Resources

The United States has committed to stabilizing greenhouse gas emissions to 1990 levels by the year 2000. To meet this goal there are a wide variety of DOE and EPA programs that have been developed to encourage businesses and communities to become more energy efficient and use renewable energy. Here is just a sampling of some of these programs. Check to see if your community and local businesses and industries are taking full advantage of these resources. You can also contact your regional DOE office to inquire about additional Climate Change Action Plan Programs that your community can tap.

DOE Energy Partnerships for a Strong Economy

To help further the goals of the Energy Policy Act of 1992 and the Climate Change Action Plan, DOE offers a series of programs known collectively as *Energy Partnerships for a Strong Economy.* These programs offer a variety of resources and assistance to businesses, industry, state and local governments, and others to remove market barriers that limit the current use of energy efficiency and renewable energy. The programs are designed to help participating partners encourage greater productivity and increase profits while meeting environmental objectives. Some of these programs are described below. For additional programs and information contact DOE Office of Energy Efficiency and Renewable Energy Customer Service Center at 1-800-363-3732.

DOE Rebuild America

Rebuild America aims to stimulate the private sector to upgrade 4 billion square feet of space while achieving an average energy savings of 25 percent. DOE will provide financial support, technical assistance and training, planning and management support to local "community partnerships" that will retrofit multiple buildings. These community partnerships may consist of local governments, utilities, trade allies, energy service companies, and building owners. The partnership will be expected to form a program team, propose a retrofit plan, find and leverage additional financial resources, implement retrofits, and track progress. For more information contact the Energy Efficiency and Renewable Energy Customer Service Center at 800-363-3732.

DOE Energy Analysis and Diagnostic Center (EADC) Program

The EADC program uses engineering faculty to direct the work of undergraduate and graduate students conducting energy efficiency audits for small and medium sized manufacturing plants located within 150 miles of their host campus. The average EADC audit recommends annual energy savings of approximately $40,000 per year. Since its inception in 1976 the program has completed 5100 assessments generating energy savings of approximately $517 million. Selected EADC's are conducting combined energy, waste, and productivity assessments. To find out if there is an EADC offering services in your area call:

Mr. Charles Glaser
U.S. Department of Energy, EE-223
1000 Independence Avenue, SW
Washington, DC 20585
(202) 586-1298
Fax (202) 586-6507
email: charles.glaser@hg.doe.gov

The Motor Challenge Program

Motor Challenge is a joint effort by the U.S. Department of Energy, industry, motor/drive manufacturers and distributors, and other key participants. Through the Motor Challenge Clearinghouse organizations can sign up as "partners" and get access to a variety of resources to increase electric motor system efficiency and improve productivity. Resources include education and training materials, workshops, an electronic bulletin board, decision tools, fact sheets, case studies, sourcebooks, and direct technical assistance from staff engineers. To find out more, contact:

The Motor Challenge Information
Clearinghouse
PO Box 43171

Olympia, WA 98504-3171
(800) 862-2086

NICE³

National Industrial Competitiveness through Energy Environment Economics

Federal grants are offered to industries that wish to design, test, demonstrate, and assess the feasibility of new processes or equipment with the potential to increase energy efficiency, reduce pollution, and decrease production costs. Grant awards average $250,000. The program is administered jointly by the U.S. Department of Energy and the U.S. Environmental Protection Agency, and is open to participants throughout the U.S. and the territories. For more information contact your state energy office or DOE at (303) 275-4755.

Climate Challenge

Through this partnership program utilities identify and implement cost-effective options for meeting greenhouse emissions. Participating utilities can receive technical assistance, help in conducting outreach, and help in monitoring results. The program also offers an Options Workbook that identifies a wide variety of options that a utility can use to fulfil its commitments to reduce, avoid, or sequester greenhouse gas emissions. For more information call 1-800-363-3732.

DOE Regional Support Offices

Atlanta DOE Support Office
730 Peachtree Street NE, Suite 876
Atlanta, GA 30308
(404) 347-2837
(AL, FL, GA, KY, MS, NC, PR, SC, TN)

Boston DOE Support Office
One Contress Street, 11th Floor
Boston, MA 12114
(617) 565-9700
(CT, MA, ME, NH, RI, VT)

Chicago DOE Support Office
9800 South Cass Avenue
Argonne, IL 60439
(708) 252-2001
(IL, IN, MI, MN, OH, WI)

Dallas DOE Support Office
1420 West Mockingbird Lane, Suite 400
Dallas, TX 75247
(214) 767-7245
(AR, LA, NM, OK, TX)

Denver DOE Support Office2801
Youngfield Street, Suite 380
Golden, CO 80401
(303) 231-5750
(CO, MT, ND, SD, UT, WY)

Kansas City DOE Support Office
911 Walnut Street, 14th Floor
Kansas City, MO 64106
(816) 426-5533
(IA, KS, MO, NE)

New York DOE Support Office
26 Federal Plaza, Room 3437
New York, NY 10278
(212) 264-1021
(NJ,NY)

Philadelphia DOE Support Office
1880 JFK Bouldevard, Suite 501
Philadelphia, PA 19103
(215) 656-6950
(DC, DE, MD, PA, VA, WV)

San Francisco DOE Support Office
1301 Clay Street, Room 1060 North
Oakland, CA 94612
(510) 637-1945
(AZ, CA, HI, NV)

Seattle DOE Support Office
800 Fifth Avenue, Suite 3950
Seattle, WA 98104
(206) 553-1004
(AK, ID, OR, WA)

U.S. Environmental Protection Agency

Green Lights Program

EPA Green Lights program helps participating companies and organizations increase lighting system efficiency, reduce electricity costs, and improve lighting quality. Through a memorandum of understanding participating organizations agree to survey their facilities and install energy efficient lighting, while Green Lights staff provide technical assistance, user-friendly information on lighting technology and financing, and public recognition. To get a Green Lights Information Pack, call:

Green Lights Hotline: (202) 775-6650

or write:

Greenlights

ICF, Inc.

9300 Lee Highway

Fairfax, VA 22031

Lines are open 8:30 as 9:00 pm EST

Energy Star Buildings

To help plan and implement building energy upgrades, the EPA's Energy Star Buildings program offers guidance packages, technical manuals, case studies, software to calculate savings, and a data base of financing programs for building-efficiency upgrades. For more information call the EPA at (202) 233-9146.

Climate Wise

Climate Wise offers assistance and recognition to enable and encourage industries to reduce greenhouse gas emissions by voluntarily adopting energy efficiency, renewable energy, and pollution-prevention technologies. Companies that commit to taking comprehensive cost effective actions to reduce emissions are offered a variety of resources and assistance through the program. For more information, contact either the EPA at (202) 260-4407 or DOE at (800) 363-3732.

U.S. Environmental Protection Agency
Climate Change Division
State and Local Outreach Program

This program offers resources to help states and local communities develop comprehensive climate change programs. State agencies can apply for grants and resources to prepare State greenhouse gas inventories, develop State action plans, and implement innovative, high-priority pilot projects. To see if or how your state is participating, contact Alexander Winslow at (202) 260-4314.

Running the Energy Planning Process

Well-run meetings and workshops are the core of the energy planning process. This section contains background on what's required to run effective workshops as well as tips on keeping people interested.

SECTION CONTENTS

1 **What's needed for meetings**

2 **Keeping people interested**

3 **Brainstorming techniques**

What's needed for meetings

This section describes the people and resources that you should have in place to make your meetings as effective as possible. Your effort will be easier if each task force selects several participants to fulfill the following roles:

Facilitators

Each task force needs a facilitator to run meetings. Ideally, this person should be experienced in conducting meetings and guiding a group through discussions and decisions. If you can't find experienced facilitators for each task force, people with leadership potential can take advantage of this opportunity to learn how to run meetings.

Facilitators will need to prepare for workshops by reading all workshop materials. Meeting preparation will also include copying worksheets and formatting results from previous workshops for participants. These responsibilities should be shared among task force members.

It's a good idea to organize a facilitators' meeting to make sure everyone understands the upcoming workshop. At this meeting, facilitators may wish to review tips on running effective meetings, workshop instructions and worksheets, and task force packets.

Each workshop section contains a Facilitator Agenda and Facilitator Directions. The facilitator agenda outlines what should happen during the workshop and provides suggested times for each activity. Facilitators should have a copy on hand to steer the workshop.

The facilitator directions contain detailed information on workshop exercises. They include step-by-step instructions on completing worksheets and other exercises. In some cases, these directions also contain variations on holding the workshop.

Recorders and mailers

Recorders and mailers should type up and send workshop results to each participant to help them prepare for the next meeting. Since this task requires time and office equipment, the steering committee should enlist staff from an organization sponsoring the planning effort.

Coordinator of workshop materials and copies

Each workshop requires copies of worksheets and supporting materials as described in each workshop section.

Callers

Callers phone participants to remind them of workshops or events.

The right workshop location

Find a meeting space large enough to accommodate your group. Each participant should have a place to sit, and if possible, table space on which to work. A school is ideal since it probably has a gym or auditorium suitable for large meetings as well as classrooms for small group discussions. Set aside at least one wall for charts. Ensure that the room has adequate lighting and temperature control.

The right time and place for meetings

Meeting times need to fit your community's schedule. It's a bad idea to schedule workshops during Monday Night Football, city council meetings, or at busy times like the holiday season.

Most become bored with meetings lasting over two hours. Since overly long meetings are a surefire way to send people packing, establish acceptable meeting times and start meetings promptly to discourage stragglers.

Materials

Bring the following to each workshop and meeting:

➤ Poster-sized easel pads/flip charts for each task force to record their findings. Provide at least one pad per task force.

➤ Colored water-base markers, that don't mark up walls, can liven up your lists.

➤ Tape or adhesive putty to hang charts and worksheets.

➤ Enough copies of the Workshop Title and Goal and a concise Agenda (found on the first page of each workbook section) for each workshop participant.

➤ Any Worksheets and Handouts from the meeting and workshop sections. Distribute them as directed.

➤ A sign-in sheet for participants.

Keeping people interested

Since the planning process involves many meetings over several months, there will be a natural attrition rate among participants. However, making meetings worthwhile and interesting will keep participation levels high. Contributing to a community effort doesn't have to be painful, and if participants feel they are making measurable progress while enjoying themselves, they will remain interested.

Reach out and touch someone

If attendance drops, personal phone calls are your best bet. You can set up a phone tree or one person can volunteer to call every task force member to remind them of upcoming meetings. A simple phone call can be a major factor in whether someone chooses to attend a meeting.

Keep the issue alive in the community

Keep the media informed of your progress and build public awareness of your work throughout the process. Constantly build on the enthusiasm and interest generated by early events such as the Energy Town Meeting.

Keep the process moving

Instead of letting the process drag on, encourage participants to promptly complete workshops. Initially, some participants may want to examine issues in microscopic detail. Resist this temptation, since a drawn-out process will deter participants from coming back.

Make meetings productive

To ensure participants' continued participation, they must feel their time has been well spent. At the end of each meeting, briefly review what the group has accomplished in that session. This review will remind participants of the progress that they have made toward their goal of developing and implementing an effective energy action plan.

Set the right tone

Primary responsibility for making meetings enjoyable falls upon the facilitator. If a facilitator cuts people off, criticizes ideas, and is a general nuisance, the session will quickly take on an unpleasant tone. While facilitators don't have to be stand-up comedians, it helps if they can create an enjoyable atmosphere where participants can freely share their thoughts.

Brainstorming techniques

Several of the workshops rely on participants brainstorming information and ideas. Brainstorming explores a range of options, and doesn't try to sell any one perspective. It offers a safe environment for participants to share their ideas with the group and stretch their imaginations. To encourage effective participation, keep these points in mind:

Appoint a recorder

Find someone who can quickly and legibly record all ideas on large sheets of paper. Use more than one recorder to allow ideas to flow quickly.

There are no wrong ideas

Criticizing ideas while brainstorming can be tempting, but at this point the name of the game is to generate as many ideas as possible and save the critical assessments for later. If some ideas are not on point, but may have value later on, you may wish to create a separate sheet, dubbed the "parking lot." The purpose of this sheet is to record ideas for future reference.

Listen to the full explanation of an idea

The brainstorming process runs more efficiently when participants resist the opportunity to interrupt or throw in their two cents. When summarizing and recording ideas, recorders and facilitators should make sure they hear what each person says, and not what they think participants are saying. If you are unsure of what participants said, ask them to repeat or rephrase their thoughts.

Encourage broad participation

Group success depends upon every group member sharing her or his ideas. Ask for contributions from those who have kept silent.

Many have great ideas, but are afraid of ridicule. Encourage people to share their creative ideas, no matter how outlandish they seem. Promote risk-taking by taking risks yourself.

Keep the discussion on track. Remind participants they don't need to go into microscopic detail regarding your ideas. Occasionally, participants will contribute ideas that have little to do with the topic at hand. By simply recording these contributions on a sheet of paper, you can briefly acknowledge the idea while keeping the discussion on track.

Additional Resources

For more information on how to run meetings and workshops see other RMI publications:
- How to Run Effective Meetings
- The Economic Renewal Guide: How to develop a sustainable economy through community collaboration

Talk to us!

We want to learn from you. Please give us your comments on this book and any thoughts you have on how to improve it. If you tried to use any part of this book in your community, please let us know what worked, what didn't, and what kind of results you achieved.

Are you a(n):
- ❒ interested citizen?
- ❒ local government staff person?
- ❒ utility staff person?
- ❒ elected official?
- ❒ state or federal government staff person?
- ❒ other? _____

How would you rate this book?
- ❒ very useful
- ❒ moderately useful
- ❒ not useful

Please tell us how it could be improved: _____

_____

What effect did this book have in your community? _____

_____

Name_____

Address _____

Phone _____

Please send your comments to:
Rocky Mountain Institute
Attn: Community Energy Staff
1739 Snowmass Creek Road
Snowmass, CO 81654-9199
(970) 927-3851 or (970) 927-4510

Order Form

Rocky Mountain Institute
1739 Snowmass Creek Road
Snowmass, CO 81654-9199
(970) 927-3851 / FAX (970) 927-3420

Please send me the following RMI publications:		
D95-2 *A Primer on Sustainable Building*	____	$16.95
E95-3 *Homemade Money: How to Save Energy and Dollars in Your Home*	____	$14.95
E92-9 *The Efficient House Sourcebook*	____	$13.95
ER95-4 *The Community Energy Workbook*	____	$16.95
ER92-23 *Economic Renewal Guide*	____	$ 15.00
Home Energy Briefs *(circle titles ordered)*		
• Lighting • Refrigerators and Freezers • Windows •		
• Water Heating • Cooking Appliances and Dishwashers •		
• Washers, Dryers, and Miscellaneous Appliances •		
• Home Office Equipment •	____	$ 2.00 *each*
RMI *Newsletter* (three issues, one year)	____	$10.00*
RMI Information Packet and Publications List	____	Free

* requested minimum donation

subtotal:	
+ 20% shipping/handling:	
+ 3% tax if shipped in Colorado	
total enclosed:	

We normally ship by U.S. Mail or UPS; for faster delivery, please call.

☐ *My check or money order is enclosed*

☐ *Please charge my:* ☐ *Visa* ☐ *Mastercard Signature:* _____

Card #: _____ *Exp. date:* _____

Please send the publications to: (please print or type)

Name: _____

Address: _____

Town/City: _____ *State:* _____

ZIP/Postal code: _____ *Country:* _____

Telephone: _____

ROCKY MOUNTAIN INSTITUTE